EXPLORE THE BOOK

Other works by

J. SIDLOW BAXTER

THE BEST WORD EVER

A captivating new presentation of John iii, 16. Theological, evangelistic, devotional, practical. In two parts—(1) The New Testament Truth, (2) The Old Testament Type.

STUDIES IN PROBLEM TEXTS

Informing, elucidatory and applicatory expositions of certain Scripture passages which have occasioned perplexity.

HIS PART AND OURS

Enriching expository and devotional studies in the Scripture usage of the possessive "My" in relation to the union of Christ and His people. "A truly great book"—*Moody Monthly*.

MARK THESE MEN

Arresting studies in striking aspects of Bible characters with special relevances for our own times and the days ahead.

EXPLORE THE BOOK

A Basic and Broadly Interpretative Course
of Bible Study from Genesis to Revelation

J. SIDLOW BAXTER

In Six Volumes

VOLUME ONE
GENESIS TO JOSHUA

MARSHALL, MORGAN & SCOTT, LTD.
LONDON :: EDINBURGH

LONDON
MARSHALL, MORGAN AND SCOTT, LTD.
1–5 PORTPOOL LANE
HOLBORN, E.C.1

AUSTRALIA
317 COLLINS STREET
MELBOURNE

NEW ZEALAND
23 MONTGOMERY ROAD
ROTHESAY BAY
AUCKLAND

SOUTH AFRICA
P.O. BOX 1720, STURK'S BUILDINGS
CAPE TOWN

CANADA
EVANGELICAL PUBLISHERS
241 YONGE STREET
TORONTO

First published in 1951
Second impression 1956
Third impression 1958

MADE AND PRINTED IN GREAT BRITAIN BY PURNELL AND SONS, LTD.
PAULTON (SOMERSET) AND LONDON

FOREWORD

THE BULK of the instalments which comprise this Bible Course were originally delivered as my Thursday evening Bible Lectures in Charlotte Chapel, Edinburgh. That accounts for their conversational mode of address in parts. They were not written as essays, but were designed for public utterance, and I have thought it wise to leave them in their first form, believing that there are certain practical advantages in so doing. I would ask that this be noted leniently, especially if the exacting eyes of some literary connoisseur or dilettante should wander over them in their now-printed fixity. Moreover, I must plead that as these studies were first prepared to be spoken, without thought of later publication, I have in various parts indulged a preacher's rather than a writer's liberty in appropriating from the writings of others. I can only hope that sheer admiration may not have betrayed me too near the dreaded boundary-line of plagiarism. If it has, then I am relieved to feel certain that it can only be with authors who are no longer with us. I can never be too grateful to dear old (and, to many, old-fashioned) John Kitto, and to John Urquhart and A. T. Pierson, and Sir Robert Anderson, and G. Campbell Morgan, and others of the same evangelical tradition. They were all masters in their own day and in their own way. To them all, and to that incomparable composite work, the *Pulpit Commentary*, I here acknowledge my repeated indebtedness, and pay my tribute to them all. This Bible Course as a whole, however, is solidly the product of my own independent study, and I gladly accept responsibility for it, believing that in every part it genuinely honours the Bible as the inspired Word of God. May God graciously crown it with a ministry of usefulness to many who live and labour for His dear Son, our Lord and Saviour.

J. S. B.

DEDICATION

These studies are dedicated with deep gratitude
and affectionate esteem to my beloved, saintly,
and now elderly friend,

JAMES ARTHUR YOXALL, ESQ.,
of Ashton-under-Lyne
and Stalybridge;

my spiritual "father" and gifted teacher in
the precious things of Christ; the inspirer of
many heavenward aspirings within me, the
one who first planted in my youthful heart a
zest for Bible study; who has always been to
me the ideal Christian gentleman, the choicest
of preachers, and, above all, a kindly,
experienced older friend ever brimming over
with the sanctifying love of the Lord Jesus.

CONTENTS OF VOLUME ONE

THE BIBLE

"Within this wondrous volume lies
   The mystery of mysteries;
   Happiest they of human race
   To whom their God has given grace
   To read, to fear, to hope, to pray,
   To lift the latch, to find the way;
   And better had they ne'er been born
   Who read to doubt, or read to scorn."

SIR WALTER SCOTT.

INTRODUCTION

No MAN's education is complete if he does not know the Bible No Christian minister is really qualified for the ministry of the Christian Church without a thorough study of the Bible. No Christian worker can be fully effective without a ready knowledge of the Bible. No Christian believer can live the Christian life to the full without an adequate grasp of the Bible.

Our Purpose

Our purpose in this present course of Bible study is to give *a grounding in the Scriptures*. Let us be frank and clear at the outset. If we really want to know the word of God better, this course of study will help us. Our effort has been to maintain the same standard of thoroughness throughout. We would emphasise, however, that it is no use reading the following studies *instead of* the Bible. To do that would be to miss the purpose altogether. What we are after is that *the Bible itself* shall be read, part by part, each part several times over, and the present scheme of studies used *along with* this. However carefully the following lessons are read, if they are read *without* the parallel study of the Bible itself, the real fascination of Bible study will be missed. Our hope is that some who have not yet studied their way right through the Bible will resolve on devoting such and such hours of their available time each week to beginning at Genesis and gradually exploring the whole Bible, book by book, as directed by this Bible study course, and using the help which is here provided at each stage.

With all too many Christians today the tendency is to read the Bible just to pick up a few good points or suggestions for addressing meetings or preparing sermons, or to pick out a few nice bits to help with the Christian life. This is bad. It results in scrappiness. It engenders superficiality both mentally and spiritually. The word of God was never meant merely for these hurried consultations. We need to study and to know the written word of God as a whole, for such study and knowledge gives depth and richness and fulness to *all* our public ministry, and stabilises our whole Christian experience. Moreover, I would remind fellow-preachers that the greatest sermons usually come when we are not looking for sermons but are studying the word of God for the sake of its own vital truth.

Now this present course of Bible study is not meant merely to yield suggestions for addresses and sermons—though it will probably do that again and again if really studied along with the Bible. It is meant to give a practical grip on the Bible as a whole. We do well to realise that those sermons or books which most stir us at the time of hearing or reading often leave us little that is of permanent value, while, on the other hand, those that teach us most may not be so immediately stirring. Quite apart from any superficial interest of the moment, such as preparing messages or seeking guidance in some crisis, we should determine to get a worthy grasp of God's book; for to know it well gives a quality to our Christian service which nothing else can, and stands us in good stead throughout our life. Every Christian minister and worker should be a specialist in the Bible.

Our Method

We ought to say a few words here about our *method*. The Bible is such an endless book, and there are so many ways of studying it, that as we launch forth into this course of studies we are reminded of the sailor who, when asked where he sailed, said: "Sir, I am restricted to the ocean!" Like a great ocean, the wonderful contents of the Bible are before us, but we do not want to be merely sailing anywhere—or we shall get nowhere! We need the chart and compass of a settled method so that we may navigate these glorious seas without unprofitable digressions to the right hand or to the left.

Much depends on our method of study. According to choice, we may study the books of the Bible spiritually, historically, typically, topically, prophetically, dispensationally, analytically, biographically, critically, devotionally, or in other ways. The method which we adopt in this present series is that which we may call *interpretative*. We shall study the books of the Bible interpretatively; that is, we shall seek to get hold of the controlling thought, the outstanding meaning and message of each book, and then see it in relation to the other books of Scripture. The importance of this kind of study will be obvious at once; for unless we grasp the *significance* of what is written we miss that which is of first concern. Moreover, this progressive, interpretative study of the Scriptures is really a necessary basis and preliminary to all the other kinds of study which we have mentioned.

Following this method, then, and with a view to determining the essential message of each book, as we take each of the different books in turn we shall set forth its *STRUCTURE*, by means of an analysis; its main movements in the form of a *SYNOPSIS*; and its special features by way of *SUGGESTION* for further study. We shall let each book tell us its secret and open its heart to us. We shall resolutely guard against forcing any artificial outline on any book of Scripture. To sacrifice exactness for the sake of smart alliteration is an impertinence when dealing with Divinely inspired writings. There are Bible teachers today, of a certain type, who excel in ingenious "skeletons." But an erroneous analysis, however adroitly drawn up, obscures the real and vital message of a book. As we proceed with our studies we shall see how often a book or passage lights up with new force or beauty when a true analysis is made of it.

It may be thought strange at first, perhaps, that we give some books fuller treatment and more detailed analysis than others. We would point out, therefore, that this variation is in accord with our purpose. The relative importance of things must not be gauged simply by the page-space which they occupy. As the one small diamond outvalues the large square of plate-glass, and as the epochal event of one day may dwarf the ordinary doings of decades, so in the Scriptures, while everything has its due place, there are things which stand out, as did Saul among the sons of Israel, head and shoulders above their fellows. Each part is important; but some parts are especially so.

Therefore our aim is to deal with each book or part in just such a way as will most effectively lay bare its special signifi-cance, and thus contribute most effectively toward a practical hold on the message of the Bible in its entirety. It is for this reason that we have given fuller treatment to the five books of Moses, which are the foundation of all else. It is for this reason, also, that we deal more in detail with a book like Leviticus, the words and symbols and types and ideas of which are interwoven with all that follows, right to the end of the Apocalypse, whereas we give comparatively brief treatment to 1 and 2 Chronicles, the contents of which, being historical, need to be grouped rather than minutely expounded. Our purpose is not that of a Commentary, in which the books, chapters, paragraphs and verses are successively annotated. Let it be borne in mind throughout that we are after the main meanings and special significances, with a view to getting the broad scope and comprehensive message of the whole.

Our Approach

A right *approach* to the Bible is of utmost importance. There is a movement today to popularise the Bible simply as *literature*. It is our careful opinion that such a movement has in it more of harm than of good. Amid the wonderful *diversity* of the Scriptures there is an even more wonderful *unity*. The sixty-six books are not simply a collection of writings; they are one book—one in the progressiveness of the revelation which they collectively unfold, one in the harmony of the structure which they collectively constitute, one in the spiritual unity of the message which they collectively declare. The Bible *as a whole* claims to be the word of God; and its claim is substantiated both by the nature of its contents and the history of its influence. If, then, this book is the word of *GOD* it cannot be read simply as literature! —not without forcing the mind to an artificial or evasive or dishonest attitude which must prove harmful. In the studies which we here commence we approach the Bible as being in its totality *the Word of God*; and in all our studying of it, therefore, we are seeking to learn, under the illumination of the Holy Spirit, the mind and the truth and the will of *God*.

In our study of the Bible, also, we need ever to guard against becoming so engrossed in the fascination of the *subject* that we lose sight of the *object*. As we have said, in these studies we want to get hold of the big, broad meanings in the wonderful old Book: but unless the meanings get hold of *us* our study will have failed of its vital objective. Our Lord Jesus Himself has taught us that *HE* is the focal theme of all the Scriptures; and everywhere, therefore, we want to see beyond the *written* word, to Him who is the *living* Word. And we want to see Him in such a way as causes us to love and trust Him the more. Dr. Jowett tells of a tourist who was travelling through some of Scotland's loveliest scenery, but who was so absorbed in his guide book that he never saw the loveliness through which he was passing. There can be Bible study of that sort, too. Our great object is to know the true God, to become more like Christ, and to be more fully possessed by the Holy Spirit. True Bible study will encompass that object, for the inspired pages of Holy writ live and thrill and glow with the presence of God!

Let us therefore come to the Scriptures very *reverently*, realising that they are inbreathed by the Holy Spirit, and that He, the Holy Spirit, "the Spirit of wisdom and unveiling" in the knowledge of God (Eph. i. 18), must be our Teacher. Let our prayer be: "Open Thou mine eyes, that I may behold wondrous things out of Thy law" (Ps. cxix. 18). And let the dominating motive in all our study of God's word be, in the words of Colossians i. 10: *"That ye might walk worthy of the Lord unto all pleasing, being fruitful in every good work, and increasing in the knowledge of God."*

This is the greatest book on earth,
    Unparalleled it stands;
Its author God, its truth Divine,
Inspired in every word and line,
    Tho' writ by human hands.

This is the living rock of truth
    Which all assaults defies.
O'er every stormy blast of time
It towers with majesty sublime;
    It lives, and never dies.

This is the volume of the Cross;
    Its saving truth is sure;
Its doctrine pure, its history true,
Its Gospel old, yet ever new,
    Shall evermore endure.

PRELIMINARY

The Bible as a Whole

WITH THE aforementioned method and motive clearly in our minds, we now open our Bible to explore this wonderful old Book of Books as far as the self-imposed limits of our present study-scheme will allow us. But before we actually make a start with Genesis, it will be helpful for us to take an anticipative view of the Bible as a whole.

Our Bible consists of sixty-six component parts. These are divided into two distinctive major collections, the Old Covenant scriptures and the New Covenant scriptures; or, as we commonly name them, the Old and New Testaments. But each of these two Testaments, the one consisting of thirty-nine books, the other of twenty-seven, is found to be arranged in certain clearly homogeneous groups; and in this connection careful investigation reveals the presence of a marvellous Divine design running through the whole.

THE OLD TESTAMENT

The First Seventeen

Take the Old Testament first. We start with Genesis, Exodus, Leviticus, Numbers and Deuteronomy. These obviously constitute a fivefold unity which marks them off at once as a separate group. They are all from one pen, that of Moses. They are all historical. They have always been known as the Five Books of Moses or the Pentateuch. Note, then, their number and their nature. As to their number, they are *five*. As to their nature, they are *historical*.

Next we find Joshua, Judges, Ruth, 1 Samuel, 2 Samuel, 1 Kings, 2 Kings, 1 Chronicles, 2 Chronicles, Ezra, Nehemiah, Esther. We instinctively stop at Esther, without going on to the Book of Job, because we are conscious that with Job we come to a very different kind of literature. Joshua to Esther are the twelve which make up the second main group of books in the Old Testament. Note the number and nature again. As to their number, they are *twelve*. As to their nature, they are again *historical*.

So, then, the first stretch of our Old Testament consists of *seventeen historical* books, falling into a natural sub-division of five and twelve. And there is a further sub-division in the twelve; for the first nine (Joshua to 2 Chronicles) are records of Israel's *occupancy* of Canaan, while the last three (Ezra, Nehemiah, Esther) concern the period after the *expulsion* from the land, and the repatriation of the "Remnant". Thus the seventeen historical books are really sub-divided into five (pre-Canaan), nine (in Canaan), and three (post-Exile).

The Middle Five

Next we find Job, Psalms, Proverbs, Ecclesiastes and the Song of Solomon. We need no telling to make another break at the end of the Song of Solomon, for immediately following it is the Book of the Prophet Isaiah, which obviously introduces another and quite different set of writings, i.e. those of the prophets. There is no doubt about it—Job, Psalms, Proverbs, Ecclesiastes and the Song of Solomon belong together and make up the third distinctive Old Testament group. All the preceding seventeen, as we have noted, are found to be historical; but these further five are not historical; they are individual and experiential. All of the foregoing seventeen historical books are national; but these five are not national, they are personal, and they deal mainly with the problems of the individual human heart. Moreover, the preceding seventeen are all written in prose, whereas these further five are not prose; they are poetry. So then, mark their number and their nature. As to their number, they are *five*. As to their nature, they are *experiential*.

The Remaining Seventeen

Finally, we come to another stretch of seventeen. This time it is the prophetical books: Isaiah, Jeremiah, Lamentations, Ezekiel, Daniel, Hosea, Joel, Amos, Obadiah, Jonah, Micah, Nahum, Habakkuk, Zephaniah, Haggai, Zechariah, Malachi. Obviously these seventeen belong together just as clearly as do the seventeen historical books. And just as we found the seventeen historical books sub-dividing themselves into five (Moses) and twelve (Joshua to Esther), so do we find it with these seventeen prophetical books. The first five are rightly termed the "*Major* Prophets", while the remaining twelve, which were always classed together as one book in the Jewish canon of the Old Testament (see Acts vii. 42), are known as the "*Minor* Prophets".

That this is no artificial distinction a moment's reflection will show. It is in Isaiah, Jeremiah, Ezekiel and Daniel that we find the basic ethical features of all Old Testament prophecy and the comprehensive scheme of Messianic prediction. In Isaiah the coming Messiah is seen both as the suffering Saviour and as the victorious Sovereign who reigns in world empire. In Jeremiah, where we also have Jehovah's full case against Israel, He is the righteous "Branch" of David and the ultimate Restorer of the judged and dispersed people. In Ezekiel, looking beyond intermediate judgments, we see Him as the perfect Shepherd-King in whose glorious reign the ideal temple of the future is erected. In Daniel, who gives us the most particularised programme of times and events in their successive order, we see the Messiah "cut off" without throne or kingdom, yet standing up at last as universal Emperor on the ruins of the crashed Gentile world-system.

The twelve "minor" prophets, though they amplify various aspects, do not determine the main shape of Messianic prophecy; they conform to the general frame already formed for us in Isaiah, Jeremiah, Ezekiel and Daniel.

Nor let it be thought that the poetic dirge, "Lamentations", is merely an addendum to Jeremiah. Not only does it have the marks of independence and separateness, but it also has a positional significance which we should not fail to note. It is the centre-point of the "major" prophets. That is, it divides Isaiah and Jeremiah on the one hand from Ezekiel and Daniel on the other. In other words, it intersects between the greatest two of the *pre*-exile prophets and the greatest two of the *post*-exile prophets. And it belongs there properly, for besides dividing them *positionally* it divides them *historically*. It monumentalises that toweringly and tragically significant event, which separates the pre-exile from the post-exile prophets, namely the destruction of Jerusalem, the abortion of the Davidic dynasty, and the scattering of the covenant people in a world-wide dispersion from which even yet, after 2,500 years, they have not been regathered, although providentially preserved as a distinct people.

Moreover, as the last twelve of the seventeen *historical* books further sub-divide themselves into nine and three, the first nine being *pre*-exilic, and the remaining three (Ezra, Nehemiah, Esther) being *post*-exilic, so is it with these twelve "minor" prophets, i.e. the first nine are all *pre*-exilic, while the remaining three (Haggai, Zechariah, Malachi) are *post*-exilic; and these two terminal trios, the last three *historical* books and the last three *prophetical*, have a reciprocal correspondence with each other.

Thus the thirty-nine books of our Old Testament fall into this orderly grouping of seventeen historical, five experiential, and seventeen prophetical, with both the seventeens sub-grouped into five and nine and three, and the five books which deal with the individual human heart placed right between the two seventeens, at the very heart of the Old Testament.

Is this accident or design? Think of it: over thirty writers contributed to the Old Testament, spaced out over twelve hundred years, writing in different places, to different parties, for different purposes, and little dreaming that their writings, besides being preserved through generations, were eventually to be compiled into that systematic plurality in unity which we now find in the Old Testament. When one reflects on this, surely one cannot be charged with fancifulness for thinking that behind the human writers there must have been a controlling divine design.

THE NEW TESTAMENT

Gospels and Acts

We turn to the New Testament now; and here we find equal order, with equally evident design. First we have Matthew, Mark, Luke, John, Acts. These are the only historical books of the New Testament, and are foundational to everything which follows, and therefore stand together. Note their number and their nature. As to their number, they are *five*. As to their nature, they are *historical*.

Christian Church Epistles

Next comes a group which just as plainly coheres as one subsidiary whole. It is that group of epistles which are all addressed to *Christian Churches*: Romans, 1 Corinthians, 2 Corinthians, Galatians, Ephesians, Philippians, Colossians, 1 and 2 Thessalonians. Note their number and their nature. As to their number, they are *nine*. As to their nature, they are *doctrinal*.

Pastoral Epistles

Then come four epistles which are another little group in themselves, namely, 1 Timothy, 2 Timothy, Titus, Philemon. These four are not written to Christian churches. They are *pastoral and personal*.

Hebrew Christian Epistles

Finally, we have another group of nine, that is, Hebrews, James, 1 Peter, 2 Peter, 1 and 2 and 3 John, Jude, Revelation (which is really an epistle of our Lord Himself: see the opening verse). These nine are not addressed to Christian churches as the other nine are; and indeed there is nothing in any of them about the Church mystical either. The first of them (Hebrews) is obviously addressed to the Hebrew nation as such. James, likewise, is addressed to "the twelve tribes which are scattered abroad". And Peter addresses his writing to "the sojourners of the Dispersion" (i.e., the Jews of the Dispersion). There is no need to go into further details to show that these nine epistles, Hebrews to the Apocalypse, are distinctively Hebrew in their standpoint and atmosphere, and they are rightly called the "Hebrew Christian Epistles".

A Wonderful Archway

Thus our New Testament consists of five historical books, making a solid, fivefold slab of basic fact beneath our feet; then, rising up on each side, like two beautifully wrought pillars, the nine Christian Church Epistles and the nine Hebrew Christian Epistles; and these two wonderful pillars are connected and arched by the four Pastoral Epistles, the whole making a wonderful archway of truth into the Church of Christ and the Kingdom of God, and reaching its high vertex in that transcendent epitome of

Christian truth, "Great is the mystery of godliness, God was mani-
fest in the flesh, justified in the Spirit, seen of angels, preached
unto the Gentiles, believed on in the world, received up into
glory". Yes, by its literary structure, the New Testament is a
wonderful *archway* into saving truth and everlasting blessedness.

The comparative and contrastive parallels between the two
ninefold groups of epistles is a study all in itself. Both groups start
with a great doctrinal treatise, Romans and Hebrews respectively.
Both groups end with an eschatological unveiling, 1 and 2 Thessalonians in the one case, and the book of the Revelation in the
other. Romans, at the beginning of the first group, shows us that
salvation in Christ is the *only* way. Hebrews, at the beginning of
the second group, shows us that salvation through Christ is the
better way. In Thessalonians, at the end of the first group, we see
the second coming of Christ especially in relation to the *Church*.
In Revelation at the end of the second group, we see the second
coming of Christ especially in relation to *Israel* and the *nations*.
And so on; for we might elaborate this much further.

This presence of plan and design does not only pertain to the
Bible in this general sense; it runs through all the different book-
groups considered separately; and the more we follow it through
in detail, so the more wonderful it becomes, until all possibility
of its being mere coincidence is eliminated by overwhelming
abundance of evidence that this is indeed the word of the living
God.

NEW TESTAMENT

EXPERIENCE : DOCTRINE		
9	4	9
CHRISTIAN CHURCH EPISTLES	PASTORAL AND PERSONAL	HEBREW CHRISTIAN EPISTLES

NEW TESTAMENT HISTORY				
5 HISTORIC FOUNDATIONS				
MATTHEW	MARK	LUKE	JOHN	ACTS

OLD TESTAMENT

HISTORY (17)			EXPERIENCE	PROPHECY (17)		
BASIC LAW 5	PRE-EXILE RECORDS 9	POST EXILE 3	FIVE INNER LIFE 3	BASIC PROPHECY 5	PRE-EXILE PROPHETS 9	POST EXILE 3
M O S E S	C A N A A N	N A N A L S	H E A R T	M A J O R	& T W E L V E	M I N O R

THE BOOK OF GENESIS (1)

Lesson Number 1

NOTE :—For this first study read the whole Book of Genesis through once or twice.

AUTHORSHIP OF THE PENTATEUCH

Again and again in these studies we shall briefly but carefully consider questions of authorship relating to different parts of Scripture. In the long-drawn-out battle between theological " Modernism " and evangelical conservatism, the biggest (as it was the first) of Bible authorship controversies has been about the authorship of the Pentateuch. Is it *Mosaic*, or a *mosaic*?

To attempt a commensurate review here is beyond our scope. Perhaps, however, it is scarcely needful; for a point is now reached historically where the controversy may be seen in comprehensive silhouette, and results may be safely judged. We believe it fair to say that the main arguments for the Mosaic authorship remain unshaken; those for composite and later authorship are now largely fallen to pieces. This is forcibly indicated in the following quotation from Sir Charles Marston.

" It is quite possible that portions of some of the books of the Old Testament are derived from earlier documents. But to suppose that a cut-and-dried method could be found of isolating them, which nevertheless was entirely useless for our contemporary literature, imposed a considerable strain on anyone's credulity. It raised questions as to how and when the original books of the Old Testament were written; and above all it raised questions of the literary facilities possessed by the Israelites from the time of Moses onwards. The critical methods met these questions by assuming that the Hebrews were more or less illiterate. The assumption has completely broken down. It will be seen, from the archaeological evidence . . . that the Israelites had, from the time of Moses onwards, at least three alphabetical scripts. First, what is known as the Sinai Hebrew; next, what is known as the Phoenician Hebrew; and lastly, after the captivity in Babylon, what is known as the Assyrian Hebrew. Those facts entirely change the whole literary problem. Oral transmission becomes inadmissible. And the theory of the institution and adoption of the Mosaic ritual many centuries after the time of Moses, becomes grotesque and absurd, in the light of what we now know of his time.

" So J., E. and P., the supposed authors of the Pentateuch, are becoming mere phantom scribes and fetishes of the imagination. They have made Old Testament study unattractive, they have wasted our time, and they have warped and confused our judgments on outside evidence. It has been assumed that they possessed some sort of prescriptive right and authority superior to the Sacred Text. In the clearer light that Science is casting, these shadows that have dimmed our days of study and devotion are silently stealing away."

THE BOOK OF GENESIS (1)

ALTHOUGH, in the sweep of its revelation, the Bible carries our minds back to patriarchal and primeval and even pre-Adamite eras of the earth, the Bible itself did not begin to be written until the time of Moses. As an *historical* revelation its commencement coincides with the third chapter of Exodus, which records the communication of God through the burning bush of Horeb, and synchronises with the eightieth year of Moses. All that precedes this chapter was already *past* when the writing of our Bible began; and all that is recorded in the foregoing chapters is designed to lead up to the great new movement in human history, and the wonderful new unfolding of Divine revelation, which here begins.

Genesis and the entire Bible.

The Bible is not the *earliest* revelation of God. Its own pages clearly convey that the first human pair and the antediluvians and the post-Flood patriarchs received Divine revelations; and it is not improbable that these were in some degree committed to written form. In Genesis we have a synopsis of all former revelation, sufficient to constitute a working introduction to the further revelation of God communicated to us in the Bible.

Moreover, besides being introductory, Genesis is *explanatory*. The other writings of the Bible are inseparably bound up with it inasmuch as it gives us the origin and initial explanation of all that follows. The major themes of Scripture may be compared to great rivers, ever deepening and broadening as they flow; and it is true to say that all these rivers have their rise in the watershed of Genesis. Or, to use an equally appropriate figure, as the massive trunk and widespreading branches of the oak are in the acorn, so, by implication and anticipation, all Scripture is in Genesis. Here we have in germ all that is later developed. It has been truly said that "the roots of all subsequent revelation are planted deep in Genesis, and whoever would truly comprehend that revelation must begin here."

Genesis and the Pentateuch.

The Bible opens with the Pentateuch, or five books of Moses, the name "Pentateuch" (Greek—*pente*, five; and *teuchos*, book) having come down from the Septuagint Version of the Old Testament (the translation of the Old Testament into Greek, which is said to have been made by seventy Alexandrian Jews about the third century B.C., and is called the Septuagint Version from *septuaginta*, the Latin for seventy). There is good reason, however, for believing that before ever the Septuagint Version was made the writings of Moses were recognised as fivefold. The Jews called them "the Law" or "the five fifths of the Law" or simply "the fifths." It is probable that originally the whole was one, divided into five sections, each having as its title its first word or words.

There is a spiritual *completeness* about the Pentateuch. Its five parts not only give us a consecutive history covering the first two thousand five hundred years of human history; they constitute a progressive spiritual unity, setting forth, in their main features, what has been described as "the order of the experience of the people of God in all ages."

In Genesis we have *ruin* through the sin of man. In Exodus we have *redemption* through the blood of the Lamb and the Spirit of power. In Leviticus we have *communion* on the ground of atonement. In Numbers we have *direction* during pilgrimage, by the overruling will of God. In Deuteronomy we have the double truth of renewed and completed *instruction*, and the pilgrim people brought to the pre-determined *destination*. Is not this truly "the order of the experience of the people of God in all ages"?

But besides this, these first five books of the Old Testament give us most unmistakably a progressive fivefold revelation of God in His relationship with His people. In Genesis we see the *sovereignty* of God in creation and in election (in the choosing of Abraham, Isaac, Jacob, and their descendants; and in covenanting the land of Canaan to them as their predestined inheritance). In Exodus we see the redeeming *power* of God in His deliverance of Israel from Egypt, "with a mighty hand and with an outstretched arm." In Leviticus we see the *holiness* of God in His insistence on the separation and sanctification of His redeemed people. In Numbers we see the *"goodness and severity"* of God, —severity toward the unbelieving generation which came up from Egypt but never entered the covenanted inheritance, and goodness toward their children, in providing, protecting, and preserving, till Canaan was occupied. In Deuteronomy we see the *faithfulness* of God,—faithful to His purpose, His promise, His people, in bringing the redeemed to the promised possession. Thus—

THE HUMAN SIDE

Genesis.   Ruin—through the sin of man.
Exodus.   Redemption—by "blood" and "power."
Leviticus.   Communion—on the ground of atonement.
Numbers.   Direction—guidance by the will of God.
Deuteronomy. Destination—through the faithfulness of God.

THE DIVINE SIDE

Genesis.   Divine sovereignty—in creation and election.
Exodus.   Divine power—in redemption and emancipation.
Leviticus.   Divine holiness—in separation and sanctification.
Numbers.   Divine goodness and severity—judging, caring.
Deuteronomy. Divine faithfulness—in discipline and destination.

Thus it is seen that these five parts of the Pentateuch are full of purpose and progress. They are the Bible in miniature.

Genesis and the Apocalypse.

It is important to recognise the relationship between Genesis and the last book of Scripture. There is a correspondence between them which at once suggests itself as being both a *proof* and a *product* of the fact that the Bible is a *completed* revelation. There is no adequate understanding of either of them without the other; but taken together they are mutually completive. There is no going back beyond the one, and no going forward beyond the other; nor is there in either case any *need* to do so. In broad outline and majestic language Genesis answers the question: "How did all begin?" In broad outline and majestic language Revelation answers the question: "How will all issue?" All that lies between them is development from the one to the other.

Note the *similarities* between Genesis and the Apocalypse. In both we have a new beginning, and a new order. In both we have the tree of life, the river, the bride, the walk of God with man; and in both paradises we have the same moral and spiritual ideals. God has never abandoned the Eden ideal for man; and although in the end the garden has given place to the city, the Eden ideal of holiness finally triumphs.

Mark the *contrasts* between the one book and the other. In Genesis we see the first paradise *closed* (iii. 23); in Revelation we see the new paradise *opened* (xxi. 25). In Genesis we see *dis*possession through human sin (iii. 24); in Revelation we see *re*possession through Divine grace (xxi. 24). In Genesis we see the "curse" imposed (iii. 17); in Revelation we see the "curse" removed (xxii. 3). In Genesis we see access to the tree of life disinherited, in Adam (iii. 24); in Revelation we see access to the tree of life *re*inherited, in Christ (xxii. 14). In Genesis we see the beginning of sorrow and death (iii. 16–19); in Revelation we read "there shall be no more death, neither sorrow" (xxi. 4). In Genesis we are shown a garden, into which defilement entered (iii. 6–7); in Revelation we are shown a city, of which it is written: "There shall in no wise enter into it any thing that defileth" (xxi. 27). In Genesis we see man's dominion broken, in the fall of the first man, Adam (iii. 19); in Revelation we see man's dominion restored, in the rule of the New Man, Christ (xxii. 5). In Genesis we see the evil triumph of the Serpent (iii. 13); in Revelation we see the ultimate triumph of the Lamb (xx. 10; xxii. 3). In Genesis we see the walk of God with man interrupted (iii. 8–10); in Revelation we see the walk of God with man resumed, and a great voice says from heaven, "Behold the tabernacle of God is with men, and He will dwell with them . . ." (xxi. 3).

Note the *completions* of the one book in the other. The Garden, in Genesis, gives place to the City, in the Apocalypse; and the one man has become the race. In Genesis we see human sin in its beginnings; in the Apocalypse we see it in its full and final developments, in the Harlot, the False Prophet, the Beast, and the Dragon. In Genesis we see sin causing *physical* death, on earth; in the Apocalypse we see sin issuing in the dread darkness of the "*second* death," in the beyond. In Genesis we have the *sentence* passed on Satan; in the Apocalypse we have the sentence *executed*. In Genesis we are given the *first promise* of a coming

Saviour and salvation; in the Apocalypse we see that promise in its final and glorious *fulfilment*. Genesis causes *anticipation*; the Apocalypse effects *realisation*. Genesis is the *foundation* stone of the Bible; the Apocalypse is the *capstone*.

THE STRUCTURE OF GENESIS

As we have said, all that goes before the third chapter of Exodus was already past when the writing of the Bible began. Let us stand, then, at that third chapter of Exodus and look back over what is recorded in Genesis, getting the main lines of perspective. It will be readily seen that Genesis is in two major divisions. All Bible students agree that the call and response of Abram constitute a quite new departure in the narrative, and mark off the two main parts of the book—the first part covering chapters one to eleven, and the second part chapters twelve to fifty.

This being so, we see how each part is arranged according to a significant fourfold plan. In the first part we have four outstanding *events*—the Creation, the Fall, the Flood, the Babel crisis. In the second part we have four outstanding *persons*—Abraham, Isaac, Jacob, Joseph. The entire contents of Genesis are arranged around and in relation to these four pivotal events in the one part, and these four pivotal figures in the other.

Seeing the pivotal events and figures of Genesis thus thrown into relief, we quickly perceive also the unifying idea running through what is recorded; and this gives us the principal significance of the book as a whole. Standing right at the beginning of the sixty-six books, Genesis would bring us to our knees in reverent obeisance before God as it exhibits to our eyes, and thunders in our ears, that truth which is to be learned before all others, in our dealings with God, in our interpretation of history, and in our study of Divine revelation, namely—*THE DIVINE SOVEREIGNTY*.

Looking back over the four great events of part one, and the four great figures of part two, we see that they constitute an impressive demonstration of the Divine sovereignty. In the first of the four *events*, we have the Divine sovereignty in *the physical creation*. In the second we have the Divine sovereignty in *human probation.* In the third we have the Divine sovereignty in *historical retribution.* In the fourth we have the Divine sovereignty in *racial distribution.* In these four great events we see the sovereignty of the Creator in His eternal priority, His moral authority, His judicial severity, and His governmental supremacy.

Turning to the second part of Genesis, we see the sovereignty of God in *regeneration.* The process of regeneration here outlined stands in sharp contrast to the process of *degeneration* in the first part of the book. From Adam to Abraham we see the course of *degeneration*: first, in the individual—Adam; then in the family —Cain and his descendants; then in the nations—the antediluvian civilisation; and then persisting throughout the race, as such, at Babel. Then there comes a new departure. We see the process of *regeneration* operating: first, in the individual—Abraham, Isaac, Jacob; then in the family—the sons of Jacob; then in the nation—Israel; all with a view to the ultimate regeneration of the race. In Abraham, Isaac, and Jacob we see Divine sovereignty in *election.* Abraham, although the youngest son, is chosen in preference to his two elder brothers. Isaac is chosen in preference to Ishmael, the elder son of Abraham. Jacob, although second to Esau, is chosen in preference to his brother. Running through it all we see the principle of Divine *election.* God chooses whom He will, in sovereign grace. Then, in the wonderful biography of Joseph, we see the sovereignty of God in *direction,*— in the overruling and infallible directing of all happenings, however seemingly contrary, to the predetermined end.

In the case of Abraham we see this sovereign election expressed by a supernatural *call*; for it is clear that God had directly intervened (see Gen. xii. 1–3).

In the case of Isaac, we see it expressed by a supernatural *birth.* Abraham had said, " Oh, that Ishmael might live before Thee! " (xvii. 18). But no! When Abraham is 100, and Sarah 90, the miracle-babe Isaac comes to them.

In the case of Jacob it is shown in supernatural *care.* First God saves him from Esau's knife; then meets him at Bethel; prospers him despite Laban's guile; saves him from the revengeful ire of his brother who comes to meet him with a band of four hundred men; and so it goes on, until at last when Jacob is dying, he blesses young Manasseh and Ephraim, "The Angel which redeemed me from all evil, bless the lads."

Finally, in Joseph, we see the Divine sovereignty in direction, exhibited in supernatural *control*, making all happenings to contribute to the predestined issue.

Thus, in these four men, we see a fourfold development—(1) supernatural call, (2) supernatural birth, (3) supernatural care, (4) supernatural control.

And so in this first book of Scripture we find that by marking the pivotal events and figures we come to understand the significance of the writing as a whole; and we may set the facts down as follows.

THE BOOK OF GENESIS

THE DIVINE SOVEREIGNTY—IN CREATION, HISTORY AND REDEMPTION

I. PRIMEVAL HISTORY (i.–xi.)

Four Outstanding Events

THE CREATION—Divine sovereignty in the physical creation.
God's eternal priority.
THE FALL—Divine sovereignty in human probation.
God's moral authority.
THE FLOOD—Divine sovereignty in historical retribution.
God's judicial severity.
THE BABEL CRISIS—Divine sovereignty in racial distribution.
God's governmental supremacy.

II. PATRIARCHAL HISTORY (xii.–l.).

Four Outstanding Persons

ABRAHAM—Divine sovereignty in election.
Supernatural *call*.
ISAAC—Divine sovereignty in election.
Supernatural *birth*.
JACOB—Divine sovereignty in election.
Supernatural *care*.
JOSEPH—Divine sovereignty in direction.
Supernatural *control*.

THE BOOK OF GENESIS (2)

Lesson Number 2

NOTE :—For this second study read thoroughly again (making notes of any impressive points) Genesis, chapters i. to xi.

In anticipation of our remarks concerning the geographical extent of the Flood, we would give a word of counsel. As we study our English Bible we should ever remember that we are dealing with a translation, not the original. A true understanding of the word used in the original may greatly affect our interpretation in many an instance. This need not discourage those who do not know Hebrew or Greek, for in these days wonderful facilities are provided. Without a doubt the greatest of these is Strong's Exhaustive Concordance, which, by a very easy system of reference, gives not only every occurrence of every word in the English, but also the Hebrew or Greek word so translated, also the English pronunciation, and every other English word, too, by which the same Hebrew or Greek word is translated in our English Bible—not to mention other excellent features. It is a possession beyond price to the Bible student. We cannot too highly recommend it. The looking up and following through of words used in the original is as enlightening as it is fascinating.

J. S. B.

THE BOOK OF GENESIS (2)

WE HAVE seen, in our first study, that the dominant idea in this Book of Genesis is *the sovereignty of God*. We have noted, also, that the book falls into two main parts. In the first part (i.–xi.) we have four outstanding *events*—the Creation, the Fall, the Flood, the Babel dispersion. In the second part (xii.–l.) we have four outstanding *persons*—Abraham, Isaac, Jacob, Joseph. We now briefly review the four super-events of part one.

The Creation

First, then, we go back to chapters i. and ii., to that transcendent initial event, *the Creation*. In the opening verse of the book we read: "In the beginning God created the heaven and the earth." This is not a human theory: it is a Divine "testimony." In Psalm xciii. 5 we read: "Thy testimonies are very sure." The word of God testifies concerning truths which are above the unaided intelligence of man, and beyond the farthest reach of human investigation. Genesis i. 1 is the first such "testimony." There is a polarity of difference between a theory and a "testimony" or "witness." A theory deals with the *interpretation* of facts. A witness deals with *the facts themselves*. It is vital to realize that this opening verse of Scripture is not merely the first postulate of a human philosophy, but the first testimony of a Divine revelation. It is the first great truth which God would have man to know: and man could not know it apart from the Divine testimony. We accept it as such, believing with the psalmist that "the testimony of Jehovah is sure, making wise the simple" (Ps. xix. 7).

This initial testimony of our faithful Creator stands sublime in its simplicity. There is no definition of God, no description of creation, and no declaration of date. Positive and complete in itself, it yet leaves room for all subsequent development in Scripture and all discovery by Science. It is axiomatic. As geometry is built upon certain axiomatic truths, so the one foundation axiom of the Bible is laid down in its first sentence.

It is fashionable today to profess disbelief in miracles. Accept this first sentence of Scripture, and there will be little difficulty in accepting all the miracles that follow; for the less are included in the greater. Note, also, that in this first, basal pronouncement of Scripture there is a denial of all the principal false philosophies which men have propounded.

> "In the beginning *God*"—that denies Atheism with its doctrine of *no* God.
>
> "In the beginning God"—that denies Polytheism with its doctrine of *many* gods.
>
> "In the beginning *God created*"—that denies Fatalism with its doctrine of *chance*.
>
> "In the beginning *God created*"—that denies Evolution with its doctrine of infinite *becoming*.
>
> "God created *heaven and earth*"—that denies Pantheism which makes God and the universe identical.
>
> "God created *heaven and earth*"—that denies Materialism which asserts the eternity of matter.

Thus, this first "testimony" of Jehovah is not only a declaration of Divine truth, but a repudiation of human error.

But what of verse 2—"And the earth was without form, and void; and darkness was upon the face of the deep"? Does this describe the first condition of the earth after its creation? And what of the six "days" which follow in this first chapter? Do they describe the *process* of the original creation? We need to think and speak very clearly here, for there is much misunderstanding. If the Bible is the inspired word of God, nothing can be more important than to understand rightly its teaching as to the origin of things. Yet the fact is, alas, that no chapters in the Bible have been more misunderstood and misrepresented than these first two chapters of Genesis. It is quite correct to say that in these two chapters we have a record of "creation" (for we have the original creation of the universe stated in chapter i. 1, and the subsequent creation of the present animal order in verse 21, and the creation of man in verse 27); yet the statement needs qualifying and explaining.

A discrimination must be made (the Bible certainly makes it) between the original creation of the earth and its subsequent *reconstruction* with a view to its becoming the habitation of *man*. It cannot be too strongly emphasised that the six "days" in this first chapter of Genesis do *not* describe the original creation of the earth. Those who suppose or assert this are obliged to treat the six "days" as vast periods of time, so as to square Genesis with what modern science has shown us concerning the vast antiquity of our earth. Yet in all truth they fail thus to reconcile Genesis and geology; and what is worse, they involve the Scripture itself in unresolvable self-contradictions. We do not purpose to go into all that just here, but we submit a brief addendum on the matter at the end of this present study.

That second verse, which says that the earth was "waste and void," does not, as the many think, describe the first condition of the earth after its creation. It alludes to a cataclysm which desolated the earth later. Verses 1 and 2 have no logical connection. There is a break between them, the duration of which is not known. Undoubtedly verse 2 should read, "And the earth *became* (not just 'was') without form and void . . . " The same Hebrew word here used is so rendered in chapter ii. 7—"Man *became* a living soul" (not to mention many other such instances, in some of which the rendering is, "it came to pass"). Modern geology furnishes data proving the immense age of our globe. Genesis has no controversy with geology on that score. Between the first two verses of Genesis there is ample scope for all the geologic eras. None can say what lapse of ages lies between them.

So, then, the first verse of Genesis simply states the fact of the original creation, and leaves it there, in the dateless past. Then verse 2 tells of a chaos which came to this earth later. And then *the six "days" which follow describe the re-formation of the earth with a view to its becoming the habitation of man*. What brought about the cataclysm which laid the earth "waste and void" we do not know with any certainty. Scripture does seem to give certain veiled indications that it had to do with a pre-Adamite rebellion and judgment of Lucifer and associated angel-beings (see Isa. xiv. 9–17; Jer. iv. 23–7; Ezek. xxviii. 12–18, where the language certainly transcends any merely local or temporal limits). It is not within our present purpose to go into these things here. What we do re-emphasise is that these six "days" in the first chapter of Genesis do *not* describe the original creation. Nowhere in Scripture are they said to be an account of the original creation. During the first four days no creative act is recorded. It is only when we come to the animals and man that the Hebrew word for "create" is used (verses 21 and 27). In a word, these six days give the account of a *new* beginning; but they are not the *first* beginning. When once this is clearly appreciated the supposed conflict between Genesis and geology dies away.

Our final remarks here about these six "days" must be to point out the *process* and the *progress* and the *purpose* which they exhibit. From the very first we find the earth swathed about by "the Spirit of Elohim" (i. 2); and at each stage of the reconstruction we read that "God *said*." Thus we have the *will* of God, expressed by the *word* of God, and executed by the *Spirit* of God. Such is the process here exhibited. And this process expresses itself in an orderly six-fold *progress* culminating in man. In man we see the crowning *purpose* of the whole.

Man the Crown

In chapter ii *the creation and first condition of Adam* are described. There are four movements—production, provision, probation, progression. The act of *production* is narrated in verse 7. Man is formed of "the dust of the ground," yet he is inbreathed of God with the "breath of lives." Behold his littleness and his loftiness!—his earthliness and heavenliness! Next, in verses 8–14, we see the Divine *provision* for man. It was provision in perfection and profusion. Next, in verses 15–17, we see man placed under *probation*. Man's liberty was to be conditioned by loyalty. Amid many provisions there was just one prohibition. This constituted the point of probation. Finally, note the *progression* as indicated in verses 18–25. Point by point there is forward movement. This is seen in the relation between man and the animals; in the calling forth of the latent faculty of speech; and supremely in the provision of Eve for that deeper need of Adam, and in that perfect first marriage-bliss of Eden. Thus there is *production* in the likeness of God; *provision* for the body, *probation* for the mind, and *progression* to the point of heart-satisfaction. In these four movements we see the *MAN*, the *SERVANT*, the *KING*, the *HUSBAND*.

The Fall

That sin, with all its attendant sufferings, exists throughout our world is plain to all. How did it get in? The Scripture explanation is given in Genesis iii. It is not our purpose here to *vindicate* the Scripture explanation against the contrary opinions of men. We are touching on it expositorily, not controversially. We accept the Scripture explanation; and there are three things which make up the account—(i) the tempting, (ii) the yielding, (iii) the results.

As for *the tempting* (verses 1–6), we note first that temptation was permitted. It is not easy to see how it could have been otherwise in the educating of a rational and volitional being such as man. The real tragedy is that there was a tempter. The fact that man was under the simple probation mentioned in chapter ii. 17 made him liable to temptation. But, mark, the tempter could *only* tempt. There *need not* have been sin. And there was *no reason* to yield. We note, too, that the temptation was introduced to Eve in solitariness. This is Satan's common method. And again, the temptation was connected with the beautiful: its real character was concealed. There was also a gradual growth in the strength of the temptation. First, God's word is merely questioned (verse 1). Then it is flatly contradicted (verse 4). And then, as the tempted one foolishly continues to listen, the very motive behind God's word is maligned (verse 5).

As for *the yielding* (verse 6), we see that Satan first captured the ear, then the eye, then the inward desire, and finally the will. Eve allowed her ear to listen to the tempter. Then she allowed her eye to feed on the object of temptation. Then she allowed desire to run away with the will. Compare verse 6 with 1 John ii. 16. "When the woman saw that the tree was good for food"—*the lust of the flesh*. "And that it was pleasant to the eyes"—*the lust of the eyes*. "And a tree to be desired to make one wise"—*the pride of life*. The first temptation, in Eden, and all the myriad temptations by which men and women have been lured into sin ever since, are fundamentally identical. And the tempter's great purpose is ever to divorce the will of man more and more from the will of God. It is important to note that God had made it as easy as could be to resist such temptation. Adam and Eve had been forewarned concerning the thing which Satan sought to make them do. See chapter ii. 17 with iii. 3. The command was plain. The warning was emphatic. Obedience was easy, for God had surrounded them with abundant satisfactions, and given them the most distinguished place in His earth creation. Finally, it is well to compare the Genesis account of the yielding with I Timothy ii. 14. Eve was "beguiled," but Adam was not. His was a clear choice, so it would seem, to be one with Eve in her fall.

As for *the results* (verses 7–24), note the following points. Satan had said that their eyes would be opened and that they should know good and evil (verse 5). There was a mocking fulfilment now. Their eyes *were* "opened"!—and they "knew"!—but what an eye-opening, and what a knowing!—"The eyes of them both were opened, and they knew that they were naked." There was innocency no longer. That was the first result. We note now the first appearance of *shame*—"They sewed fig leaves together, and made themselves aprons." Thank God for the sense of shame which He has put in human nature! It has saved mankind from many evils. A sense of shame—that was the second result. But note also that there was evidently a change in *the human body*. In Romans viii. 3 we read that Christ came "in the likeness of sinful flesh." That cannot mean that our Lord's human nature was in any way infected by sin. How then was He in the likeness of *sinful* flesh? The answer is that although our Lord was absolutely sinless He did not have about His body the pristine glory, the original glory of unfallen man, in Eden. The inference is that before the Fall there was a radiant glory about the bodies of Adam and Eve which was itself their resplendent covering. We are told that the very skin of Moses' face shone after his forty days of communion with God on Sinai. What then must have been the shining beauty of that as yet sinless pair in lovely Eden? Bathed in the glory-light of that unsullied communion with God, their whole bodies must have shone. But immediately upon the Fall that glory departed, and "they knew that they were naked." That was the third result.

Nor was that all. There was a tragic *inward* change. There suddenly sprang into consciousness a strange war within where all had hitherto been love and joy and peace. There came the terror of a newly-awakened faculty—the faculty of *conscience*. Thus, with the first sin came the first *fear*: Adam and his wife fled from God and tried to hide from Him! That was the fourth result—and note that there does not seem to have been any humble contrition, even when the sin was exposed before God. There had come about a spiritual alienation of man from God. The reign of spiritual death had set in. And besides all this, man is now expelled from the Garden wherein is the Tree of Life; the ground is cursed; the Serpent is cursed; man is given the headship over woman; and God provides clothes for Adam and Eve. Yet, amid judgment, God remembers mercy, and the first great promise of the coming Saviour is given in verse 15. The full music is to be developed as time goes on and as the Scripture revelation unfolds; but here in Genesis iii. 15 the first few notes are struck, in the promise that the "seed of the woman" should break the head of the serpent.

The Flood

If there is one period of history more than another about which we could wish for fuller information, it is the antediluvian, the period between the Fall and the Flood. The Genesis narrative is severely reticent, and that for a plain reason. Sixteen hundred years are packed into two pages, so that, whatever else we may or may not see, we may not miss the significant connection between the Fall and the Flood. The inspired writer omits all that is not vital to his purpose. Biblical narrative is never concerned with the mere lapse of time, but with the moral significance of events. There is an almost dramatic development from the Fall to the Flood. Let us mark it clearly. In chapter iii. we have the Fall. In chapter iv. we have Cain and the Cain line—"the sons of men." In chapter v. we have Seth and the Seth line— "the sons of God." In chapter vi. the two lines cross, with tragic moral results. In chapter vii. judgment falls—the Flood. This dramatic sequence, once seen, can never be forgotten. The separation of the two lines was vital. Their confusion was fatal. The resultant moral condition was appalling. The corruption was extreme. Divine intervention became unavoidable. Retribution was inevitable. The Flood came, both as an act of judgment and as a moral salvage measure. This is the first great Bible lesson on the indispensability of separation and no-compromise. The Divine insistence all the way through is that the spiritual seed shall "come out and be separate."

There are those who have held that "the sons of God" spoken of in chapter vi. were fallen angels, that is, the "angels which kept not their first estate, but left their own habitation," who are referred to in Jude 6. The late Dr. E. W. Bullinger, that able but all-too-often fanciful and unreliable exegete, sponsors this idea. A little reflection will show how preposterous it is. The angels are spirit beings. They are sexless, and therefore are not capable either of sensuous experience or of sexual processes: nor are they capable of reproduction. As for the suggestion that these evil angels somehow took human bodies to themselves and thus became capable of sex functions, it is sheer absurdity, as anyone can see. Both on psychological and physiological grounds it is unthinkable. We all know what an exquisitely delicate, sensitive, intricate inter-reaction there is between the human body and the human mind or soul. This is because soul and body came into being together and are mysteriously united *in one human personality*. Thus it is that the sensations of the body become experiences of the mind. Now if angels merely took bodies, and indwelt them for the time being, their doing so could not have made them in the slightest degree able to experience the sensations of those bodies, for the angels and those bodies were not united in one personality, as is the case with the human mind and body. Indeed, the bodies could not have been bodies of flesh and blood, for without being inhabited by the human spirit the human flesh-and-blood body dies. When our Lord Jesus came into this world to be our Saviour, He did not merely take to Himself a human body and inhabit it for the time being. That would not have made Him human. That would not have been real incarnation. The Son of God not only took a human body, He took to Himself our human *nature*; and to do this He had to be *born*. If, then, these "sons of God" in Genesis were the fallen angels, the only way they could have become human and have married and have had children (vi. 1, 4) is by their having undergone a real human *birth*—that is, by their having been incarnated and born of human mothers but without human fathers! To think that this happened is preposterous. Bullinger asserts that "sons of God" is a description only used of those who are *direct* creations of God—that is, of the angels, of the first man, Adam (Luke iii. 38), and of those in the present dispensation who are a "new creation" in Christ (2 Cor. v. 17;

Rom. viii. 14, etc.): but he surely forgets verses like Isaiah xliii. 6 and xlv. 11, where the expression "My sons" is equivalent to "Sons of God." Let us dismiss completely from our minds, then, the strange idea that these "sons of God" in Genesis were the fallen angels, who left "their first estate" in order to cohabit with women of the earth. Besides the objections which we have already raised to it, surely the impression which Scripture conveys to us is that the fall of these angels—like that of Satan—occurred before ever man was created upon the earth.

Was the Flood in Noah's day universal? As to the *fact* of the Flood, the testimony of universal tradition and of twentieth-century archaeology have put that finally beyond doubt: but was the Flood *universal*? To discuss this question adequately would require space far exceeding the limits of our present purpose; but there are two or three basically important facts which we cannot leave unmentioned. First, let us clearly understand that it is not vital to the inspiration of the Scriptures to maintain that the Noachian Flood was universal. That expression "the earth," which comes so often in the Biblical account, does not bind us to this, for the Hebrew word (*eretz*) which is translated as "earth" frequently means one country or locality merely. For instance, in the Divine call to Abram, "Get thee out of thy country," the word is *eretz*; and in very many other places *eretz* is given as "land." Similarly, the Hebrew word (*har*) which is translated as "mountain" (vii. 20) is a word of variable connotation. It may mean little more than hillocks, or uplands, as well as mountains proper. It is the word which is used again and again in the title, "Mount Zion." Clearly, we are not intended to picture Noah and the Ark as borne aloft above Alps and Himalayas, where through sheer weight the waters would become part of the everlasting snows and ice, where the Ark, in fact, would have become buried in ice for several thousands of feet, and where, even if such ice-burial could have been somehow overcome, life in the Ark would have been impossible apart from some miraculous system of "central heating"! There is a legitimate and idiomatic use of hyperbole in the Hebrew language of the Old Testament, just as there is in the English of today. When the cricket spectator tells us that the batsman sent the ball spinning "miles away" we appreciate the meaning at once. Even so, when Moses speaks of cities "fenced up to heaven"

(Deut. ix. 1) we recognise legitimate hyperbole; and similarly, when he says that the waters of the Flood covered all the hills that were "under the whole heaven" (Gen. vii. 19) we recognise the same hyperbolic usage as in Deuteronomy ii. 25, where the very same expression, "under the whole heaven," occurs with an obviously limited connotation. As a matter of fact the depth of the waters is given to us in Genesis vii. 20; and hyperbolisms must always be read in the light of literal statements and figures. (See our note concerning Strong's Exhaustive Concordance, preceding this present study.) Much more might be said along this line, but we have said enough to show that the inspiration of the Scripture is not at the mercy of our proving that the Flood was universal.

Another word which we must add is that the Noachian Flood must not be confounded with *the prehistoric flood* of which our geologists speak. All round the crust of this planet there are the marks of a vast flood; but these are not such as could have been left by an inundation of such short duration as that in Noah's day, even if that in Noah's day was universal. The flood to which geology bears witness is that of Genesis i. 2. It is to this, also, that 2 Peter iii. 5 refers.

And we note, finally, that when the whole Adamic race was destroyed, there was one man and his family who "found grace" in the sight of God. "Noah was a righteous man, and pure in his generations; and Noah walked with God." This man and his family were spared: and this man, be it noted, was the *vital* man. He was the tenth man from Adam *in the Messianic line,* from which the world's Saviour was to come in "the fulness of the time." Satan may do his worst, and man may sink to his lowest, and judgment may fall to the utmost; but the ultimate purpose of Jehovah cannot be thwarted. It moves on, and will yet triumph in a "new heavens and a new earth" wherein shall be righteousness and undimmed glory.

The Babal Dispersion

We must not think of the pre-Flood age as one of primitive crudity. The indications are that it was the most remarkable civilisation our race has ever known. Human longevity in that era, uniformity of language, nearness to the original Divine revelation, and the freer communication between God and men—think what these must have meant. We get significant hints as to the arts and industries of that time in Genesis iv. 20-4. But that first civilisation, with its accumulations of knowledge and experience, its treasures of art and literature, its agriculture and industries, is now gone, and the Adamic race is to have a new start in Noah and his three sons with their families.

Marked restraints are now imposed. The duration of human life is now greatly curtailed. The length of a generation is much shorter. The soil takes more toil now and gives less in return; and "flesh" is therefore now included in man's diet. A restraint of "fear" towards man, also, has to be put upon the beasts. The restraint of the death-penalty is put upon the slaying of man by man (which "violence" had become rife in the pre-Flood days: vi. 11, 13). Amid these restraints the faithfulness of God stands out in the sign of the rainbow. The Divine promise was necessary. It gave man an assured hope for the future.

But there was another restraint to be imposed, namely, *the confusion of tongues* (xi. 1-9). The essential fact to grasp is that the pluralising of human language was a culminating restraint-measure. It was precipitated by a human confederacy to establish a big racial centre, with a high astral tower. We must not attribute to those long-ago builders the stupidity of imagining that they could build a tower right up to heaven. In chapter xi. 4 the words *"may reach"* are in italics, indicating that they do not come in the original. The verse does not really relate to the height of the tower. What it says is, *"And his top with the heavens"*, that is, with an astronomical planisphere, Zodiac pictures, and drawings of the constellations—just such as we find in the ancient temples of Esneh and Denderah in Egypt. Perhaps we ought to give the late Lieut.-Gen. Chesney's corroboration of this. After describing other discoveries among the ruins of Babylon, he says: "About five miles S.W. of Hillah, the most remarkable of all the ruins, the *Birs Nimroud* of the Arabs, rises to a height of 153 feet above the plain from a base covering a square of 400 feet, or almost four acres. It was constructed of kiln-dried bricks in seven stages to correspond with the planets to which they were dedicated: the lowermost black, the colour of Saturn; the next orange, for Jupiter; the third red, for Mars; and so on. These stages were surmounted by a lofty tower, on the summit of which, we are told, were the signs of the Zodiac and other astronomical figures; thus having (as it should have been translated) *a representation of the heavens*, instead of 'a top which reached unto heaven.'" We ourselves would not go so far as to claim that these are the remains of the original tower; but beyond a doubt they illustrate its nature and dimensions.

The Babel crisis probably occurred some three hundred years after the Flood. In chapter x. 25 we are told that it was in Peleg's days that "the earth was divided" (as happened at the confusion of tongues: xi. 9). Peleg died 340 years after the Flood, as can easily be reckoned in chapter xi. 10–19. The Babel tower was designed to hand down antediluvian traditions. Its wrongness lay in the fact that its builders were defying the Divine command to spread abroad and replenish the earth. "Let us make us a name!" exclaim the builders. "Let us not be scattered abroad upon the face of the whole earth." Dr. Alfred Edersheim comments: "Such words breathe the spirit of 'Babylon' in all ages. Assuredly their meaning is 'Let us rebel!'—for not only would the Divine purpose of peopling the earth have thus been frustrated, but such a world-empire would have been a defiance to God and to the kingdom of God, even as its motive was pride and ambition."

We cannot stay here to discuss the greatness of Babel, the capital of Nimrod's kingdom; but from this time onward Babel, or Babylon, becomes the symbol-city of "this present evil world," energised, as it is, by the arch-rebel, Satan. The utter destruction of the historic Babylon, which duly happened in fulfilment of predictions like that in Isaiah xiii. 19–22, is one of the wonders of Biblical prophecy. But Babylon lives on in "mystery" form, as we find in the Book of the Revelation; and the destruction of the *historic* Babylon typifies the coming crash of the "*mystery*" Babylon and the present world system.

NOTE. It occurs to us to mention that those who may be interested in a further consideration of those "sons of God" in Genesis vi will find a much fuller treatment of the subject in the last chapter of the author's book, *Studies in Problem Texts.*

ADDENDUM TO LESSON 2

Genesis i. 2, and the six "days"

It is supposed by many that the words, "without form, and void," in Genesis i. 2, describe the first condition of the earth after its creation, and that the six "days" of chapter i. are therefore the six successive stages of the original creation-process; but the more one examines this the less tenable it becomes.

To begin with, *it occasions needless conflict between Scripture and Science*. According to reckoning based on Bible chronology, the race of Adam did not appear on this earth until six or seven thousand years ago; but modern geology has now shown beyond doubt that the earth existed immense ages before then. How are we to account, then, for that vast period of the earth's existence before the time when, according to the Bible, the Adamic race first appeared? If we say there is no break between the first two verses of Genesis, and that the words, "without form, and void," in verse 2, describe the first condition of the earth at its creation, away back beyond all the geologic ages, then, of course, the only way we can fit in the vast expanse of time between the creation of the earth and the comparatively recent appearance of man is to say that the six "days" of Genesis i. were six great *ages*, and that man appeared somewhere in the sixth.

But this lands us in a difficulty. These great ages, we are assured, would cover tens of thousands of years each, which means that man, if created somewhere in the sixth, must have been at least some thousands of years old at the time when, according to Genesis Adam was in Eden; whereas the clear teaching of Genesis is that even as late as the birth of Seth, Adam was only 130 years old (Gen. v. 3). So, then, on this score alone, if we are to accept the plain words of Scripture, yet at the same time avoid hopeless disagreement with the well-established findings of modern geology, we simply cannot hold that Genesis i. 2 describes the original state of the earth at its creation. Genesis and geology are reconciled, however, when we see that between verses 1 and 2 there is a gap sufficient to cover all the geologic ages, and that the six "days" describe, not the original creation of the earth, but its reconstruction, ages later, to become the habitation of man.

This geological difficulty increases upon further consideration. Vegetable remains from pre-Adamite ages are found in the earth's strata, as also are fossils of animals which had eyes. It is noteworthy that in the six days of Genesis no beings having eyes were created until after the fourth day, when the sun was caused to shine on the earth. *How shall we explain these pre-Adamite vegetables, and these*

45

animals having eyes? If we deny the break between the first two verses of Genesis, and say that the words "without form, and void" describe the earth at its original creation, we are shut up to three expedients, each of which is untenable.

First, we may say that the six days were six ordinary days of twenty-four hours each, *immediately following* the creation of the earth in its waste and void condition. But in that case Genesis is made to teach that the earth is only six or seven thousand years old (seeing that man was created on the sixth of those days, and the human race is only six or seven thousand years old), and at once geology parts company with Scripture.

Second, we may say that the six days were six ordinary days, but *not* immediately following the original creation of the earth in its waste and void condition. But in that case, during the vast period between the original creation of the earth and those six days of only a few thousand years ago, the earth must have *remained* in its condition of chaos and emptiness and darkness; and this again puts us at war with geology; for how can we account for that pre-Adamite vegetation, and the animals having eyes, in that dense, ages-long chaos and darkness?

Third, we may say that the six days were immense ages which followed upon the earth's original creation in its waste and void condition. But in that case the beginning of the present order of the animals and man is carried thousands and thousands of years farther back than any fair dealing with the language of Scripture allows.

If, however, we reject these three expedients, recognising that there is a break between the first two verses of Genesis, so that verse 1 refers to the original creation, and verse 2 refers to a desolation which occurred later, all such difficulty is removed. There is ample and intelligent play for all geological discoveries, and at the same time we do justice to the language of Scripture.

Still further, to say that verse 2 describes the state of the earth as originally created seems *incompatible with the wording of Genesis concerning the third and fourth days*. We read that on the third day God said: "Let the earth bring forth grass, the herb yielding seed, the fruit tree yielding fruit after its kind whose seed is in itself upon the earth." The wording here does not imply any creative act. The word "create" is not used. It is simply "bring forth." The life-germs of vegetation were already in the earth. Now if the earth was created "without form, and void," it is surely very difficult to account for this latent vegetation, unless we are thorough-going evolutionists holding the absurd idea that matter can produce life. Whether we say that the six days were six ordinary days of twenty-four hours each or six long ages, this difficulty remains. But the difficulty disappears as soon as we recognise that this second verse of Genesis refers to the wreck of an anterior creation in which both vegetable and animal life flourished. The "Scofield" Reference Bible well says on this point: "It is by no means necessary to suppose that the life-germ of seeds perished in the catastrophic judgment which overthrew the primitive order. With the restoration of dry land and light the earth would 'bring forth' as described. It was *animal* life which perished, the traces of which remain as fossils. Relegate fossils to the primitive creation, and no conflict of science with the Genesis cosmogony remains."

So with the fourth day: "God made two great lights." No creative act is here implied. The word "create" is not used. The Hebrew word translated as "made" does not involve origination. Sun, moon, stars were already there. How shall we explain this? If the second verse of Genesis adverts to the original creation, then there are difficulties right and left. We cannot say that the six days were ordinary days of twenty-four hours each, for that brings down the creation of the sun and moon and stars to the time when Adam was created, some six or seven thousand years ago, merely, and thus puts us hopelessly wrong on the age of the solar and sidereal systems. Yet neither can we say that the six days were long ages, for that would make the vegetation which thrived through that sunless *third* age an enigma. No such problem remains, however, when we see that although the first verse of Genesis refers to the original creation, the second verse refers to a subsequent disruption. Needless opposition to science is removed, and at the same time we pay a proper respect to the language of Scripture.

But now, quite apart from geological considerations, surely the Bible itself makes quite plain that the words "without form, and void" do not refer to the earth's first condition. Turn to Isaiah xlv. 18 —"Thus saith Jehovah that created the heavens, God Himself that formed the earth and made it: He hath established it: He created it not in vain, He formed it to be inhabited." The Hebrew word here translated "in vain" is that which is translated "without form" in Genesis i. 2. Isaiah xlv. 18 says that God did *not* create the earth "without form." Surely such a statement is conclusive. The prophet's argument is that the Jehovah of Israel is the Elohim of the creation: He did not create the *earth* a desolation, nor was the desolation of *Israel* the design of His providence, but the outcome of Israel's sin; and as the desolated earth was restored, so would a repentant Israel be restored. The reference to Genesis is incidental but none the less conclusive. God "did *not* create" the earth "without form"; therefore it must have become so at a *later* time. This at once implies that between the first two verses of Genesis there is an indefinite interval.

Besides this, the very wording of Genesis i. 2 gives evidence that it does not refer to the earth as it was originally. As we have already mentioned (in Lesson 2), the word "was," in our English version, should be "became." Undoubtedly, we should read it: "And the earth *became* waste and empty." Again and again, in the Old Testament, the same Hebrew verb is translated as "became," or even as "it came to pass." This is the verb in Genesis ii. 7—"Man *became* a living soul." Surely, then, when we read in Genesis i. 2, that "the earth *became* without form, and void," we are to understand that this desolation befell the earth at some point of time *after* its original creation, and that the six "days" which now follow on from verse 3 describe, not the original creation, but a process of *reconstruction*.

An ancillary argument to the same effect may also be drawn from the two Hebrew words which are here translated as "without form" and "void." The two Hebrew words are *tohu* and *bohu*; and it is noteworthy that the only two other places where the double expression occurs in Scripture are prophetic passages depicting terrible divine judgments. The first is Isaiah xxxiv. 11, where the two Hebrew words are translated "confusion" and "emptiness." The second is Jeremiah iv. 23, where the translation, like that in Genesis, is "without form" and "void." Examination of the context shows that, in the first passage *certainly*, and in the second *probably*, the prophet is describing calamity which envelops *the whole earth*. The prophets, of course, knew full well that the double expression, *tohu and bohu*, was used in the opening lines of Genesis; and since they now use the same expression to describe colossal crises of Divine retribution and desolation, is there not strong suggestion that they understood the occurrence of the expression in Genesis i. 2 similarly to indicate judgment and destruction, and *not* to refer to the earth's first condition after its original creation?

It is noteworthy, too, that the six days of Genesis i. are nowhere said in Scripture to be an account of the original creation. On the other hand, a careful differentiation is observed. During the first four of the six days no creative act is recorded. We are not told that God "created" the light. What is light? It is not a substance: it is the effect of ethereal vibrations; and modern science has shown how accurate are the words used in Genesis about it. We are not told that God "created" the waters: He "*divided*" them. We are not told that God "created" the "land," but that, having gathered the waters, He let the land "*appear*." We are not told that God "created" new vegetation, but that He said, "*Let the earth bring forth*." The Hebrew word for "create" is not once used until we come to the fifth and sixth days, when *sentient* life is introduced, in the creation of the animals and man. The Hebrew word for "create" is *bara*, and there are only three places in the first chapter of Genesis where it occurs—in verse 1, to describe the original act of creation; in verse 21, where we have the creation of the "living creatures" other than man; in verse 27, where we have the creation of man. Thus, there is not one place in these six days where the word "create" is used of mere matter —of the earth itself.

Now all this leads to a further important point. That is, it settles *the question as to whether the six "days" were ordinary days, or long ages.* When once we recognise the break between the first two verses of Genesis we can dispense with the artifice of forcing the six days to mean six geological ages. It is regrettable that some of our leading evangelical expositors should have resorted to this expedient. They have done so—with good motive, no doubt—to escape certain supposed geological difficulties. Apart from this these six days would have continued to be understood simply as six ordinary days of twenty-four hours each. There is certainly no *Scriptural* warrant for making them into periods; though, of course, those who adopt the period theory now try to make out that there *is*. What, then, are their pleas?

First, they say that the word "day" is frequently used in Scripture to mean a period. To this the answer is clear. Where the word is so used, its symbolic meaning is so plain that it can scarcely be misunderstood; and, further, the word is never so used when a *number* of days are being recorded—whether it be the hundred and fifty days of the Flood (Gen. viii. 3), or the forty days that Moses spent on the Mount (Exod. xxiv. 18) or the three days that Jonah was inside the great fish (Jonah i. 17), or the six days in which the Lord made heaven and earth (Exod. xx. 11), or other numbers of days.

Second, they say that ordinary days cannot be meant because the sun was only placed in relation to our earth on the fourth day. Again the answer is clear. Not only was there *light* before the fourth day, but we read, in connection with the very first day, "And God called the light *day*, and the darkness He called *night*" (i. 5). Sir Robert Anderson, who tried to uphold the period theory, was obliged to admit that "*this passage clearly indicates our ordinary day.*" Besides, men of science now know that the sun is not the only source of light.

Third, they say that the *seventh* day still continues (because the words, "the evening and the morning," are not used of it as of the other six), and that if the seventh day be thus a long period, then so must be the preceding six. But again the answer is clear. The words, "the evening and the morning" do not describe the *close* of each day. If they were meant to do that, the order would be inverted to "the morning and the evening." They rather describe the *commencement* of each day (and the Jews still reckon their days to commence from six o'clock in the evening). After describing each day's proceedings, the inspired writer goes back to the beginning of the day, to number it—"the evening and the morning were the first day," and so on. Those who argue that the seventh day still continues point us to Hebrews iv. 9—"There *remaineth* therefore a Sabbath rest to the people of God"—which is supposed to confirm their theory. But in all truth it is no confirmation at all, for it certainly does not teach or even suggest that God's seventh-day rest in Genesis still continues. On the contrary, it merely says "God *did* rest (not *does* rest) on the seventh day"; and our Lord's own word is "My Father *worketh* (not resteth) *even until now*, and I work" (John v. 17, R.V.)! The simple truth about that Hebrews passage is that there are *three* rests there mentioned—(1) God's seventh-day rest in Genesis: see chapter iv. 4,

(2) the Canaan rest which God provided for Israel: see chapter iii.
11, iv. 8, R.V.), and (3) the spiritual rest which is provided for ourselves in Christ, and of which the other two were types: see chapter
iv. 9–11. Now it is this *third* "rest" which *"remaineth"* (not God's
seventh-day rest in Genesis) as verses 8 and 9 make absolutely clear.

Thus fall to pieces the efforts to supply Scripture support for making
the six days of Genesis i. into six long periods. Mr. Sydney Collett has
well said, "Four things are mentioned in connection with these days
—viz. there was *light* and there was *darkness*, there was *evening* and
there was *morning*; and I contend that in the absence of any inspired
word to the contrary, we are bound by all known phenomena to
regard such words as defining natural days as we know them, of
twenty-four hours, one part of which was dark and the other part
light. It is to be feared that the period theory expositors scarcely
realise what the consequences would have been had those days of
Genesis i. really been long periods, as they suggest; for, taking a very
moderate estimate, each day is supposed to have occupied a period
representing ten million years of our time. Now let it be carefully
noted that, according to the Scriptures, those 'days' had only two
divisions—viz. darkness and light, intersected by evening and morning
i.e. the part that was called 'day' was *all light*, and that part which
was called 'night' was *all darkness*. There is no escape from this. So
that, according to the most recent of estimates, each 'day' must have
consisted of about five million years of unbroken darkness, followed
by about five million years of unbroken light! Now, seeing that the
trees and shrubs and grass were made on the third day, and the fowls
and other living creatures on the fifth day, one naturally asks what
became of these things after they were created, for it is certain that
no vegetable creation could possibly live—much less animal life—
through five million years of unbroken light, any more than it could
survive a similar period of unbroken darkness. And yet, if we accept
the period theory, this is what we should have to believe took place!"
There are other grotesque problems, also, involved in the period theory,
but we must leave them. Let it be settled in our minds that between
the first two verses of Genesis there is a break sufficient to cover all
the geologic ages, and that the six days of the earth's reconstruction
to become the abode of man were six days of twenty-four hours each.
We shall thus maintain a harmony both with Scripture and Science.
The six days of Genesis i describe a *new* beginning; but they are not
the *first* beginning. That vast, remote act by which the universe began
is summarised in the one brief, august, initial sentence—"In the
beginning God created the heaven and the earth."

THE BOOK OF GENESIS (3)

Lesson Number 3

NOTE :—For this third study read again Genesis, chapters vi. to ix. and xxxvii. to l.

"To constitute one thing the type of another, something more is wanted than mere resemblance. The former must not only resemble the latter, but must have been designed to resemble the latter. It must have been so designed in its original institution. It must have been designed as something preparatory to the latter. The type as well as the antitype must have been pre-ordained; and they must have been pre-ordained as constituent parts of the same general scheme of Divine providence. It is this previous design and this pre-ordained connection (together, of course, with the resemblance) which constitute the relation of type and antitype."

BISHOP MARSH, *Lectures*.

THE BOOK OF GENESIS (3)

THE TYPE-TEACHING OF GENESIS

(a) Old Testament Types in General

It is a fact that in no little degree the Old Testament Scriptures are permeated by latent typical meanings. Instances of their typical content are cited again and again in the New Testament, the following being specimens:

Persons
> "Adam . . . is a figure (*tupos* = type) of Him that was to come."—Rom. v. 14.
> "Melchizedek . . . made like unto (*aphomoioō* = made to resemble) the Son of God."—Heb. vii. 3.

Objects
> "That rock (of which the Israelites drank: see Exod. xvii.) was Christ."—1 Cor. x. 4.
> "The first Tabernacle . . . was a figure (*parabolē* = a parable or comparison)."—Heb. ix. 8–9.

Events
> "Noah . . . saved by water: the like figure (*antitupos* = antitype) even baptism, doth now save us."—1 Pet. iii. 21.
> "Abraham . . . received him (Isaac) from the dead, in a figure (*parabolē* = a simile)."—Heb. xi. 19.

But besides these and other similar instances, in which particular persons, objects, and events are said to be types, or figures, there are passages in the New Testament which equally clearly assert the *general* presence of types and symbols in the Old Testament Scriptures. Note the following:

"Now these things (see context) were our examples (lit:—
types for us)."—1 Cor. x. 6.

"All these things happened unto them for ensamples (*tupoi*=
types)."—1 Cor. x. 11.

"The Law . . . a shadow (dark outline or silhouette) of . . .
things to come."—Heb. x. 1.

Still further, there are other chapters, passages, and verses, in
the New Testament, which, while they do not actually assert the
fact of Old Testament typology, unmistakably *imply* it. We
think, for example, of our Lord's great discourse on the Manna,
in John vi.; Paul's contrastive exposition of the two ministrations—the "Letter" versus the "Spirit," in 2 Corinthians iii.–iv.;
the argument based upon Ishmael and Isaac, in Galatians iv.;
the Melchizedek and Aaronic passages in the epistle to the
Hebrews; our Lord's words about the Brazen Serpent; His
reference to Jonah's three days in the great fish; and the various
New Testament references to Christ as the Passover, the Firstfruits, the Mercy Seat, and the Lamb. Who can read the many
such passages without seeing in them the implication of Old
Testament typology?

Indeed, quite apart from this unanswerable New Testament
warrant for our belief in the typology of the Old Testament, such
are the circumstantial data in some cases that we could not fail
to perceive the presence of typical meanings, the similitudes
being far too clear and numerous to be merely coincidence. For
example, we are nowhere told that Joseph is a type of Christ,
yet who can read that wonderful Old Testament record, in the
light of New Testament history, without recognising in Joseph
—beloved, humiliated, exalted (not to mention the variety of
contributory details)—one of the clearest and fullest types of
Christ anywhere in the Scriptures?

Notwithstanding such circumstantial data, however, it is well
to be clear on this point, that the one all-sufficient authority for
Old Testament typology is the clear warrant of the New Testament—a warrant which, as we have shown, is clearly there. We
hold that the writers of the New Testament, like those of the
Old, were men inspired by the Spirit of God; and because of this
their word has a unique authority with us.

Values of Typology.

Now the presence of this latent typical content invests the Old Testament Scriptures with a wonderful new wealth of meaning; and it is regrettable, therefore, that the study of types has fallen into considerable disfavour in some quarters, because allegorical and mystical interpretations have been carried to foolish extravagances which are without any New Testament warrant whatever. Studied with good sense and a careful eye to New Testament teaching, the typology of the Old Testament is a priceless treasure-mine to the Bible student, and should on no account be neglected.

Besides this, the typology of the Old Testament furnishes a grand proof of its Divine inspiration. If this typical import does indeed inhere, how unanswerably it argues superhuman wisdom and foreknowledge!—for not only do the Old Testament types exhibit the consummate skill of the Divine Workman, they are a form of *prophecy*, forepicturing persons and things which were yet to be, and revealing the Divine anticipation of all future events. Indeed, they are the most wonderful kind of prophecy, for they give a colour and fulness and vividness of presentation which cannot be given in direct, unfigurative prediction.

Principles of Interpretation.

In our interpretation and application of types there are two precautions which should always be borne in mind. First: no doctrine or theory should ever be built upon a type or types independently of direct teaching elsewhere in Scripture. Types are meant to amplify and vivify doctrine, but not to originate it. They are illuminative but not foundational. Their purpose is to illustrate, not to formulate.

This is obvious in the very nature of the case, for if they are types, then they are not originals, but representations of things other than themselves; and unless the realities which they typify existed, the types themselves could not exist. Thus, types are dependent, and must not be used independently to authenticate doctrine.

Some time ago a preacher was heard advocating an elaborate theory, that at the Second Coming of Christ the saints must pass through successive heavens to undergo a process of purification before being presented at the throne of God, the whole theory being construed from a passage of somewhat doubtful import in Leviticus. That kind of thing is wrong and should be avoided.

Second: the parallelism between type and antitype should not be pressed to fanciful extremes. Types, it would seem, are not meant to be exact replicas of those things which they typify, but to enrich and illumine our understanding of the more essential features in the antitype. When the interpretation of types is carried into insignificant minutiae it degenerates into imaginative allegorising, which has many dangers.

Definition and Classification.

A type may be said to be any person, object, event, act, or institution Divinely adapted to represent some spiritual reality, or to prefigure some person or truth to be later revealed. Or, to put it another way—God has been pleased to invest certain persons, objects, events, acts, institutions, with a prefigurative meaning, so that besides having a real relationship with their own times they have had a significance reaching far forward into the future. (The word "institutions" in the above definitions covers all rules, rites, ceremonies, organisations, offices, times, places, instruments, implements, structures, furniture, robes, forms, colours, and numbers, which may be invested with a typical value.)

It is thus seen that types fall into four classes—persons, objects, events, institutions. It may be wise, also, to add here that no Old Testament person, object, event, or institution should be dogmatically asserted to be a type without clear New Testament warrant. It has been well said that types which are not thus authenticated have merely the authority of analogy and congruity.

(b) Types in Genesis

The foregoing remarks about Old Testament typology in general are made for two reasons—(1) it is well that while we are still in the early stages of this Bible Course we should have clear ideas regarding the presence and purpose of types; and (2) the book of Genesis, which we are now studying, is singularly rich in types. We submit, below, a catalogue of the more prominent types found in Genesis; and it will be seen that this first book of Scripture is specially marked by the prevalence of typical *persons*.

Persons.

Adam—type of Christ.
Eve—type of the Church.
Cain and Abel—carnal *v.* spiritual.
Enoch—the coming Translation.
Flood-survivors—the Church.
Lot—type of worldly believer.
Melchizedek—type of Christ.
Hagar and Sarah—Law *v.* Grace.
Ishmael and Isaac—Flesh *v.* Spirit.
Abraham—the Father (xxii. and xxiv.).
Isaac—Christ (xxii. and xxiv., etc.).
The Servant—the Spirit (xxiv.).
Rebekah—the Church (xxiv.).
Joseph—type of Christ.
Asenath—type of the Church.

Objects, Events, etc.

The Sun—type of Christ.
The Moon—type of the Church.
The Stars—type of saints.
The Six days—regeneration.
The Sabbath—spiritual rest.
Coats (iii. 21)—imputed righteousness.
Abel's lamb—type of Calvary.
The Flood—type of Judgment.
The Flood—regeneration (1 Pet. iii. 21).
The Ark—type of Christ.
The raven—the old nature.
The dove—the new nature.
Sodom Fire—final Judgment.
Ram (xxii.)—Christ our Substitute.
Egypt—type of the "World."

All of these are deep wells of truth; truth which, when it is brought to the surface, is as clear and fresh as it is deep and hidden. We recommend a careful consideration of them. Meanwhile we here pick out just two of them for brief treatment, as examples.

SPECIMEN TYPES IN GENESIS

(1) The Flood Survivors—a Type of the Church

Noah and those who were saved with him in the Ark are remarkably typical of Christian believers, and of the Church as a whole, in seven outstanding ways. (See Gen. vi.–ix.)

1. *Chosen.*

They were made party to a covenant (vi. 18). This covenant, in which they were chosen to salvation, was made 120 years before the Flood came, as it would seem from chapter vi. 3 with vi. 8.

Even so, Christian believers are a chosen people. "God hath from the beginning chosen you to salvation" (2 Thess. ii. 13). "He hath chosen us in Christ before the foundation of the world" (Eph. i. 4).

2. *Called.*

The Ark was entered in response to a Divine call. "The Lord said unto Noah: Come thou and all thy house into the Ark" (Gen. vii. 1).

Similarly, the true people of Christ, besides being eternally chosen in Him, are brought into their vital union with Christ by a Divine call. Thus we read in Romans viii. 30, "Moreover, whom He (God) did predestinate, them He also called." And in 1 Corinthians i. 9, we read, "God is faithful, by whom ye were called into the fellowship of His Son."

3. *Believers.*

Noah built the Ark, and entered it with his family, because he believed God (vii. 4 with vii. 7). See also Hebrews xi.—"By faith Noah . . . prepared an Ark."

So the people of Christ are distinctively *believers*. See Hebrews x. 39—"We are of them who believe to the saving of the soul"; (and many other passages). Note: Noah's faith made him *obedient* (Gen. vi. 22; vii. 5). So is it with the Christian (1 Pet. i. 22; Rom. xvi. 26; etc.). Noah's faith also brought him *imputed righteousness* (Heb. xi. 7 with Gen. vii. 1). So is it with the faith of the Christian believer (Rom. v. 1; x. 4).

4. *Separated.*

The Ark which effected salvation also involved separation. Noah was already separated from his wicked generation, in the spirit and tenor of his life. His entering the Ark was the outward culmination of it.

Christians also are a separated people. "They are not of the world" (John xvii. 16); "A people for God's own possession" (1 Pet. ii. 9, R.V.); and accordingly we are exhorted to make our separation a practical and obvious thing,—"Wherefore come out from among them, and be ye separate, saith the Lord" (2 Cor. vi. 17).

5. *Sealed.*

Besides being told that "they went in" to the Ark, we are told that "the Lord shut him in" (Gen. vii. 16). Thus were the occupants of the Ark inviolably sealed by God Himself unto the day of salvation after the Flood.

So are Christian believers sealed. "After that ye believed, ye were sealed with that Holy Spirit of promise" (Eph. i. 13). "Ye are sealed unto the day of redemption" (Eph. iv. 30). "He which stablisheth us with you in Christ, and hath anointed us, is God, who also hath sealed us" (2 Cor. i. 22).

6. *Risen.*

The higher the Flood prevailed the more the Ark rose above it. When the guilty world was beneath the Flood of judgment and death, those in the Ark were risen above it and were alive! (Gen. vii. 17–19). Thus in a remarkable figure the Ark meant life out of death.

This has its counterpart in the experience of the Christian. "The Ark was . . . the like figure whereunto baptism doth also now save us *by the resurrection of Jesus Christ*" (1 Pet. iii. 21). "Risen with Christ" (Col. iii. 1).

7. *Rewarded.*

They not only survived the Flood, they became the possessors of a new world (Gen. viii. 15–19). So is it to be with the redeemed in Christ. "We, according to His promise, look for new heavens

and a new earth, wherein dwelleth righteousness" (2 Pet. iii. 13).
See also Rev. xxi. 1–4.

Note the outstanding facts about Noah's occupation of the new
world: (1) Fragrant fellowship (viii. 20); (2) The "curse" stayed
(viii. 21); (3) A perpetual covenant (ix. 12, etc.). Even so is it in
the "new heaven and new earth" for which Christian believers
look (Rev. vii. 15–17; xxii. 3–5, with iv. 3).

(2) Joseph—a Type of Christ

A more intriguing story than that of Joseph was never written.
What makes it the more wonderful is that it is true. The supposition that it is a mythological post-Mosaic invention has now
been flung to the rubbish-heap of discredited modernist pre-
sumptions, by the spade of the archæologist. The story is true:
and one cannot read it thoughtfully without exclaiming, "Truth
is stranger than fiction!" It has been truly said that while we
are nowhere specifically notified that Joseph was a type of Christ,
"the analogies are too numerous to be accidental."

The life of Joseph runs in three periods. We see him first as
the beloved son, supreme in the regard of his father; then as
the suffering servant, rejected by his brethren; and, finally, as
the exalted saviour, lifted high over all in princely splendour and
administrative authority. Thus, in this triple way, Joseph becomes
the most complete single type of Christ anywhere in the Bible.

The Beloved Son.

1. *Pre-eminent in the love of the father.*—See xxxvii. 3. "Israel
loved Joseph more than all his children." So is Christ the well-
beloved Son in whom the Divine Father specially delights. See
Matt. iii. 17; Col. i. 13 (R.V.).

2. *Pre-eminent in filial honour.*—See xxxvii. 3. The tunic of
distinction and heirship was the outward attestation of the father's
regard. See John v. 37 (which probably refers to Voice and Dove
at Baptism): John v. 36; iii. 35.

3. *Pre-eminent in the Divine purposes.*—This is clearly revealed
in Joseph's dreams which were prophetic, as Jacob himself per-
ceived (xxxvii. 5–11). So is it with Christ. In Him God "framed
the ages" (Heb. i. 2). Also Eph. i. 9–10.

4. *Pre-eminent as the father's messenger.*—See xxxvii. 13–14.
"I will send thee unto them . . ." So is Christ the pre-eminent
Messenger of the Father. See Isaiah xlii. 1; Luke iv. 18 ("He
hath sent Me"); Heb. i. 1–2.

The Rejected Servant.

1. *Hated.* Joseph was hated by his brethren. Alas, this is also
true of Christ. Almost the same words are used of both. Compare xxxvii. 4 with John xv. 24; xxxvii. 8 with Luke xix. 14;
xxxvii. 18 with Matt. xxvi. 3–4; xxxvii. 19–20 with Matt. xxi. 38;
xxxvii. 11 with Matt. xxvii. 18.

2. *Sold.* Joseph was sold by his brethren for twenty pieces of
silver (xxxvii. 27–28) to Gentiles. Christ was sold for thirty
pieces of silver (Matt. xxvii. 9) and delivered to the Gentiles.
Joseph was stripped of his "coat." (See Matt. xxvii. 28.)

3. *Suffering.* How Joseph must have suffered! Compare
xxxvii. 23–4 with xlii. 21. See Joseph in the slave-market, then
under temptation (xxxix. 7–12), in further adversity (xxxix. 20).
All this has its counterpart in the gracious Antitype.

4. *Dead (in intent and figure).* About twenty years elapsed
between the selling of Joseph and the re-union. He was accounted
dead (xxvii. 31–4; xlii. 13 and 38; xliv. 20). So Christ, in actuality,
suffered death for our sakes.

The Exalted Saviour.

1. *Exalted as the wisdom and power of God to salvation.* See xli.
38–9, and Joseph's new name (xli. 45). Becomes the world's
bread-supplier (xli. 57). Administrator of affairs (xli. 40 with
xlvii. 14–26). So Christ (1 Cor. i. 24; Acts v. 31; John vi. 51;
v. 22).

2. *Exalted to the right hand of the throne.* See xli. 39–44. So is
Christ exalted to right hand of Majesty on high (Eph. i. 20–1;
Heb. i. 3). Joseph given Gentile bride (xli. 45). So bride of Christ,
the Church, during this age (Rom. xi. 25; Eph. iii. 6).

3. *Exalted among his own brethren.* See xlii. 6; xliii. 26. Revealed
to penitent brethren after sin brought home to them (xlv).
Becomes special succourer of Israel (xlvii. 11–12). Consummates
wonderful Divine plan (xlv. 5–9). Becomes (virtually) resurrected

(xlv. 28). All this paralleled in Antitype (Rev. i. 7; Jer. xxiii. 5–6; Eph. i. 9–10; Rev. i. 18).

4. *Exalted to an everlasting pre-eminence.* See xlix. 26. He was "separate from his brethren" in *character*, as records show. Scripture levels not one charge against Joseph, although more space is given to him than any other in Genesis. His exaltation was both a vindication and a reward. So with Christ. "He humbled Himself . . . wherefore God also hath highly exalted Him, etc." (Phil. ii. 5–11).

THE BOOK OF GENESIS (4)

Lesson Number 4

NOTE:—For this fourth study in Genesis re-read chapters xii. to l. Make notes of any striking bits or special thoughts in connection with the four outstanding characters, Abraham, Isaac, Jacob, Joseph.

"The scientific method is applicable to Scripture. First we trace scattered facts and truths, and then gather them up and arrange them. Like things are put together under a common designation, a process, based on similarities of nature and feature, attributes and characteristics, structure and relations, with a view to discovering what general law pervades them all, and supplies a broad basis for inference and deduction. This, the Baconian method of inductive philosophy which revolutionized scientific study is the true principle in Scripture research."

ARTHUR T. PIERSON, D.D.

THE BOOK OF GENESIS (4)

WE HERE reach our fourth and final study in the Book of Genesis. Thus far we have not given separate consideration to the four pivotal persons—Abraham, Isaac, Jacob, and Joseph, around whom the whole of the narrative revolves in the second part of the book (xii.–l.): but in this present study they come under review, though as part of a larger theme. We here give a final example of the type-teaching of Genesis, and then make certain closing suggestions about the further study of the book.

THE SEVEN GREAT MEN OF GENESIS

The principal personalities which are brought successively before us in the Book of Genesis all have a typical significance. That this is so seems clearly shown by New Testament references such as that in which Paul speaks of Ishmael and Isaac as representing the two covenants (Gal. iv. 22–7), and at the same time representing the two natures—that which is "after the flesh," and that which is "after the Spirit" (Gal. iv. 29). The priest-king Melchizedek is another example (Heb. vii.); and the first man of all, Adam, is declared to be a "figure (type) of Him that was to come" (Rom. v. 14).

Turning, then, to the main figures in Genesis, we observe that not only are some of them types of *persons* (as, for instance, Isaac and Joseph are types of Christ), but when viewed collectively they typify *progressive stages of spiritual experience.*

It goes almost without saying that the first man, Adam, besides being (in his relationships) a type of Christ, is (in his fallen state) a type of the natural man, or of unregenerate human nature. Again and again in the New Testament he is thus alluded to (Rom. vi. 6; Eph. iv. 22; Col. iii. 9). Now one of the leading purports of Genesis seems to be that of showing us all that which springs from the first Adam—all that which *can* spring from him, both of good and ill, both by nature and through the influence of Divine grace. This corresponds with the work of God's Spirit in our own hearts. The Holy Spirit first shows us what we are in Adam—what we are in ourselves, by nature, with a view to creating a sense of need, so that as the prodigal first "came to himself" and then came to the father, we also might know ourselves, and seek God. So then, in Genesis, we are first shown that which is in Adam, and that which naturally and normally springs from him.

If we want to know the awful capabilities of evil which are within Adamic human nature, we only need to trace the Cain line through its records of godless culture, earthly-mindedness, vanity, violence, and rebellion against God.

If we would know what can come from the same human material when under the renewing and transforming power of Divine grace, we need to follow the line of *the men of faith*.

There are seven such men in Genesis, standing out in unmistakable prominence. They are Abel, Enoch, Noah, Abraham, Isaac, Jacob, Joseph. That these seven do indeed have a peculiar prominence and significance is indicated by the fact that, under the guidance of the inspiring Spirit, the writer of the epistle to the Hebrews picks them out, as distinct from all others, for inclusion in that classic New Testament catalogue of Old Testament worthies, Hebrews xi. Let us note the *outstanding* characteristics of these men.

Abel.

What is the marked characteristic of Abel? His name, his choice of occupation, his sacrifice, and the reflective comments of the New Testament concerning him, together mark him out as being distinctively and representatively *the man of spiritual desire*.

Cain, the man of earthly desire, is the first-born. Abel, the man of spiritual desire, comes afterwards. The order is ever thus. "That is not first which is spiritual, but that which is natural; and afterward that which is spiritual" (I Cor. xv. 46). The name "Cain" means *possession*, pointing, as did Cain's life, to hopes fixed on earthly things. The name "Abel" means *exhalation* (or vapour), speaking of ascent to higher regions.

Cain was a "tiller of the ground"—with earthward interests and holdings. Abel was a "keeper of sheep"—the tent-dwelling pilgrim, desiring something beyond. Cain goes "out from the presence of the Lord," and busies himself with "cities" and with works "in brass and iron." Abel reaches after better things (Heb. xi. 16), seeking rest in God; suffering and dying in hope of the "better resurrection." Cain, ignoring sin and the Fall, is all for a religion of self-culture, offering the fruit of that which is under a curse. Abel, the man of spiritual aspiration, offers a sacrifice which is at once a confession of sin, and the expression of strong desire for fellowship with God on the ground of for-giveness through sacrifice and faith. Abel is *the man of spiritual desire*.

Enoch.

Next comes Enoch. What is the distinguishing characteristic here? Enoch is forever immortalised as the man who "walked with God." But what is the inner meaning of his walk with God, so far as the man himself is concerned. *Why* did Enoch walk with God? There was no compulsion about it. There was no *need* for him to walk with God, whether he wished to do so or not. The inner truth is that behind the *walk* was the *will*. There was a blending of Enoch's will with the will of God. It was this that made the walk possible. "Can two walk together except they be agreed?" (Amos iii. 3). Enoch put from him all controversy with the will of God, and accepted it in preference to his own.

But if behind the walk was the will, behind the will was the activity of that strange and vital faculty in human nature which we call *choice*. While it is true that God and Enoch walked together in a wonderful fellowship, yet the basic truth is not that God walked with Enoch, but (as indeed Genesis puts it) that "Enoch walked with God." It was not God going Enoch's way, but Enoch going God's way. Behind this walk with God was Enoch's full and final *choice* of God's will and way. His name means *dedicated*. Enoch is the man who chooses God's way— *the man of spiritual choice*.

Noah.

And now comes Noah. As a type-figure among the seven out-standing men of Genesis, the special significance attaching to Noah is unmistakable. From the New Testament we learn that

Noah's experience of being "saved through water" is a typical anticipation of *regeneration*, of which Christian baptism is the symbol (I Pet. iii. 21).

Of Noah, as well as of Enoch, it is written that he "walked with God"; but the type-emphasis is shifted a further stage forward in the account of Noah, so that now, consequent upon the spiritual *choice* indicated in the words "Noah walked with God," we see spiritual *renewal*, typified in Noah's passing through the waters of the Flood. First, in chapter six, we see Noah, the man of spiritual choice, still on the ground of the old world. Then, in chapter seven, we see him separated from the old world, in the ark (Christ), and by the water (regeneration). Then, in chapters eight and nine, we see him going forth into a new life in a new world—which speaks of newness of life through regeneration. Thus, in Noah, we see, typically, *spiritual renewal*.

Abraham, Isaac, Jacob, Joseph.

We come now to the post-Flood patriarchs, and to save space we group them together, though there is much we should like to have said about them separately. These four, following the typifying of regeneration, in Noah, exhibit, in a typical way, the qualities and characteristics of the regenerate life. They show us those forms of life which are known after regeneration.

In ABRAHAM we see *the life of faith*. He stands out as the supreme exemplar of the faith-life. In him we see the man of faith going forth, trusting in the Divine guidance, believing the Divine promises, receiving Divine assurances, inheriting the Divine blessing, undergoing sharp testings, and—despite occasional failures—being "accounted righteous" through faith, and being called "the friend of God."

In ISAAC we see *the life of sonship*. The Genesis account clearly puts the emphasis upon Isaac's unique sonship. He is the son of special promise, of special birth, of special preciousness, the only son of his mother, and the only heir of his father, the son at whose weaning a great feast is made, and through whom the promises are to be realised, and for whom a special bride must be chosen. In Isaac, then, dwelling in the land of inheritance, biding by the wells of water, with many joys and few conflicts, we see the typified privileges and joys of sonship.

In JACOB we see *the life of service*. Jacob is that life which (as at his birth) "takes hold with the hand." Jacob is the worker throughout, busy with his hands. Here is untiring service. There are mistakes in method and manner, yet there is blessing, for at heart the motive is good. The busy worker would even help God to work the Divine purposes out the more expeditiously, until God has to touch His servant's thigh, and teach him, also, to be a prince in prayer. Yet Jacob is spiritual at heart, as all his words show. Esau will give up the birthright for meat. Jacob will give up his meat for the birthright, if by any means he might obtain the inheritance. Here, then, in Jacob, is eager activity, work, service.

Finally, in JOSEPH, the finest and highest type of regenerate life is set forth. The biographical sketches of the Bible are unflatteringly true to fact, yet although more space is devoted to Joseph than to any other single subject in Genesis, in all the record God does not speak one word of reproof against Joseph. In him we see *the life of suffering and glory*. Here faith and sonship and service are blended in something deeper and grander, issuing in complete rule over the world and the flesh. Here Egypt (type of the world and the sense-life), which had been a snare to Abraham and Isaac, is completely ruled. Here is "the fellowship of His sufferings and the power of His resurrection." Here is the character of the regenerate made "perfect through sufferings." Here is suffering and reigning with Christ, and being "glorified together"!

These, then, are the marked characteristics exhibited by the seven outstanding men of Genesis.

> Abel—spiritual desire.
> Enoch—spiritual choice.
> Noah—spiritual renewal.
> Abraham—the life of faith.
> Isaac—the life of sonship.
> Jacob—the life of service.
> Joseph—the life of suffering and glory.

Is there not clear and wonderful typical teaching here? Note the progressive order. First comes spiritual *desire*, then spiritual *choice*, then spiritual *renewal*. After this we see life lived by a new principle—that of *faith*. Then faith brings the sense of *sonship*, out of which grows *service*. Finally, we have the deeper depths and higher heights of fellowship with the life of God, in *suffering* and *glory*. Obviously, this is the *true* order, and must not be altered.

Truly there is fascinating type-teaching here! Let these seven characters be studied in this light, and they become rich with suggestions that fill out our ideas of the great truths which they typify. This is the genius of typology. Truths of which we should have a very limited apprehension if they were only communicated to us by plain didactic language, are made to live and grow before us when we see them in the picturesque and vivid setting of type and symbol.

For instance, if we were merely told in so many words that there must be spiritual desire and choice and renewal, followed by faith, sonship, service, suffering and glory, how limited would our idea of these things be! But when we see them illustrated and exemplified in the living and fascinating characters of these seven men, our understanding of the truths thus typified is incalculably enriched.

Of course, it must be clearly realised that we are here viewing these seven men *typically*, and not biographically. Because Noah here typifies, in a unique way, spiritual renewal, this must not be taken to imply that Abel and Enoch, who went before him, were *not* spiritually renewed men! And because Abraham here typifies, in a unique way, the life of faith, this must not be taken to imply that the three before him and the three after him were not men of faith! All the seven were men spiritually renewed, men of faith. Each of the seven, considered *individually*, shows his experience, in measure, of the whole seven-fold truth set forth by all the seven *collectively*. Yet each of the seven is nevertheless marked by the one outstanding characteristic, which invests him with a special *typical* significance, and gives him his place in the completed type constituted by all the seven together.

Finally, let it be our prayer that *we* may be men and women of spiritual desire, spiritual choice, and spiritual renewal, walking by faith, realising our heavenly sonship, serving the Lord from a sense of filial devotion, knowing "the fellowship of His suffering," and ever rejoicing in the prospect of glory yet to be!

CONCLUDING SUGGESTIONS

The Book of Genesis should also be studied *biographically*. It is rich in human characters. Study, for instance, the seven great men before-mentioned, noting the dominant feature or determining crisis in the recorded history of each—Abel the worshipper, Enoch the walker, Noah the worker, Abraham the wanderer, Isaac the watcher, Jacob the wrestler, Joseph the waiter. What character studies are Esau, Lot, Cain!—illustrating, respectively, "the lust of the flesh, and the lust of the eyes, and the pride of life" (1 John ii. 16). Nimrod, Sarah, Laban, Judah, and others, well repay study.

Genesis should be specially studied *spiritually*. No book of the Old Testament is richer in spiritual values. Here is a life-time of rewarding study in itself! Its spiritual teachings fall into two categories—(1) truths to enlighten the mind; (2) lessons to regulate the life. As to the former, we may mention—the presence and gracious purposes of God in human history; the presence and evil purposes of a personal devil; the origin and progress of sin in the human race; the depravity of fallen human nature; the Divine prevision and provision; the ministry of angels; the Divine sovereignty and condescension; these being but a few of many tremendous truths. As for the *lessons* which abound here—to cite only one of many fruitful instances—what illuminating spiritual lessons we find in the records pertaining to the rise and progress of faith in the soul of Abraham! Take, for instance, ʌe very first records concerning him—chapter xii. 4 to xiii. 4. See here (1) faith *responding* (xii. 4–9); then faith *receding* (xii. 10–20); then faith *returning* (xiii. 1–4). The lessons associated with these early experiences of the pilgrim believer are important beyond expression.

Then, again, Genesis should be studied *prophetically*. The whole of subsequent revelation and history is really the unfolding of the prophecies in this first book of Scripture. Here are great prophecies, concerning *Christ* (iii. 14–15), concerning the *Earth* (iii. 17–18; viii. 21–2), concerning the *Race* (ix. 25–27), concerning *Israel* (xiii. 14–17; xxii. 15–18), concerning other nations and tribes (xvii. 19–20; xxv. 23; xlviii. 17–20; xlix. 1–28). In the light of many wonderful fulfilments these prophecies constitute unanswerable evidence of the superhuman origin of the Scriptures.

Genesis should be studied *dispensationally*. In His dealings with mankind, it has pleased God to adopt different methods suited to different times. These periods are conveniently termed "dispensations." A dispensation has been defined as "a period of time during which man is tested in respect of obedience to some *specific* revelation of the will of God." Seven such are distinguished in the Scriptures; and four of these we find in Genesis. They have been well expressed as: (1) the period of *Innocence*, in which God tested man; (2) that of *Conscience*, in which God suffered man; (3) that of human *Government*, in which God restrained man; (4) that of *Promise*, in which God wrought for man.

There are other ways of studying Genesis, such as geographically, critically, textually; but the above-mentioned supply enough suggestion to occupy us profitably for a long while.

PAUSE HERE!—AND TEST YOUR STUDY THUS FAR

1. What are the main groups of books in the Old Testament? (Give number and nature of each.)
2. What are the main groups of books in the New Testament? (Give number and nature of each.)
3. What are the progressive truths which run through the Pentateuch?
4. What are the similarities and contrasts between Genesis and the Apocalypse?
5. What is the structure of Genesis, and how does it suggest the principal lesson of the book?
6. What is our authority for asserting the presence of types in the Old Testament? What is a type? Define and classify.
7. What are the grounds for saying that the six days of Genesis describe the re-formation of the earth, and not its original creation?
8. What were the main results of the Fall?
9. Were the "sons of God" in Genesis vi. the fallen angels? If not, why not?
10. What suggestions are there that the Noachian Flood may not have been universal?
11. When did the Babel crisis probably occur? What were its main significances?
12. Who are the seven outstanding "men of faith" in Genesis? And what may they be said progressively to typify?

THE BOOK OF EXODUS (I)

Lesson Number 5

NOTE:—For this study read the whole book of Exodus through once or twice, and the first eighteen chapters a third time.

THE BOOK OF EXODUS

THE DIVINE POWER, HOLINESS, AND WISDOM

I. THE EXODUS (i.–xviii.).

Projected—i.–iv.
Obstructed—v.–xi.
Effected—xii.–xviii.

II. THE LAW (xix.–xxiv.).

"Commandments"—(Moral).
"Judgments"—(Social).
"Ordinances"—(Religious).

III. THE TABERNACLE (xxv.–xl.).

Designed—xxv.–xxxi.
Delayed—xxxii.–xxxiv.
Completed—xxxv.–xl.

THE BOOK OF EXODUS (1)

WE TURN now to the second book of Scripture, namely, Exodus; and we have good reason to approach our study of it with real eagerness, for never was there a more striking or vital record written for our learning.

It is here that we see the outgoing of Israel from Egypt—an entire race of people suddenly and forever flinging away the shackles of a generations-long servitude, and migrating to a new country and a new corporate life. It is here that we have the giving of the Law, and the enunciating of the Mosaic Covenant. It is here that we see the erecting of that marvellously symbolical structure, the Tabernacle. It is here that Moses grows up before us and goes forth to his mighty task. It is here that we mark the transition of the Israelites from being merely a plurality of kindred tribes into one nation, Divinely adopted, constituted, and conditioned, as such, at Sinai.

Is there in all history a more amazing spectacle than the Exodus?—a more august and solemn revelation of God than at Sinai?—a more significant piece of architecture than the Israelite Tabernacle?—a greater human figure than the man Moses?—a more influential national epoch than the founding of the Israel theocracy? All these are fou ᵈ in this second book of Scripture. It is the *fons et origo*—the very fount and origin of the national life, law, and organised religion of Israel.

The title "Exodus," which means "outgoing," accurately conveys the main subject of the book; but two other subjects are associated with the Exodus, as being the direct outcome of it, and complimentary to it, namely, the *Law,* and the *Tabernacle.* The book quite naturally divides thus—

1. THE EXODUS—i.–xviii.

2. THE LAW—xix.–xxiv.

3. THE TABERNACLE—xxv.–xl.

Each of the three main divisions of the book breaks up into three further subsidiary parts—(see preceding diagram on p. 74).

The Divine Power, Holiness, Wisdom.

This threefold plan at once suggests the principal significance of the book. Observe, first, the teaching here concerning *GOD*. In the Exodus (i.–xviii.) we see the *power* of God. In the Law (xix.–xxiv.) we see the *holiness* of God. In the Tabernacle (xxv.–xl.) we see the *wisdom* of God. We have seen that the outstanding message of Genesis is the Divine sovereignty. How fitting that now, in this Book of Exodus, we should see the Divine power and holiness and wisdom outstandingly exhibited to us!

Life, Law and Love.

Note, also, the teaching here regarding *ISRAEL*. In the Exodus we see Israel being brought to a new *condition*—of freedom. In the Law we see Israel being brought to a new *constitution*—that of the theocracy. In the Tabernacle we see Israel being brought to a new *conception*—of worship, and of God. By the Exodus they are brought *out*—to new liberty. By the Law they are brought *under*—a new government. By the Tabernacle they are brought *into*—a new fellowship.

These things speak to the people of God, in all times, of the basic principles underlying the Divine dealings with us. Here, in the Exodus, the Law, and the Tabernacle, is redemption, reconstruction, reconciliation. Here is life, law, love. The Exodus leads to a new and fuller *life*. Sinai conditions the new life by the one perfect *law*. The Tabernacle leads to the sublime *love* behind both.

Liberty, Responsibility, Privilege.

Fundamentally, the problem with which the various philosophies of life seek to deal is that of human freedom, responsibility, and privilege. Liberty without law is licence. Responsibility without freedom is bondage. Liberty and responsibility together, without privilege—without rewards and punishments—lack motive and meaning. Here, in the Exodus, the Law, and the Tabernacle, we see these three things—in the Exodus, *liberty*; in the Law, *responsibility*; in the Tabernacle, *privilege*.

Thus in these three parts of this book—historical, legislative, ecclesiastical—we are touching wonderful teaching. Let us now explore part one. It opens up as follows—

I. THE EXODUS (i.–xviii.).

PROJECTED—THROUGH MOSES (i.–iv.).

How necessitated—
  (a) Israel's expansion in Egypt (i. 1–12).
  (b) Israel's oppression by Egypt (i. 13–22).
How anticipated—
  (a) Moses' preparation in Egypt (ii. 1–15).
  (b) Moses' preparation in Midian (ii. 16–25).
How precipitated—
  (a) The New Message from God (iii. 1–iv. 17).
  (b) The New Mission of Moses (iv. 18–31).

OBSTRUCTED—BY PHARAOH (v.–xi.).

The eight requests—
  v. 1–3; vii. 10; vii. 15–18; viii. 1–4; viii. 20–3; ix. 1–4; ix. 13–19; x. 1–6.
The eight refusals—
  v. 2; vii. 13; vii. 22–3; viii. 15, 19; viii. 32; ix. 7, 12; ix. 34–5; x. 11, 20, 27.
The ten requitals—
  vii. 20; viii. 6; viii. 16; viii. 24; ix. 3; ix. 10; ix. 22; x. 12; x. 21; xi. 5.

EFFECTED—BY JEHOVAH (xii.–xviii.).

Goshen to Red Sea—
  (a) The Passover and memorials (xii. 1–xiii. 16).
  (b) The Leading out of Israel (xiii. 17–22).
Through Red Sea—
  (a) Egyptian pursuit of Israel (xiv. 1–12).
  (b) Israel saved: pursuers dead (xiv. 13–31).
Red Sea to Sinai—
  (a) One month: to Desert (xv. 1–xvi. 1).
  (b) Two weeks: to Sinai (xvi. 1–xviii. 27).

In these three movements the three great actors in this drama of ancient history are emphasised respectively—ISRAEL, EGYPT, GOD.

THE EXODUS—AND ISRAEL

Think what the Exodus meant for Israel. It meant four things specially. First, it marked the beginning of a new *LIFE*. In chapter xii. 2, we read: "This month (Nisan) shall be unto you the beginning of months: it shall be the first month of the year to you." April becomes January. The new life is marked by the beginning of a new calendar. They are to reckon anew from this event which marks their birth as a nation.

Second, the Exodus meant the beginning of a new *LIBERTY*. As the great host came forth from Egypt Moses thus addressed them: "Remember this day in which ye came out from Egypt, out of the house of bondage; for by strength of hand the Lord brought you out from this place" (xiii. 3). That grim word "bondage" was to be associated with Egypt for ever afterward in the memory of Israel. Egypt was distinctively "the house of bondage." But at the Exodus Israel went out to liberty.

Third, the Exodus meant the beginning of a new *FELLOW-SHIP*. This is symbolised in the "feast" which was instituted in connection with the Passover. "This day shall be unto you for a memorial; and ye shall keep ' feast to the Lord through-out your generations" (xii. 14). In the Old Testament the feast is ever the symbol of fellowship (see xxiv. 11).

Fourth, the Exodus marked the beginning of a new *ASSUR-ANCE*. When God announced His purpose to bring about the Exodus, He thus addressed the people through Moses: "I will take you to Me for a people, and I will be to you a God: and ye shall know that I am the Lord your God, which bringeth you out from under the burdens of the Egyptians. And I will bring you into the land concerning the which I did swear to give it to Abraham, to Isaac, and to Jacob; and I will give it you for an heritage: I am the Lord" (vi. 7-8).

All this has its counterpart in the Gospel of Christ. Luke tells us that when Moses and Elijah appeared with Christ on the Mount of the Transfiguration they "spake of His decease (lit.—'His Exodus') which He should accomplish at Jerusalem." Christ is the Leader of an Exodus far greater than that under Moses. The exodus under Moses is indeed a *type* of that which Christ has wrought for us, as we see from 1 Corinthians v. 7–8—"For even Christ our Passover is sacrificed for us." As the Exodus under Moses meant a new life, a new liberty, a new fellowship, and a new assurance for Israel, so the Gospel of Christ means all this to the believer.

THE EXODUS—AND EGYPT

Think what the Exodus meant in relation to Egypt. It meant three things specially. First, it was the first big-scale exposure of the falsity of idolatry. The primal revelation of Himself, and of Divine truth, which God had given to the early fathers of the race, had been more and more obscured or perverted as time had elapsed, through the perverted mind and will of fallen man; and systems of idolatry had grown up (Joshua xxiv. 2, 14, 15), man having made all manner of gods for himself. Egypt at the time of the Exodus was probably the greatest kingdom on earth, and its gods were considered correspondingly great. When God would call out the people of Israel to their new life and their intended national mission of restoring the knowledge of the one true God, He would, at the same time, expose the falsity of all man-concocted deities. Thus we find God saying: "Against all the gods of Egypt I will execute judgment: I am the Lord" (xii. 12) (see also Num. xxxiii. 4). This smash-up of Egypt's gods not only compelled even the magicians of Egypt to confess: "This is the finger of God (i.e., of the *true* God)," but, being so conspicuous, it was a lesson to all the nations of that day (xv. 14–15; xviii. 11; and see Joshua ix. 9). It duly impressed, also, the minds of the Israelites; and we hear them singing, from the farther bank of the Red Sea: "Who is like unto Thee, O Lord, among the gods?"

Second, the overthrow of Egypt demonstrates the uselessness, sin, and folly of attempting to resist Jehovah, the God of Israel, the one true God. At the beginning of the contest Pharaoh contemptuously asked: "Who is Jehovah, that I should obey Him?" The Exodus was designed to answer that question in a way which should be a lesson to all men for all time. Indeed, God announced to Pharaoh, through Moses: "In very deed for this cause have I raised thee up, for to show in thee My power, and that My Name may be declared throughout the earth" (ix. 16).

Third, it is to be remembered that all the principal features of the Exodus possess a typical import, and that in line with this, Egypt, the scene of the Exodus, is a type of "the world," in the morally evil sense. Egypt is a type of the world (1) in its material wealth and power (Heb. xi. 26); (2) in its fleshly wisdom and false religion (Exod. viii. 7, etc.; 1 Kings iv. 30); (3) in its despotic prince, Pharaoh, who himself is a figure of Satan; (4) in its organisation on the principles of force, human aggrandisement, ambition, and pleasure; (5) in its persecution of the people of God (Deut. iv. 20); (6) in its overthrow by Divine judgment (xii. 29; xv. 4–7). In the plagues, the smiting of the firstborn, and the drowning of the Egyptian host, we see the final tribulation, judgment and destruction of the present world-system.

THE EXODUS—AND GOD

Supremely, the Exodus was an expression of the Divine power. It was as such that it made its outstanding impact on the Hebrew mind. It became for ever afterwards, to Israel, the standard of God's power to deliver His people. Scores of times it is thus referred to in the Old Testament, Micah vii. 15 being representative—"According to the days of thy coming out of the land of Egypt will I show unto him marvellous things." Note the "according to," indicating the unit of measurement.

That the Exodus should thus become the Old Testament unit of measurement is no surprising thing when we consider what a complex marvel it was. It was (1) a marvel of *judgment*—in the miraculous plagues, the smiting of the firstborn, and the over-whelming of the Egyptian host in the sea; (2) a marvel of *grace*—in the exempting of the blood-marked dwellings, and the delivering of the Israelites; (3) a marvel of *might*—in the clearing of a way through the Red Sea; (4) a marvel of *guidance*—in the pillar of cloud and of fire; (5) a marvel of *provision*—in the miraculous supplying of food and drink; (6) a marvel of *faithfulness*—in the Divine honouring of the Abrahamic covenant and the further covenant with the nation at Sinai; (7) a marvel of *condescension*—as seen in the Tabernacle, by means of which the infinite, holy God abode, in a special way, among His redeemed people.

It is an interesting point, in the *comparative* study of the Scriptures, to note the change-over from this Old Testament standard to a new unit of measurement in the New Testament. The New Testament standard of God's power to deliver His people is seen in Ephesians i. 19–21:

> *"That ye may know . . . what is the exceeding greatness of His power to us-ward who believe,* according to *the working of His mighty power which He wrought in Christ when He raised Him from the dead, and set Him at His own right hand in the heavenlies, far above all principality and power and might and dominion and every name that is named, not only in this age, but also in that which is to come."*

The Old Testament unit of measurement is thus superseded by the greater manifestation of the Divine power through Christ.

In comparing the new standard with that of the Old Testament, however, it is instructive to observe that the New Testament standard repeats the seven wonderful characteristics marked in the Exodus. Like the Exodus, it is (1) a marvel of *judgment*—in the judicial dealing of God with human sin, at Calvary, and in the overthrow of Satan, with the "principalities and powers" of evil; (2) a marvel of *grace*—in the exempting of the blood-sealed believer from judgment and punishment, on the ground of identification with the Cross; (3) a marvel of *might*—in the raising up of Christ from the dead and His exaltation as Prince and Saviour far above all the powers of heaven and earth and hell; (4) a marvel of guidance—in the giving and ministry of the Holy Spirit as the new pillar of cloud and fire; (5) a marvel of *provision*—in the blessing of the believer with "all spiritual blessings in the heavenlies in Christ," and the supplying of all need "according to God's riches, in glory, by Christ Jesus"; (6) a marvel of *faithfulness*—in the further developing of the Abrahamic covenant, through Christ, in whom all kindreds of the earth are blessed, in the honouring of the later covenant through Moses, which disobedient Israel had broken, and in the revelation of the New Covenant, in Christ's blood; (7) a marvel of *condescension*—in the abiding of the Holy Spirit within the believer, transforming the human personality into a "temple of the living God."

THE EXODUS—AND THE GOSPEL

Finally—as already noted—the Exodus under Moses is a graphic type of that greater exodus in Christ: it is meant to speak to us of this; and it is well, therefore, to fix in mind the points of comparison and contrast.

Main Points of Comparison.

1. The Exodus brought a mighty emancipation for Israel. The Gospel brings deliverance from the guilt and penalty and bondage of sin.

2. The Exodus centred in the Passover and the slain lamb. The Gospel centres in the great passover of Calvary and "the Lamb slain from the foundation of the world."

3. The Exodus became for ever afterwards commemorated in the Passover Feast. So "Christ our Passover is sacrificed for us; therefore let us keep the feast" (1 Cor. v. 7).

Main Points of Contrast.

1. (In means.) The sheltering blood, in the Exodus, was merely that of an animal. In the Gospel it is "the precious blood of Christ." In the one case *many* lambs are slain; in the other, One for all.

2. (In extent.) The Exodus was national and therefore limited. The Gospel is universal, its characteristic word of address being "whosoever."

3. (In effects.) The one was deliverance from physical bondage; the other is from spiritual. The one deliverance was temporal; the other is eternal. The one opened up the way to an earthly Canaan; the other to a heavenly.

THE BOOK OF EXODUS (2)

Lesson Number 6

NOTE :—For this study read three times over chapters xix. to xxiv.

II. THE LAW (xix.–xxiv.)

"COMMANDMENTS" (governing *Moral* Life—xix.–xx.).

The terms of the Sinai Covenant submitted (xix. 3-6).
The terms of the Sinai Covenant accepted (xix. 7–8).
The two parties to the Covenant meet—(1) Israel (xix. 9–17)
The two parties to the Covenant meet—(2) God (xix. 18–25).
The ten commands—spiritual basis of Covenant (xx. 1–17).
The earthen altar—outward symbol of Covenant (xx. 18–26).

"JUDGMENTS" (governing *Social* Life—xxi.–xxiii.).

Concerning masters and servants (xxi. 1–11).
Concerning physical injuries (xxi. 12–36).
Concerning property rights (xxii. 1–15).
Concerning various evil practices (xxii. 16–xxiii. 9).
Concerning national Sabbaths and Feasts (xxiii. 10–19).
Concerning national relationships (xxiii. 20–33).

"ORDINANCES" (governing *Religious* Life—xxiv.).

NOTE: The "Ordinances" (which are contained in the instructions regarding the Tabernacle), really begin in the next chapter (xxv.). We include them here to set off the threefold nature of the Law, and because they also were part of the Divine communications to Moses during the forty days in the Mount, mentioned at the end of the present section (xxiv. 12–18).

THE BOOK OF EXODUS (2)

THE LAW (xix.–xxiv.)

THE SECOND of the three main parts of Exodus runs from the beginning of chapter xix. to the end of chapter xxiv. It is occupied with the giving of the Law, and the enunciating of the Mosaic Covenant. The Law is in three parts—"Commandments," "Judgments," "Ordinances." (See across.)

There are certain important considerations which we must bear in mind if we would truly understand the giving of the Law, marking, as it does, that new relationship between God and Israel which we speak of as the Mosaic Covenant.

HOW THE LAW CAME IN

First, the Mosaic Covenant, strictly speaking, is not a new covenant, but a development in and of the Abrahamic Covenant. The subject of the Covenant is thus introduced to Israel at Sinai:

"*Ye have seen what I did unto the Egyptians, and how I bare you on eagles' wings, and brought you unto Myself. Now, therefore, if ye will obey My voice indeed, and keep My covenant, then ye shall be a peculiar treasure unto Me above all people; for all the earth is Mine. And ye shall be unto Me a kingdom of priests, and an holy nation*" (Exod. xix. 4–6).

What is meant here by "My covenant"? It is referred to without explanation, as something known already by Israel. We can only know by turning back to earlier occurrences of that word "covenant." We find it twice before this in Exodus. First, in chapter ii. 24 we read: "God heard their groaning, and God remembered His covenant with Abraham, with Isaac, and with Jacob." Then in chapter vi. 4–5 we read: "I have established My covenant with them (Abraham, Isaac, Jacob), to give them the land of Canaan. . . . I have also heard the groaning of the Children of Israel, whom the Egyptians keep in bondage, and I have remembered My covenant." In both these references the word "remembered" looks back to the Abrahamic Covenant, and specially, therefore, to Genesis xv. and xvii., in which chapters we have the seal (xv. 17–18) and sign (xvii. 10) of the Abrahamic covenant. Between Genesis xvii. and Exodus ii. 24 there is no mention whatever of any other Divine covenant. Thus it is perfectly clear that when God says to Israel, at Sinai, "Keep My covenant," the reference is to the Abrahamic covenant.

Now the giving of the Law at Sinai, and the forming of the Mosaic covenant, are often misunderstood because their relationship with the Abrahamic covenant is not clearly grasped. There are two basically important facts to realise about the Abrahamic covenant—(1) the ground of Abraham's acceptance was his *faith* (Gen. xv. 6); and (2) Abraham's part in the keeping of the covenant was simply a sincere continuance in faith and uprightness,—"Walk before Me, and be thou perfect (sincere, upright), and I will make My covenant between Me and thee" (Gen. xvii. 1–2). When the keeping of the covenant was again enjoined at Sinai, the giving of the Law did not intend a change-over from this faith-basis of the Abrahamic covenant to a works-basis. Knowing the heart of fallen man, God did not now impose the keeping of the moral law as a new basis of acceptance. Nay, going with the commandments, in the Sinai elaboration of the Abrahamic covenant, was the provision of the "ordinances" which pointed to the atonement of Christ, and showed the real basis of acceptance through faith. Canaan was to be possessed, and the nation still to be blessed, on the promise-and-faith basis. The reason why the Mosaic covenant brought Israel under "the curse of the law," instead of into fuller benediction, lay in the wrong reaction of the people themselves to it; for, as the narrative apparently indicates, and as Israel's subsequent history confirms, the Hebrew people themselves seem from the first to have shifted the emphasis from the faith-basis to that of acceptance on a works-basis, so that for ever afterward, in the words of Paul, they were "going about to establish their own righteousness" (Rom. x. 3). See their self-confident response at Sinai—"All the people answered together, and said: All that the Lord hath spoken we will do" (Exod. xix. 8); "And they said: All that the Lord hath said we will do, and be obedient" (Exod. xxiv. 7). Surely there is grave presumption in this self-confident vow.

In sovereign wisdom, and knowing the end from the beginning, God forbearingly received the people on their own standing, gave them the Law, and promised abundant blessing upon their obedience: but in the light of Israel's wrong attitude, at and after Sinai, we can see how their experience under the Mosaic Covenant developed into the saddest tragedy in Hebrew history.

WHY THE LAW WAS GIVEN

If, then, the giving of the Law was not meant to displace the faith-basis of the Abrahamic Covenant, why was the Law given? It was given for three reasons.

1. *To provide a standard of righteousness.* Whereas periodic oral communications were sufficient in the Divine dealings with Abraham and the first fathers of the Hebrew race, it became necessary, now that the people were constituted a nation and a theocracy, to furnish a written and permanent standard of morality, expressing the Divine ideal for character and conduct (Deut. iv. 8; Ps. xix. 7–9; cxix. 142).

2. *To expose and identify sin.* As solid objects become black when silhouetted against a bright background, so sin—unrecognised as such in the comparative obscureness of fallen man's perverted conscience—becomes at once shown up and sharply marked off against the light of the Law. Thus, we find Paul saying: "The Law entered that the offence might abound (or become obvious)" (Rom. v. 20); "By the Law is the knowledge of sin" (Rom. iii. 20); "I had not known sin but by the Law" (Rom. vii. 7); "It (the Law) was added because of transgressions"—i.e., that sin might be exposed as offence against God (Gal. iii. 19).

3. *To reveal the Divine holiness.* It was absolutely indispensable that the unique privileges conferred upon the elect nation, for the fulfilling of its high vocation, should be safeguarded by a reverential recognition of the inviolate holiness of God, lest privilege should lead to presumption. It is not without significance that the Biblical revelation, considered as a whole, presents first the *power* of God (as seen specially in the Creation, the Flood, the Babel dispersion, the overthrow of Sodom, the Exodus); then the *holiness* of God (as

seen specially in the Mosaic Law and the subsequent Divine dealings with Israel); and *then* the *love* of God (as seen specially in the Gospel of Christ);—the truth being at once suggested that the revelation of the *love* of God must be safeguarded by a due recognition of His awful power and holiness.

The characteristic word for God, on the lips of Jesus, is "Father"; but let it be remembered that *not until* Christ came, as the crowning revelation of God, was the Divine fatherhood given prominence. The truth of the Divine fatherhood is not safe for man without earlier revelation of the Divine power and holiness. One of the faults of certain modern theology is the mental divorcing of the Divine love from the Divine power and holiness.

The symbol of holiness is fire. Thus the Law is given amid fire on Sinai (xix. 18; xxiv. 17), and with strictest prohibitions (xix. 10–13, 21–5). Israel ever realised that the Law enshrined a God of awful holiness (Deut. xxviii. 58; xxxiii. 2; Ps. lxviii. 17; Heb. xii. 18 and 29). As an expression of the Divine holiness, the Law given through Moses is unapproachable. In the "Commandments"—especially when spiritually interpreted, as Christ interpreted them (Matt. v. 21–8),—we see the holiness of God in its sublimity. In the "Judgments," with their intolerance of all wrongdoing and compromise, we see the holiness of God in its awful severity. In the "Ordinances," with their exhaustive prescriptions covering Israel's worship, we see the holiness of God in its utter inviolateness. The God of Sinai is a holy God; and truly, in His holiness, "our God is a consuming fire"!

THE LAW AND THE ABRAHAMIC COVENANT

A further question now arises, namely: What then, really, is the relationship between the Law of Moses and the covenant through Abraham?

1. The Law was *added to* the Abrahamic Covenant. "It was added because of (i.e.—to mark) transgressions till the Seed should come to whom the promise was made" (Gal. iii. 19). This, in itself, shows that the Law was not meant to delete the faith-feature of the Abrahamic Covenant. It came by

way of insertion, not deletion. It was meant to mark an addition not a subtraction.

2. The Law *does not disannul* the Abrahamic covenant. "The covenant that was confirmed before of God, in (to) Christ, the Law, which was four hundred and thirty years after, cannot disannul, that it should make the promise of none effect. For if the inheritance be of the Law, it is no more of promise; but God gave it to Abraham by promise" (Gal. iii. 17–18).

3. The Law, as wrongly accepted by Israel, passed its death-sentence on guilt, and thus inflicted a curse *which held back the blessing* of the Abrahamic Covenant: but in Christ the curse was removed, that the Abrahamic blessing might be released to faith. "Christ hath redeemed us from the curse of the Law . . . that the blessing of Abraham might come on the Gentiles through Jesus Christ, that we might receive the promise of the Spirit through faith" (Gal. iii. 13–14).

THE LAW AND THE HISTORY OF ISRAEL

Israel, as a *nation*, broke the Law and the Mosaic Covenant (see 1 Kings xix. 10; 2 Kings xvii. 15; xviii. 12; Ps. lxxviii. 37; Jer. xi. 10; xxxi. 32; Ezek. xvi. 59; Hos. viii. 1; Heb. viii. 9, etc.). But what do we really imply by this? Do we mean, simply, that the individuals who composed the nation failed to measure up to the requirements of the ten commandments, and that it was for this reason alone that the captivities and exile took place? No, for have we not seen that when God gave the ten "Commandments" He also gave the "Ordinances" which pointed to Christ, and showed the true ground of acceptance, through vicarious atonement, and by faith?

It is of vital importance to understand how the word "law" is used in the Old Testament. First, it is used just once or twice to denote the ten "Commandments" (Exod. xxiv. 12; see R.V.). Second, it is used of individual "judgments" and "ordinances" —"This is the law of the burnt-offering," etc. (Lev. vi. 9, 14, 25; xxiv. 22, etc.). Third, it is used by far the most commonly to denote the whole of the Mosaic economy, comprising "Commandments," "Judgments" and "Ordinances" alike. This, its general use, is shown with absolute conclusiveness in such passages as

Deuteronomy iv. 8, 44–5; Joshua viii. 34; 1 Kings ii. 3; Daniel
ix. 11–13; Malachi iv. 4.

Now when it is asserted that Israel broke the Law, and thus
violated the Covenant, it is not meant simply that individual
Israelites, few or many, broke the ten "Commandments," but
that the nation as a whole fell foul of the major obligations of
the Covenant contained in the "Judgments" and the "Ordinances." The following are notable instances:

1. Israel was to keep a Sabbatic year every seventh year, and
   the Jubilee Sabbatic year every fiftieth, when all slaves
   were to be freed, and all debts cancelled. See Leviticus xxv.
   for interesting details and promised blessings. The Sabbaths
   were covenant "signs" between God and Israel (Exod.
   xxxi. 13). In them the land was to be rested, in grateful
   acknowledgment of the Divine ownership and goodness;
   and wonderful blessing was to attend their due observance.
   Yet from the first Israel disobeyed. Where is there anywhere in Scripture any record of Israel's keeping these
   Sabbaths? (see Jer. xxxiv. 8–22). It was because of Israel's
   unfaithfulness here that the seventy years of desolation
   came as a long Sabbath of judgment (see the remarkable
   connection between Jer. xxv. 11 and 2 Chron. xxxvi. 21;
   and then read Lev. xxvi. 32–5 as explaining both).

2. Israel was not to make any covenant with the surrounding
   nations, but was to be completely separate—and that for
   benign reasons. (see Exod. xxiii. 24–33; xxxiv. 12–17;
   Deut. vii. 1–6, etc.). Yet from the first we find Israel
   defaulting here (see Joshua ix. 14–16; Judges ii. 2; iii. 5–6;
   and many similar references).

3. Israel was to shun idolatry and the use of religious images
   (Exod. xx. 2–5; Deut. iv. 12–20; xvii. 2–7). Yet from the
   first Israel disobeyed (see Judges ii. 11–23; Jer. ii. 28;
   xi. 10; and the awful account in 2 Kings xvii. 17–23).

Other examples of Israel's grievous default might be given as,
for instance, failure in the matter of Passover observance (2 Chron.
xxx. 5), the weekly Sabbath (Ezek. xx. 13), and Tithing (Mal.
iii. 8).

It was in these ways that Israel, as a nation, broke the Law, violated the Covenant, and fell foul of the high calling of God.

THE LAW AND THE GOSPEL

Finally, a brief word about the Law in relation to the Gospel of Christ. The Law is done away, in Christ, in three ways.

1. The performing of the *"Commandments"* as a condition of personal justification is emphatically and conclusively done away; for "Christ is the end of the Law for righteousness to every one that believeth" (Rom. x. 4). Although all of the Ten Commandments, except the fourth, are included in the ethics of the New Testament, they are included as independent principles, and not as part of the Mosaic system. The keeping of them is not *obligatory to* salvation, but the spontaneous *result of* salvation.

2. The performing of the *"Ordinances"* of the Law, as a way of acceptance with God, is now superseded, inasmuch as the religious ordinances of the Mosaic dispensation were but the types and shadows of which Christ is the fulfilment and substance (Col. ii. 17; Heb. ix. 22–x. 18).

3. The Law, as a *Dispensation*, or method of Divine dealing, is now done away, inasmuch as the Gospel introduces a new dispensation for Israel and Gentiles alike. The old dispensation was that of "the Letter"—*an outward command*. The new dispensation is that of "the Spirit"—*an inward power* (see 2 Cor. iii.–iv.). The one was an objective code. The other is a subjective change. The one was a condemning ethic. The other is a transforming dynamic. "What the Law could not do, in that it was weak through the flesh, God sending His own Son in the likeness of sinful flesh, and for sin, condemned sin in the flesh; that the righteousness of the Law might be fulfilled in us who walk not after the flesh but after the Spirit " (Rom. viii. 3–4).

THE BOOK OF EXODUS (3)

Lesson Number 7

NOTE:—For this seventh lesson read again chapters xxv. to xxxiv.; and, of course, turn to them again and again to compare the details given in the lesson with the Scripture references.

MEASUREMENTS OF TABERNACLE

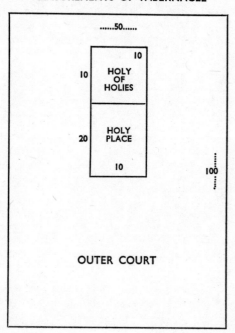

NOTE:—The figures in this simple diagram are the measurements in cubits. In the actual structure the Outer Court was larger in proportion than is shown here, and the "Holy Place" rather longer.

THE BOOK OF EXODUS (3)

THE TABERNACLE (xxv.–xl.)

THE THIRD of the three main parts of Exodus covers chapters
xxv. to xl., where the book ends. It is occupied with the construction and appointments of the Tabernacle. First, the pattern
of the Tabernacle is given to Moses during his forty days in the
Mount (xxv.–xxxi.). Then, in the episode of the golden calf, we
see the execution of the plan temporarily suspended through
Israel's lapse into idolatry (xxxii.–xxxiv.), during which interval
a temporary substitute for the Tabernacle is provided in a tent
pitched "without the Camp" (xxxiii. 7). Finally, the Tabernacle
is completed and erected (exactly one year after the Exodus—
xl. 2), and the glory of the Divine presence descends upon it
(xxxv.–xl.). The chapters thus naturally break up into three
groups (for fuller analysis see end of lesson):

THE TABERNACLE DESIGNED (xxv.–xxxi.)
THE TABERNACLE DELAYED (xxxii.–xxxiv.)
THE TABERNACLE COMPLETED (xxxv.–xl.)

The Scriptures devote more room to the description of the
Tabernacle and its appurtenances than to any other single subject. Its details are described with noticeable particularity; and
no less than seven times in Scripture we find reference to God's
solemn charge to Moses that he should make all things according
to the "pattern" which was shown to him "in the Mount"
(Exod. xxv. 9, 40; xxvi. 30; xxvii. 8; Num. viii. 4; Acts vii. 44;
Heb. viii. 5). Must there not be some special meaning behind
this? There must; and there is. The Tabernacle was not designed
with a view to any merely architectural impressiveness. It was
designed to be a symbolical and typical expression of wonderful
spiritual truth; and herein lies its significance.

To attempt anything like an exhaustive elucidation of the
Tabernacle, with its many symbolical and typical meanings, is

95

quite outside the scope of our present study. In the first place, it would require a book all to itself; and, in the second place, so many books have now been written about the Tabernacle that lengthy expatiation here is uncalled for. Our purpose is to deal with the subject summarily, yet in suchwise as to help towards a clear perception of its latent treasures.

What, then, are the principal features pertaining to the Tabernacle? They are four—

> The Structure;
> The Furniture;
> The Priesthood;
> The Offerings.

The last-mentioned of these four, however—the system of offerings—is a subject all in itself, and is given special treatment in the book of Leviticus to which we shall come later. Let us briefly consider here, therefore, the other three—the Structure, the Furniture, the Priesthood.

THE STRUCTURE

The structure, all told, was in three parts—the Outer Court, the Holy Place, the Holy of Holies. The one entrance to the Outer Court was called the "gate" (xxvii. 16). The one entrance to the Holy Place was called the "door" (xxvi. 36). The one entrance to the Holy of Holies was called the "veil" (xxvi. 31).

The Outer Court

The Outer Court was a large, oblong, rectangular enclosure with the two longer sides facing north and south, and the two shorter facing east and west. The two longer sides were 100 cubits each, and the two shorter were 50 cubits each. As a cubit is approximately eighteen inches, the Outer Court was therefore about 150 by 75 feet. Its construction was very simple from an architectural point of view, the four sides consisting of "pillars" equally spaced from each other, with curtains hung upon them and filling the spaces between them—twenty "pillars" to each of the longer sides, and ten to each of the shorter, making sixty pillars in all, erected at intervals of five cubits, and each pillar being five cubits, or seven and a half feet high. At the top, these pillars had each a capital overlaid with silver, also silver hooks and rods which connected the pillars, and to which the hangings were attached. At the base, the pillars were shod with sockets of brass, while ropes and pins were also used to give the structure firmness. The hangings which composed the screen were made of "fine linen." The entire circumference of the Outer Court was (100 + 100 + 50 + 50 = 300) three hundred cubits, or about four hundred and fifty feet.

The Sanctuary

The sanctuary or dwelling-place itself, consisting of the Holy Place and the Holy of Holies, was, like the Outer Court, rectangular and oblong, being thirty cubits long by ten cubits wide. As with the Outer Court, the two sides running lengthwise faced north and south, while the two ends, or smaller sides, faced east and west. A veil divided the Tabernacle into its two parts, the Holy Place being twenty cubits long, or two-thirds the length of the whole, and the Holy of Holies taking the remaining ten cubits, and both apartments being ten cubits wide, the uniform width of the structure. Unlike the Outer Court, the walls of the Tabernacle were completely of wood—not merely of pillars standing apart from each other—the pillars being in close contact, and bound together by transverse rods or bolts passing through rings fixed on the pillars for this purpose. Four large and beautiful curtains covered the whole structure above, roofing it in and thus making it a "dwelling."

For fuller treatment of the many interesting details, the student is advised to consult some standard Bible Dictionary. For our present purpose the simple diagram on page 94 must be sufficient. Further, it goes almost without saying that there is considerable symbolical and typical import in the materials and parts of the Tabernacle structure, into which we cannot go here; and for an interpretation of all this we refer the student to the good books on this subject which are obtainable at small cost through any evangelical publisher. We must content ourselves here by speaking about one part only of the Tabernacle structure, and even about that part very briefly, though it is perhaps the most interesting part of all—the Holy of Holies. (See the diagram above-mentioned: preceding present chapter.)

D

The Holy of Holies

There are three intensely interesting things about the Holy of Holies which impress us right away. First, we note its *dimensions*. It measured 10 × 10 × 10 cubits. That is to say, its breadth and length and height were each an exact ten cubits, and were therefore all equal with each other. Thus, the Holy of Holies was a *cube*. Later, when the Tabernacle gave place to the magnificent Temple built by Solomon, the Holy of Holies was made *twenty* cubits long; but the breadth and height were similarly doubled (1 Kings vi. 20), so that it had now become 20 × 20 × 20 cubits. Turning right over to the last two chapters of the Bible, we find that the heavenly city is described as being similarly foursquare—"The city lieth foursquare . . . the length and the breadth and the height of it are equal" (Rev. xxi. 16). What is the symbolism behind this use of the cube? Dr. A. T. Pierson tells us that among the Hebrews the cube was the old-time symbol of perfection, because of its absoluteness of symmetry. Every side of a cube is a perfect square, and each of the six sides is exactly equal with all the others. Turn the cube about any way we will, it is still the same in appearance—just as high and deep and broad. Thus we have a symbol of perfection. The Holy of Holies must be a cube, speaking at once, and before all else, of the infinite perfection of Israel's God. The heavenly city must be represented as a cube, indicating the glorious perfection of that city yet to be, "whose builder and maker is God." Is it not this significance of the cube which Paul has in mind when he speaks of "the *breadth* and *length* and *depth* and *height*" of "the love of Christ which passeth knowledge"? (Eph. iii. 18). O the wonder of that perfect love!—and, still more, of a heart-felt experience of it!

Second, note the *purpose* served by the Holy of Holies. It was to be a dwelling-place for God among His people. Have we grasped the wonder and significance of this? The Tabernacle in the wilderness was God's *first* dwelling-place on earth. He had *walked* with Adam in Eden; He had *spoken* to the Patriarchs; He had visibly *visited* Abraham; but He had made Himself no special dwelling-place on earth. Now, however, He comes down to *dwell* among His redeemed people; and onward from then till now He has had a dwelling on earth. After the Tabernacle came the Temple. After the Temple there came forth the Son from the bosom of the Father—"the Word became flesh, and *tabernacled* among us" (John i. 14, R.V. margin). Then, following the Incarnation, came the Church—a spiritual house, a "holy temple . . . builded together for an habitation of God through the Spirit" (Eph. ii. 21–2). This is God's present tabernacle, or dwelling-place on earth, and will be until that coming consummation of which it is written—"Behold, the tabernacle of God is with men, and He will dwell with them, and they shall be His people" (Rev. xxi. 3).

Third, observe the special *sacredness* of the Holy of Holies. When the people of Israel brought their offerings to the Tabernacle, they were allowed into the Outer Court, but were not allowed into the Holy Place, which was for the priests alone; and even the priests who ministered in the Holy Place were not allowed into the Holy of Holies. Only the High Priest was permitted into this inmost shrine, and even he only on special occasions, and after due preparation. The same applied to the Temple when, later, it took the place of the Tabernacle. That which God indwells is unspeakably sacred—a lesson which the people of God were meant to learn deeply and for all time. There cannot possibly be acceptable worship or true fellowship without a reverent recognition of the sacredness of that which is Divine. Now there were two Greek words which came to be used to denote the Temple, the one word meaning the entire precincts of the Temple buildings, while the other was used only of *the sanctuary itself*, the Holy of Holies; and it is a solemnly impressive fact that in every instance in the New Testament where the expression "temple of God" is used of Christian believers, either collectively or individually, the Greek word is that which refers to the Holy of Holies itself. Sacred privilege and responsibility, to be Christ's, and to be thus indwelt!

As the Tabernacle of old was a three-fold structure, so indeed are we by our very constitution as human beings. Corresponding to the "Outer Court" is the *body*. Corresponding to the "Holy Place" is the *soul*. Corresponding to the "Holy of Holies" is the *spirit*; and it is here in the inmost part of our being that God has taken up His dwelling, transforming us into His living temples.

There was once an old sculptor who had, among many other pieces of work in his workshop, the model of a beautiful cathedral.

Yet although it was an exquisitely finished, exact model, nobody admired it as it lay there, covered with the dust of years. Then, one day, the old attendant placed a light inside the model, and its gleams shone through the beautiful stained-glass windows, giving a new beauty to the whole thing; and all who came near stopped to admire it. The entire transformation was wrought by the shining out of the new light within. So may it be with the consecrated temples of these human personalities of ours!

> O joy of joys, O grace of grace,
>   That God should condescend
> To make my heart His dwelling-place
>   And be my dearest Friend!

III. THE TABERNACLE (xxv.–xl.)

DESIGNED (xxv.–xxxi.).

Ark—Table—Candlestand (xxv.).
Curtains—Boards—Veils (xxvi.).
Brazen Altar—Hangings—Oil (xxvii.).
Priests' Garments and Consecration (xxviii.–xxix.).
Incense Altar—Laver—Anointing Oil (xxx.).
The Workmen—The Sabbath Sign (xxxi.).

DELAYED (xxxii.–xxxiv.).

Israel's lapse into idolatry (xxxii. 1–14).
Disciplinary Judgment (xxxii. 15–29).
Intercession of Moses (xxxii. 30–5).
Israel rebuked and tested (xxxiii. 1–11).
Moses reassured (xxxiii. 12–23).
The further 40 days in the Mount (xxxiv.).

COMPLETED (xxxv.–xl.).

The materials subscribed (xxxv.).
The framework and hangings (xxxvi.).
The Tabernacle furniture (xxxvii. and xxxviii.).
The Priesthood garments (xxxix. 1–31).
Work Finished: Tabernacle erected (xxxix. 32–xl. 33).
The Tabernacle filled with Divine presence (xl. 34–8).

THE BOOK OF EXODUS (4)

Lesson Number 8

NOTE:—For this eighth study read again chapters xxv. to xxxi. and xxxv. to xl., looking up the references as they occur in our comments, so as to fix them the more clearly in mind.

DIAGRAM of the TABERNACLE
AND ITS FURNITURE

THE BOOK OF EXODUS (4)
THE FURNITURE OF THE TABERNACLE

THE FURNITURE of the Tabernacle is a really fascinating study. It consisted of seven carefully described articles, the nature of which leaves little room for us to doubt their intended symbolical and typical meaning, while their number—as in many other occurrences of the number seven—conveys the idea of completeness. Let us, in imagination, enter the sacred enclosure through the "gate" of the Outer Court, and reverently pass through the Tabernacle, pausing in turn at each of these seven objects, and noting the order in which they occur. A glance at the diagram on the opposite page will reduce this to the utmost simplicity.

First, then, on passing through the "gate" into the large Outer Court, we come to the brazen altar of sacrifice (xxvii. 1–8; xxxviii. 1–7), which is intended to teach us, at the very threshold, that the only way for sinful man to approach his holy God is through atoning sacrifice—a sacrifice which is at one and the same time a confession of man's sin on the one part, and a satisfaction to God on the other.

Moving on from the brazen altar, we next come to the laver, also of brass (xxx. 17–21; xxxviii. 8), containing the sacred water for the cleansing of those who ministered in the things of the Sanctuary; and this speaks to us of the need for spiritual renewal (hands and feet were to be washed before every act of ministering, speaking of holy conduct and walk).

Next we reach the "door" of the Sanctuary itself; and, passing through, we find ourselves in the "Holy Place." Here, on our right hand (the north side), we find the table of the shewbread (xxv. 23–30; xxxvii. 10–16), with its oblations (food) and libations (drink), speaking of sustenance for the spiritual life. On the left hand (the south side) we see the seven-branched candelabrum (xxv. 31–40; xxxvii. 17–24), speaking of spiritual illumination. Then, in front of us, and standing just before the "veil" of the "Holy of Holies," is the golden altar of incense, fragrantly symbolising acceptable supplication (xxx. 1–10; xxxvii. 25–28).

Finally, passing through the "veil" into the "Holy of Holies," we see that most sacred gold-covered acacia chest, the ark, speaking of covenant relationship between God and His people; and, above it, on the lid, the mercy seat, with the two cherubim, one at each side, facing each other and touching their outstretched wings above the mercy seat and the shekinah fire which burned just over it—the blood-sprinkled, shekinah-lit mercy seat speaking of intercession in the very presence of God, and of the very life of God imparted.

See, then, the remarkable progress and completeness of symbolical teaching in this sevenfold succession of objects—atonement, regeneration, spiritual sustenance, illumination, supplication, complete access and reconciliation through covenant relationship, and identification with the life of God, manifested and symbolically imparted in the shekinah flame.

For the sake of clarity, this, along with the *typical* meanings of these seven objects, may be set out as follows:

THE FURNITURE	SYMBOLICAL MEANING	TYPICAL MEANING
(1) Brazen Altar.	Atonement through sacrifice.	The Atonement of Christ.
(2) Brazen Laver.	Spiritual renewal.	Regeneration and renewal by the Holy Spirit.
(3) Table of Shewbread.	Spiritual sustenance.	Christ the Bread of Life the Holy Spirit the Water of Life.
(4) Candlestand.	Spiritual illumination.	Christ the Light of the world, and especially of His own people.
(5) Altar of Incense.	Acceptable supplication.	Prayer in the name of Jesus (see John xiv. 13, with Rev. v. 8).
(6) The Ark.	Access through Covenant relationship.	Christ as the covenant-ground of our access to God.
(7) Mercy Seat and Shekinah.	The very presence and life of God.	Christ as "Mercy Seat" (Rom. iii. 25), and (Shekinah) Holy Spirit as the imparted life of God.

A remarkable parallel has been traced between the order of this furniture in the Tabernacle and the order of the Gospel according to John. It is as though John were leading us, in exactly the same order as found in the Tabernacle, to the great spiritual *realities* which the seven articles of furniture in the Tabernacle typified. He begins by leading us to the Brazen Altar of Sacrifice; for twice over in chapter i he bids us "Behold the Lamb of God, which taketh away the sin of the world." Then, in chapter iii, he takes us to the Laver, telling us that

"Except a man be born of water and of the Spirit, he cannot enter into the kingdom of God."

Next, in chapters iv to vi, he takes us to the Table of the Shewbread, with its food and drink—recording for us the Lord's discourse to the woman concerning "the living water," of which if a man drink he shall never thirst again, and the great discourse on "the living bread," of which if a man eat he shall live for ever. Next, in chapters viii and ix, he takes us to the golden candlestand. Twice over we hear Christ saying: "I am the light of the world"; "He that followeth Me shall not walk in darkness, but shall have the light of life"; and the man born blind is given sight by the great Lightbringer.

Then, in chapters xiv to xvi there come those wonderful new lessons about praying in the name of Jesus, and we find ourselves at the golden Altar of Incense, offering prayers that became as fragrant odours by the breathing of that Name which, above all others, is dear to the heart of God.

Then, in that wonderful prayer of the Lord Jesus which is recorded in the seventeenth chapter, we are taken through the veil into the Holy of Holies and are given a glimpse of His high-priestly ministry of intercession for us in the presence of God. Nor do we see Christ there only as our High Priest, but as both the Ark and the Mercy Seat also—the covenant-ground of our access and acceptance by a new relationship, for in chapter twenty the risen One says: "I ascend unto My Father and *your* Father, and to My God and *your* God."

Finally, the reality which corresponds with the symbolic meaning of the Shekinah is disclosed. "He breathed on them, and saith unto them: *Receive ye the Holy Ghost.*" The very life of God becomes imparted to the blood-bought believer by the Holy Spirit (see John xx. 22).

How wonderful is all this correspondence of order between the long-ago Tabernacle in the wilderness and John's new pen-and-ink tabernacle of testimony! Shall we put it down to accident or Divine design? How much more wonderful still is that dear Saviour in whom we have all these seven Divine provisions, from the altar of atonement to the Pentecostal Shekinah!

THE PRIESTHOOD

We must now refer to the Priesthood, the provisions and regulations concerning which are a subject of rich interest. As we can give but the briefest treatment to this subject before passing on from Exodus to Leviticus, we must confine ourselves to one part of it, and deal with that as being representative of the whole. We shall consider the High Priest's *garments*. These are carefully described in chapter xxviii.

Turning to that chapter, we find, first, that the garments prescribed for the High Priest were to be *"for glory and beauty"* (verse 2). Arrayed with these adornments of gold and blue and purple and scarlet and fine linen and flashing gems, Israel's High Priest must indeed have looked glorious and beautiful; but who shall tell the glory and beauty of heaven's Beloved as *He* represents *us* on high?

The prescribed articles of wear for the High Priest were seven in number (see verses 4, 36, 42). They were the "breastplate," the "ephod," the "robe," the "coat," and the "linen breeches," while for the head there were the "mitre" and the "holy crown" (verses 4, 36, 42, xxix. 6).

The "breeches" were linen shorts. The "coat"—unlike our western garment of that name—was a long linen garment worn next to the body. The "robe" was a long, seamless dress worn over the "coat." It was of blue linen, and embroidered round the edge of the skirt with alternate bells of gold and pomegranates of blue and purple and scarlet. A beautifully wrought girdle secured it about the waist. The "ephod" was a short garment from the shoulders down to the waist or perhaps a little lower. The "breastplate" was a square linen container worn in front of the ephod. The "mitre" was a white linen turban; and the "holy crown" was a golden plate on the front of the mitre, inscribed with the words: "Holiness to the Lord."

Thus, these "garments" would be put on in practically the reverse order of that in which they are specified—first the "breeches," then the "coat," then, over these, the "robe," then the "ephod," then the "breastplate," and finally the "mitre" bearing the "holy crown."

Strictly speaking, the under-garments, namely, the "breeches" and the "coat," were the *ordinary* garments of the High Priest as distinct from his others, which were "for glory and beauty." Three of these latter are given special emphasis, and it is obvious that they are meant to represent great truths to us. They are the "ephod," the "breastplate," the "holy crown."

The Ephod

As already mentioned, the "ephod" (xxviii. 5–14) was a short garment from the shoulders down to the waist or perhaps a little lower. It consisted of two pieces, back and front, "joined together" at the shoulders by two "shoulder pieces" (verse 7). It was made of fine-twined linen, and embroidered with gold and blue and purple and scarlet (verse 6). It was held to the body by an artistically wrought girdle intertwining the same colours (verse 8). In line with the typical meanings everywhere present in this part of Scripture, the gold and blue and purple and scarlet and fine white linen speak, respectively, of our Lord's deity, heavenliness, royalty, sacrifice, and perfect righteousness; but most significant of all is what we are told about the two "shoulder pieces" (verses 9–12).

Two onyx stones were to be set in sockets of gold on these shoulder pieces; and in these were to be engraved the names of the twelve tribes of Israel—six on the one stone and six on the other. The reason for this is given in verse 12:

> "Thou shalt put the two stones upon the shoulders of the ephod for stones of memorial unto the children of Israel: and Aaron shall bear their names before the Lord upon his two shoulders for a memorial."

Thus the names of Israel were enshrined in precious stones, set in sockets of pure gold, to be borne upon the High Priest's *shoulder*, and memorialised before the Lord.

The Breastplate

The "breastplate" (xxviii. 15–29) was a piece of finely woven linen about 17 inches long by 8½ inches wide, doubled over so as to make a kind of square bag 8½ by 8½ inches. It displayed the same colours as the "ephod," and must have been exceedingly beautiful, for in it, also, there shone twelve precious jewels, in four rows of three each—each of the twelve bearing the name of one of the tribes of Israel, and all twelve being enclosed in settings of pure gold. The breastplate was held in position by two chains of wreathen gold which hung it on to the shoulder pieces of the "ephod" (verses 22–5), and by a "lace of blue" (at the two lower corners) which fastened it to the "ephod." The reason for all this is given in verse 29:

"And Aaron shall bear the names of the children of Israel in the breastplate of judgment upon his heart, when he goeth in unto the holy place, for a memorial unto the Lord continually."

Thus, again, are the names of God's own written in jewels and set in gold, to be memorialised before Him—but this time they are upon the High Priest's *heart*.

The Holy Crown

This was a "plate of pure gold" fastened to the front of the "mitre," and bearing the inscription: "Holiness unto the Lord" (verses 36–7). The meaning of it is explained in verse 38:

"It shall be upon Aaron's forehead, that Aaron may bear the iniquity of the holy things which the children of Israel shall hallow in all their holy gifts; and it shall be always upon his forehead that they may be accepted before the Lord."

The point in this verse is that, despite the ceremonial cleansings associated with Israel's worship, both offerings and offerers, in themselves, were really unholy in the all-holy eyes of God; yet in the High Priest, who gathered up all the people into one in himself, as it were, and at the same time bespoke the atoning sacrifice which covered them all—in him, with his garments of "glory and beauty" (typifying the glorious merit and atonement of Christ), the unholiness of the people became changed into "holiness unto the Lord," and thus the people were "accepted before the Lord."

Glorious type-teaching

Now what is the meaning of all this for *us*? Why are all these details given so carefully about the "ephod" and the "breast-

plate" and the "holy crown"? It is because there is glorious
type-teaching in it all. Here are earthly things with heavenly
meanings; physical objects setting forth great spiritual realities.

Aaron the High Priest is a type of the Lord Jesus as our High
Priest. First, in the "ephod," the High Priest bears Israel's
tribes collectively upon his *shoulders*. Then, in the "breastplate,"
he bears them individually upon his *heart*. Then, as he bears
them thus before God, he bears all their imperfection, and completely covers it all up in his own "glory and beauty," so that,
instead, God sees "Holiness to the Lord" shining from the High
Priest's brow, and the people are accepted in him. See verse 38:
"It shall be always upon *HIS* forehead, that *THEY* may be
accepted."

Three times in these three key verses (12, 29, 38) we have it
that the High Priest shall "*bear*" his people and their interests
—on his *shoulder*, on his *heart*, on his *brow*; and each time they
are represented as beautiful gems and pure gold!

We see in all this a picture of Christ and His people. First, we
are borne upon His great *shoulders*. The shoulder is the place
of upholding power. Here, then, we see our mighty Saviour's
all-sufficient power to uphold us and all our concerns, both in
the presence of God and through all the experiences that come
to us.

Then, we are borne upon His *heart*. The heart is the place of
love. As each of Israel's tribes was named in those precious
stones of long ago, so each blood-bought Christian is forever in
the heart, in the love and tender thought of Christ as He stands
before God on our behalf. Moreover, as those jewels shone from
Aaron's breast, so do the people of Christ shine forth from the
heart of Christ like precious gems in the presence of God.

Again, as our Lord represents us on high, "Holiness to the
Lord" flashes from His *brow*. The brow is the noblest and most
distinguishing feature of man. Holiness must be written here,
to be seen before all else as the High Priest enters the most holy
Presence. This is the first thing God beholds in *our* glorious High
Priest in the heavenly sanctuary. He bears it on *HIS* forehead
that *WE* may be accepted! As Aaron was to bear the "holy
crown" *always* (see verse 38), so Christ bears it always for us, so
that in Him *we* become *ALWAYS ACCEPTED*!

All this is taught *doctrinally* in the New Testament—especially in Ephesians and Hebrews. We are "accepted *in the Beloved*" who bears us on His heart before God. We are chosen "*in Him*" to be "holy and without blame," for He is our holiness. We are told of the Divine "*power* to us-ward who believe"—and that power is seen in Christ who bears His people on His mighty shoulder, "far above all principality and power and might, and every name that is named"! Well may our praise forever flow to God for such a Saviour!

Here we must break off, and leave all the many other wonderful typical teachings embodied in the Aaronic Priesthood to the joyous investigation of the reader.

CAN YOU ANSWER THESE?

1. What are the three principal subjects in the Book of Exodus, and what three attributes of God do they express?
2. What is the general structure of the book? What are the three parts of the Law, and what three aspects of life do they cover?
3. What four things did the outgoing from Egypt mean for Israel?
4. What are the main points of comparison and contrast between the Exodus and the Gospel?
5. Why was the Law given to Israel? Was it meant to be a *new* covenant, displacing the Abrahamic?
6. What is the relation between the so-called Mosaic covenant and the Abrahamic covenant?
7. What were the three parts of the Tabernacle, and what were their dimensions?
8. What were the articles of furniture in the Tabernacle, and their typical meanings?
9. What symbolic meaning is suggested as being latent in the dimensions of the Holy of Holies?
10. What were the High Priest's adornments, and what type-teaching do we find in them?

THE BOOK OF LEVITICUS (1)

Lesson Number 9

NOTE.—For this study read once the first seven chapters of Leviticus, and chapters xviii. to xx.

"The versatile ne'er-do-well is often castigated by the taunt, 'Jack of all trades and master of none.' In reality, however, that saying is a perversion. What the famous Benjamin Franklin actually said was that a man should be 'Jack-of-all-trades and master of *one*.' A really cultured man has been described as one who knows something about everything, and everything about something. So far as the Christian worker is concerned, and most of all the Christian minister, the specialisation-point must be the Bible. Other knowledge may be interesting, useful, important; but to be a master in Bible knowledge is *vital*."

J. S. B.

THE BOOK OF LEVITICUS (1)

A CERTAIN lady, on being asked if she had ever read the Bible right through, replied: "I have never read it right through, though I have read much of it consecutively. Three times I have started to read it through, but each time I have broken down in Leviticus. I have enjoyed Genesis and Exodus, but Leviticus has seemed such dull reading that I have become discouraged and have given up." Which did that friend the more deserve—sympathy or rebuke? To speak of Leviticus as "dull reading" misses the point of the book completely. How could we expect a book like Leviticus, which is occupied throughout with regulations, to provide exciting reading? Obviously, it is not meant just to be read, but to be *studied*. It yields little of its treasure to a mere reading; but a reasonable concentration transforms it into one of the most intriguing articles in the Scriptures.

Clearing the Ground

At the outset, let us clear away certain discouraging misunderstandings about the book. There appear to be four such. First, there are those who think it impossible for them so to master all the ritual and symbol in Leviticus as to get much spiritual profit. Second, there are those who suppose that since the Levitical prescriptions have now long passed away, with the Mosaic dispensation, they cannot sustain any living relation to the present day. Third, there are others who profess difficulty, inasmuch as certain of the Levitical commands, in their severity or seeming triviality, seem at variance with what else we know of God. Fourth, still others are discouraged because, whereas in Genesis and Exodus the main outline is easily found, there seems no such clear outline here, in this third book of Scripture.

Now, any fair study of Leviticus will quickly dispel these misgivings; for, as we shall see, it simply abounds in spiritual values; it has a living voice to our own day; its revelation of the Divine character is unique; and it is built together according to a clear plan. Its Mosaic authorship and Divine inspiration are attested by the Lord Jesus. It is referred to over forty times in the New Testament. All that follows it in the Scriptures is coloured by it; and, therefore, a clear knowledge of it contributes greatly towards comprehending the message of the Bible as a whole.

Much depends on a right approach to the book; and with a view to this we need to see its main purpose, its abiding value, its peculiar viewpoint and its structure.

Its Main Purpose

Leviticus was written to show Israel how to live as a holy nation in fellowship with God, and thus to prepare the nation for the high service of mediating the redemption of God to all the nations. Above all, then, Israel must be taught the holiness of God, and Leviticus reveals this in three ways: (1) in the *sacrificial system*, which insisted that "without the shedding of blood there is no remission," thus pressing on the most obtuse conscience the seriousness of sin; (2) in the *precepts* of the law, which insisted on the one Divinely revealed standard for character and conduct; (3) in the *penalties* attaching to violations of the law, which sternly proclaimed the inflexibility of the Divine holiness.

Involved in this revelation of Israel's holy God is the imperative insistence on Israel's *separation* from the other nations; and the laws of Leviticus are intended to ensure this separation, and to prepare the nation for the fulfilling of its high vocation. It may be added, also, that Leviticus was designed to prepare Israel for the coming Christ, by awakening a sense of need, and at the same time pointing forward, through the Tabernacle ritual, to the one all-atoning offering on Calvary.

Its Abiding Value

First, Leviticus is a revelation of the Divine character to ourselves today, as much as it was to Israel of old. God has not changed.

Second, it is a symbolic exposition of the basic principles which underlie all dealing between God and men, just as truly today as in the past; for although the Levitical priesthood and sacrifices are now done away, the spiritual realities which they pictorially declare abide for all time. Nowadays, even among professing

Christians, it is common to belittle the idea of atonement through propitiatory sacrifice: but over against this stands Leviticus, endorsed by the clear-cut witness of our Lord Himself and the inspired writers of the New Testament.

Third, Leviticus provides a body of civil law for the theocracy; and although some of the details in it are now otiose, the principles of it are such as should guide legislation today. Religion and State, Capital and Labour, land-ownership and property rights, marriage and divorce—these and other matters, which are all to the fore today, are dealt with in Leviticus. It has been truly said that "there is not one of these questions on which the legislation of Leviticus does not shed a flood of light into which our modern law-makers would do well to come and walk."

Fourth, Leviticus is a treasury of symbolic and typical teaching. Here are the greatest spiritual truths enshrined in vivid symbols. Here are the great facts of the New Covenant illustrated by great types in the Old Covenant. Supremely, it is in these ways an advance unveiling of Christ. It is a "treasury of Divinely chosen illustrations as to the way of a sinner's salvation through the priestly work of the Son of God, and as to his present and future position and dignity as a redeemed man." Moreover, in some of the figure-language of Leviticus there lie great prophecies of things which even to ourselves are still future. Dr. S. H. Kellogg says: "We must not imagine that because many of its types are long ago fulfilled, therefore all have been fulfilled. Many, according to the hints of the New Testament, await their fulfilment in a bright day that is coming. Some, for instance, of the feasts of the Lord have been fulfilled, as Passover and the feast of Pentecost. But how about the day of atonement for the sin of corporate Israel? We have seen the type of the day of atonement fulfilled in the entering into heaven of our great High Priest; but in the type He came out again to bless the people: has that been ful- filled? Has He yet proclaimed absolution of sin to guilty Israel? How, again, about the Feast of Trumpets, and that of the in- gathering at full harvest? How about the Sabbatic years, and that most consummate type of all, the year of Jubilee? History records nothing which could be held a fulfilment of any of these; and thus Leviticus bids us look forward to a glorious future yet to come, when the great redemption shall at last be accomplished, and 'Holiness to Jehovah' shall, as Zechariah puts it (xiv. 20), be written even 'on the bells of the horses.'" Thus we see something of the abiding value of Leviticus!

Its Standpoint

Perhaps the first simple step toward understanding the message of Leviticus is to appreciate its standpoint. This is indicated in the first words of the first chapter—"And the Lord called unto Moses, and spake unto him *out of the tabernacle of the congregation.*"

Before this, a distant God has spoken from "the mount that burned with fire"; but now—as we see at the end of Exodus—the Tabernacle is erected "according to the pattern showed in the mount," and a God who dwells among His people in *fellowship* with them speaks "out of the Tabernacle." The people, therefore, are not addressed as sinners distanced from God, like those of other nations, but as being already brought into a new relationship, even that of *fellowship*, on the ground of a blood-sealed covenant.

In line with this, the sacrifices in Leviticus do not mean to set forth how the people may *become* redeemed (for their redemption has already been wrought through the paschal lamb of the Exodus, and is now to be forever memorialised in the Passover feast). No, the Levitical sacrifices are prescribed in such wise as to set forth *how the new relationship may be maintained.*

In their *typical* interpretation the Levitical sacrifices are a wonderful unfolding of the sacrifice of Christ in its many-sided efficacy toward those of us who have *already entered* into the new relationship of justification by faith.

This is the point at which Leviticus begins. It thus follows Genesis and Exodus with obvious sequence. In Genesis we see God's remedy for man's ruin—the Seed of the woman. In Exodus we see God's answer to man's cry—the blood of the Lamb. In Leviticus we see God's provision for man's need—a Priest, a Sacrifice, and an Altar. (It is from this that Leviticus gets its name. Israel's priests were the Levites, and the word "Leviticus" comes from the Greek *Leuitikos*, meaning, "that which pertains to the Levites.") With good reason Leviticus holds the central place among the five books of Moses, for, with its doctrine of mediation through a priest, absolution through a sacrifice, and reconciliation at the altar, it is the very heart of the Pentateuch—and of the Gospel.

As C. I. Scofield observes, "Leviticus stands in the same relation to Exodus that the Epistles do to the Gospels." In the Gospels we are *set free*, by the blood of the Lamb. In the Epistles we are *indwelt*, by the Spirit of God. In the Gospels God speaks to us *from without*. In the Epistles God speaks to us *from within*. In the Gospels we have the *ground* of fellowship with God—redemption. In the Epistles we have the *walk* of fellowship with God—sanctification. As in Leviticus, so in the Epistles, there is exhibited to us the *many-sidedness* of the work of atonement as it bears on those who are already redeemed.

This, then, is the standpoint of Leviticus, and it thus becomes of special relevance to those of us who have found redemption in Christ Jesus; for, as one has said, these Levitical sacrifices are perhaps "the most complete description" of our Saviour's atoning work anywhere given to us.

As we survey these Levitical sacrifices we gain a fuller view and a bigger conception of what happened on Calvary. The different facets of the incomparable diamond are turned successively to the eye. The matchless miracle of grace is seen in its complexity and all-sufficiency, until we break forth into singing:

Dear dying Lamb, Thy precious blood
    Shall never lose its power
Till all the ransomed Church of God
    Be saved to sin no more.

E'er since by faith I saw the stream
    Thy flowing wounds supply,
Redeeming love has been my theme,
    And shall be till I die.

Then, in a nobler, sweeter song,
    I'll sing Thy power to save,
With sinless heart and raptured tongue,
    In triumph o'er the grave.

THE STRUCTURE

And now, what about the *structure* of Leviticus? In our examination of Genesis and Exodus we have seen that to appreciate their structure is to be guided safely to their central message and permanent value. The same thing—unless we are strangely mistaken—is true of Leviticus.

Our reason for the qualifying words, "unless we are strangely mistaken," is that analyses of Leviticus, which well-known Bible teachers have issued, vary considerably. One tells us that the book is in nine divisions, another says seven, another six, another five, another two (the two parts being chapters i. to x., and xi. to xxvii.). When the doctors disagree, what shall the plain man do?

Well, in the first place, we must resolutely hold to our determination not to *make* any of the books of Scripture divide up, for this is simply to force an artificial analysis—a convenient procedure which is all too often followed by would-be Bible teachers who have an aptitude for dividing subjects under alliterative headings. We must look at each book fairly and squarely, as it lies before us. Let us try to deal in this way with Leviticus.

The Two Major Parts

What then do we find? Why, this—that whatever *sub*-divisions there may or may not be, the book is certainly in *two main parts* which are marked off in an unmistakable way, the first part covering chapters i. to xvii., the second part covering chapters xviii. to xxvii. And what is it that so clearly breaks the book up into these two parts? It is this—that throughout these first seventeen chapters we are dealing with *non*-moral regulations, whereas in the remaining ten we are dealing with regulations concerning *morals*. The first part has to do with *worship*. The second part has to do with *practice*. In the first part all relates to the *Tabernacle*. In the second part all pertains to *character and conduct*. Part one shows the *way to* God—by sacrifice. Part two shows the *walk with* God—by sanctification. The first part deals with *ceremonial* and *physical* defilement. The second part deals with *moral* and *spiritual* defilement. In the first part *purification* is provided. In the second part *punishment* is to be inflicted. The first part has to do with the people's *cleansing*. The second part has to do with the people's *clean living*.

The Central Message

Now before ever we start asking whether there are any *sub-divisions* in Leviticus, this one simple division of the book into its two major parts suggests the main idea here. We have seen, in considering the *standpoint* of Leviticus, that God here speaks "out of the tabernacle," having come down to dwell in *fellowship* with His redeemed people, and that He addresses the people as being now already brought into the new relationship of *fellowship* on the ground of the blood-sealed covenant. This idea of new relationship, of fellowship, is the key to Leviticus. In the two main parts of the book we see first (i.–xvii.) the *basis* of fellowship, in propitiatory sacrifice; then, second (xviii.–xxvii.), the *obligations* of fellowship, in practical sanctification. In other words, part one shows us the Godward *foundation* of fellowship; and part two shows us the manward *condition* of fellowship.

Thus Leviticus is concerned with fellowship; and it is the supreme Old Testament illustration of that great New Testament truth expressed in I John i. 7—"*If we walk in the light as He is in the light, we have fellowship one with another, and the blood of Jesus Christ, His Son, cleanseth us from all sin.*" The first part of Leviticus says: "The blood cleanseth us." The second part of Leviticus says: "Yes, the blood cleanseth us, but only if we walk in the light." The message of the whole book is that through these two things together—cleansing and walking in the light—we have fellowship one with another, and truly our fellowship is "with the Father."

Let us therefore get this much clearly fixed in our minds, that Leviticus is in these two broad divisions:

1. THE GROUND OF FELLOWSHIP—SACRIFICE
   (i.–xvii.).

2. THE WALK OF FELLOWSHIP—SEPARATION
   (xviii.–xxvii.).

Our next step is to explore these two parts; and here we find orderly design as beautiful as it is clear. Take the first part (i.–xvii.). The first seven chapters are exclusively occupied with the *offerings* which are to be offered. The next three chapters are all about the *priests* who were to officiate in connection with the offerings. The next six chapters are all about the physical and ceremonial cleansing of the *people*, both individually and nationally; while the final chapter in this part is given to emphasising the one *place* to which the offerings might be brought, namely, the altar within the gate of the Tabernacle. Thus we have Offerings, Priesthood, People, Altar.

Turning to the second part (xviii.–xxvii.), we find the same kind of orderly progress. In chapters xviii. to xx. we have regulations concerning the *people*. In chapters xxi. and xxii. we have regulations concerning the *priests*. In chapters xxiii. and xxiv. we have regulations concerning the *feasts*, with a closely-connected word in xxiv. about the light and the shew-bread in the Sanctuary. (The feasts were a *periodic* memorial of Israel before God: the light and the bread were a *perpetual* memorial.) Finally, in chapters xxv. to xxvii., we have regulations concerning Israel's occupancy of *Canaan*. Such is the order in part two: People, Priests, Feasts, Canaan. Here is a general analysis:—

THE BOOK OF LEVITICUS

FELLOWSHIP THROUGH SANCTIFICATION

I. THE GROUND OF FELLOWSHIP—SACRIFICE

(i.–xviii.).

THE OFFERINGS (ABSOLUTION)—i.–vii.
THE PRIESTHOOD (MEDIATION)—viii.–x.
THE PEOPLE (PURIFICATION)—xi.–xvi.
THE ALTAR (RECONCILIATION)—xvii.

II. THE WALK OF FELLOWSHIP—SEPARATION

(xviii.–xxvii.).

REGULATIONS CONCERNING THE PEOPLE—xviii.–xx.
REGULATIONS CONCERNING THE PRIESTS—xxi.–xxii.
REGULATIONS CONCERNING FEASTS, ETC.—xxiii.–xxiv.
REGULATIONS CONCERNING CANAAN—xxv.–xxvii.

THE BOOK OF LEVITICUS (2)

Lesson 10

NOTE.—For this study read chapters i. to vii. (marking off the different offerings), then chapters viii. to xvii.

"Keep the Incense burning."
On the altar fire
Let thy heart's petition,
Let thy deep desire,
Be a cloud of incense
Wreathing heaven's throne,
Till God's power within thee
Shall be fully known.

"Keep the incense burning."
Hourly let it rise,
Till from opened heavens,
Till from flame-swept skies,
Fire thy heart shall kindle
To a joyous flame,
Making thee a glory
To the Saviour's Name.

THE BOOK OF LEVITICUS (2)
PART I (i.–xvii.)

(1) The Offerings (i.–vii.)

THE FIRST seven chapters of Leviticus are occupied with the *Offerings*. Detailed study of these offerings finds in them a resistless fascination. Here we can only speak of them collectively; yet even this will be enough to indicate their richness of spiritual meaning. The section divides up as follows:

> Chapter i.—The Burnt Offering.
> ,,   ii.—The Meal Offering.
> ,,   iii.—The Peace Offering.
> ,,   iv.—The Sin Offering.
> ,,   v.—The Trespass Offering.

The remainder of the section is taken up with the "laws" conditioning these offerings (see vi. 8 to vii. 38).

Thus there were five kinds of offering prescribed; and the first thing that strikes our notice is that they are divided into three and two. The first three are "sweet savour" offerings (i. 9, 13, 17; ii. 2, 9; iii. 5, 16). The remaining two are *non*-sweet savour offerings. The first three are voluntary. The other two are compulsory. The first three comprise the first utterance of Jehovah with which the book of Leviticus opens (i. 2). The other two are introduced by the second utterance, which begins iv. 2. Let this division fix itself clearly before the eye:

> The Burnt Offering
> The Meal Offering   } Sweet Savour;
> The Peace Offering   } Voluntary.
>
> The Sin Offering   } Non-Sweet Savour;
> The Trespass Offering   } Compulsory.

These offerings abound in spiritual significances; but their supreme value lies in their typical unfolding of the supreme sacrifice on Calvary. The sweet-savour offerings typify Christ in His own meritorious perfections. The non-sweet savour offerings typify Christ as bearing the *de*merit of the sinner. The sweet-savour offerings speak rather of what the offering of Christ means to *God*. The non-sweet savour offerings speak rather of what the offering of Christ means to *us*—and it is in connection with these that we here find the nine occurrences of the words, "It shall be forgiven" (iv. 20, 26, 31, 35; v. 10, 13, 16, 18; vi. 7).

Note the distinctive aspects of these offerings. The *Burnt*-offering typifies Christ's "offering Himself without spot to God." It foreshadows Christ on the Cross, not so much bearing sin as *accomplishing the will of God*. We are shown the perfection of Christ's *offering* of Himself, as God sees it.

The *Meal*-offering (not "meat," as in A.V.) exhibits typically the perfect manhood of Christ. The emphasis here is on the *life* which was offered. It sets forth the perfection of character which gave the offering its unspeakable value.

The *Peace*-offering speaks of restored *communion*, resulting from the perfect satisfaction rendered in Christ. God is propitiated. Man is reconciled. There is peace.

As for the non-sweet savour offerings, the *Sin*-offering typifies Christ as Sinbearer—"made sin for us" (2 Cor. v. 21), while the *Trespass*-offering speaks of sins (plural), and typifies Christ as Expiator, making restitution for the injury caused by our wrongdoing.

And now observe the *order* of these offerings. In our study of the Tabernacle we saw that the furniture of the Tabernacle is given in the reverse order of human approach. God begins with the Ark in the Holy of Holies, moving outward from Himself toward man. The same order is followed in these Levitical offerings. God begins with the *Burnt*-offering and ends with the *Trespass*-offering. He leaves off where we begin. If we take these offerings in their reverse order, therefore, they exactly correspond with the order of our spiritual apprehension of Christ.

When we first come, as awakened and believing sinners, to the Cross, the first thing we see in it (answering to our first-felt need) is forgiveness for our many *trespasses*. But scarcely have we begun to rejoice in the forgiveness of our sins before we realise that there is a further and deeper need, namely, *sin* in our nature. This further need is met by a deeper insight into the meaning of the Cross. Christ not only "died for our sins"; He bore our *sin*, as typified in the *Sin*-offering. It is then, when we realise that both sins and sin have been dealt with in the Cross, that we enter into wonderful peace with God, as set forth in the *Peace*-offering. Then, still further, we find rest and joy and complete acceptance with God in the glorious perfections of Christ as typified in the *Meal*-offering; while more and more we come into fellowship with God through the fulness of that one perfect Offering to God on our behalf which is set forth in the *Burnt*-offering. Is there not wonderful Divine design in all this?

(2) The Priests (viii.-x.)

The section about the priests is of unexcelled interest. The point of it is that if fellowship between the redeemed and their holy God is to be maintained, there must not only be a *sacrifice* (as in chapters i.–vii.), but a *priest* (as in these chapters viii.–x.). Besides absolution from guilt there must be *mediation*. Thank God, the Lord Jesus is both sacrifice and priest in one, to His believing people, so that we have access to God by "a new and living way" (Heb. x. 20)—a "new" way because it is the way of the *Cross*, which speaks of the one final sacrifice for sin; and a "living" way because it is the way of the *Resurrection*, which speaks of the one ever-living Priest on high.

The three chapters in this section run as follows:

Chapter viii. *CONSECRATION*—the priests set apart for God;

  „ ix. *MINISTRATION*—the priests start their serving;

  „ x. *VIOLATION*—Nadab and Abihu offer "strange fire."

Take that wonderful eighth chapter in which we have the *consecration* of the priests. Is there anywhere a chapter richer in typical meanings and spiritual suggestions? Consecration means set-apart-ness. The priests are now set apart for God, and are *claimed* by Him as such in this consecration ceremony. In the first part of the chapter we have the *order* of consecration (verses 1–13.). Then we have the *basis* of consecration—the blood (verses 14–36). Observe the order of consecration:

THE HIGH PRIEST.	THE OTHER PRIESTS.
Cleansed—verse 6.	Cleansed—verse 6.
Clothed—verses 7–8.	Clothed—verse 13.
Crowned—verse 9.	Claimed—verse 30.
Claimed—verse 12.	Charged—verse 35.

The beautiful typical import in all this is too clear to need comment.

Look now at the *basis* of consecration (verses 14–30)—sacrifice. A sin-offering, a burnt-offering, and a "ram of consecration" are to be offered. Aaron and his sons are to lay their hands on the head of the sacrifice, by which *they* become identified with *it*; and then the blood of sacrifice must be sprinkled on them by which *it* becomes identified with *them*. Thus by a double identification the priests become associated with the atoning sacrifice on the ground of which they are accepted and consecrated. The right ear, the thumb of the right hand, the great toe of the right foot, must be blood-sealed (verses 23–24). "A blood-sealed *ear* was needed to hearken to the Divine communications; a blood-sealed *hand* was needed to execute the services of the Sanctuary; and a blood-sealed *foot* was needed to tread the courts of the Lord's house." The altar itself must be sprinkled (verses 15, 19, 24). The blood is the one grand foundation of all.

It will be noticed that a difference is made between the anointing of Aaron and that of his sons. Aaron is anointed *before* the slaying of the sacrifice (verse 12). His sons are anointed *after* the slaying, along with the sprinkling of the blood upon them (verse 30). True to its characteristic precision, the Scripture makes this distinction with good reason. In the type-teaching of this chapter, Aaron, the High Priest, prefigures the Lord Jesus, while his sons typically anticipate the believer-priests of the present dispensation. The sinless Lord Jesus needed no blood-sprinkling before receiving the anointing of the Holy Spirit; and in Aaron's being anointed alone, before the blood-shedding, we see a discriminating type-picture of the incarnate Son of God, Who, until He gave Himself on Calvary, stood absolutely alone. Without the blood-shedding, Aaron and his sons could not be together in the anointing. But *after* the blood-shedding, Moses anoints "Aaron . . . and his sons . . . *with him*" (verse 30). When once the blood had been shed, Aaron and his sons—typifying Christ and His priestly house—are united in the one priestly ministry: and, united as such, they all stand before God by virtue of the same sacrifice. There is now fullest identification. In the words of Hebrews ii. 11, "Both He that sanctifieth and they who are sanctified are all of one."

We can merely add a word about chapters ix. and x. In chapter ix. we see the first actual *ministration* of the priesthood; and this is set forth in such a way as to become forever afterwards a type of true priestly ministry. After offering sacrifice for the people, Aaron goes into the Holy Place as the representative of the people, and then returns with uplifted hand of benediction as the communicator of the Divine blessing to the people (verse 23). The whole of the ministry was "as the Lord commanded" (verse 10). It was therefore accepted by the Lord, and was attested by the appearing of the Divine glory (verses 23-4)—

"And Moses and Aaron went into the tabernacle of the congregation, and came out, and blessed the people: and the glory of the Lord appeared to all the people. And there came a fire out from before the Lord, and consumed upon the altar the burnt-offering and the fat: WHICH WHEN ALL THE PEOPLE SAW, THEY SHOUTED, AND FELL ON THEIR FACES."

Alas, this glorious scene at the end of chapter ix. quickly changes. In chapter x. the same fire which has gone forth and consumed the burnt-offering on the altar now leaps forth and devours two of the priests! Nadab and Abihu offer "strange fire" before the Lord, "which He commanded them not." Here is the sin of *presumption*; and it is visited with sudden and awful judgment. Over against chapter ix., with its approbation and *attestation* of the priesthood, we now see *presumption* and *rejection*! The offering of the "strange fire" by Nadab and Abihu was "will-worship." It was "of the flesh." It had no warrant in the revealed will of God. It was a vain intruding, a violating of priestly privilege, and was utterly repudiated. Israel's priests must learn at once and forever to walk by the inflexible rule of undeviating adherence to the will and word of God.

There are many Nadabs and Abihus today. Their presumption often goes long unpunished—for the present dispensation is that of *grace*; but the tenth chapter of Leviticus is a solemn warning that though judgment tarry, it will surely fall at last. God is not mocked!

(3) The People (xi.-xvi.)

If any Scripture confirmation were required for the old proverb, "cleanliness is next to godliness," Leviticus xi. to xvi. would be quite enough. These chapters tell us that God's people must be a *clean* people. They must be clean both inwardly and outwardly. There must be physical cleanliness; and there must also be ceremonial cleansing from that which defiles them morally and spiritually in the eyes of God. They are to be both sanitarily clean and sacrificially cleansed.

The purpose of the teaching in this section is to "make a difference between the unclean and the clean" (xi. 47), and to "separate the children of Israel from their uncleanness" (xv. 31). See also xvi. 30—"The priest shall make an atonement for you to cleanse you, that ye may be clean from all your sins before the Lord." Here, in this section, we have the "categorical imperative" of cleansing.

The subjects dealt with are: flesh-diet (xi.), child-birth (xii.), leprosy in bodies, garments, and dwellings (xiii.-xiv.), sex-hygiene (xv.), and national cleansing by expiatory sacrifice (xvi.). We may classify the contents of these chapters in a more easily rememberable way by saying that this section insists on—

clean foods	— xi.
clean bodies	— xii.-xiii. 46.
clean clothes	— xiii. 47-59.
clean houses	— xiv. 33-57.
clean contacts	— xv.
a clean nation	— xvi.

We cannot here discuss the contents of these chapters. They are a separate study in themselves. They should be read carefully with the aid of a good commentary (and we would recommend, in particular, Dr. S. H. Kellogg's book on Leviticus). Chapter xvi., the great chapter about the annual Day of Atonement, we shall consider by itself later.

(4) The Altar (xvii.)

The first of the two main parts of Leviticus ends with this brief section about the Altar (xvii.). No observant reader can fail to be impressed by the solemnly emphatic language of this seventeenth chapter, concerning the one place of sacrifice. Five times, and with severe explicitness, the one Divinely ordained place is stipulated.

"What man soever there be of the house of Israel, that killeth an ox or lamb or goat in the camp, or that killeth it out of the camp, and bringeth it not unto THE DOOR OF THE TABERNACLE of the congregation, to offer an offering unto the Lord before THE TABERNACLE OF THE LORD, blood shall be imputed unto that man; he hath shed blood; and that man shall be cut off from among his people: to the end that the children of Israel may bring their sacrifices, which they offer in the open field, even that they may bring them unto the Lord, unto THE DOOR OF THE TABER-NACLE of the congregation, unto the priest, and offer them for peace-offerings unto the Lord. And the priest shall sprinkle the blood upon the altar of the Lord at THE DOOR OF THE TABERNACLE of the congregation, and burn the fat for a sweet savour unto the Lord. Whatsoever man there be of the house of Israel, or of the strangers which sojourn among you, that offereth a burnt-offering or sacrifice, and bringeth it not unto THE DOOR OF THE TABER-NACLE of the congregation, to offer it unto the Lord, even that man shall be cut off from among his people" (xvii. 3–9).

The meaning of this for ourselves is clear. There is one place, and only one, where God, in sovereign grace, has elected to meet with penitent sinners, and that is the Cross—of which the altar at the door of the Tabernacle was a type. None other sacrifice! None other priest! None other altar! "None other name under heaven given among men whereby we must be saved!" "There and there alone"—if we may borrow the words of another—"has God's claim upon life been duly recognised. To reject this meeting-

E

place is to bring down judgment upon oneself—it is to trample under foot the just claims of God, and to arrogate to oneself a right to life which all have forfeited."

Fittingly accompanying this emphasis on the one place of sacrifice, the remaining verses of chapter xvii. explain the sanctity of blood, and the meaning of blood-sacrifices. In verse 11 we read: "*For the life of the flesh is in the blood, and I have given it to you upon the altar, to make an atonement for your souls; for it is the blood that maketh an atonement for the soul.*"

It is well to note, however, that even the blood has no atoning value unless it be on the altar. God says: "I have given it (the blood) to you *upon the altar*, to make an atonement for your souls." It must be the blood; and it must be the one altar.

The Scofield note on this verse says: "The meaning of all sacrifice is here explained. Every offering was an execution of the sentence of the law upon a substitute for the offender, and every such offering pointed forward to that substitutional death of Christ which alone vindicated the righteousness of God in passing over the sins of those who offered the typical sacrifices" (Rom. iii. 24, 25). And again: "The value of the 'life' is the measure of the value of the 'blood.' This gives the blood of Christ its inconceivable value. When it was shed the sinless God-man gave his life."

The shed blood is the basis of all. It is through the shed blood of Calvary's Lamb—nothing more, nothing less, nothing else— that we have our reconciliation and salvation.

Thus, in the first half of Leviticus, we have—(1) the Offerings, (2) the Priests, (3) the People, (4) the Altar.

Let us lay well to heart the great truths in these chapters!

> "The life is in the blood,"
> And must for sin atone
> "One sacrifice" and "once for all,"
> The blood of Christ alone.

> Oh, see the guilt of sin
> Which needed such a price,
> And see the marvel of that Love
> Which made the sacrifice!

THE BOOK OF LEVITICUS (3)

Lesson Number 11

NOTE.—For this study read very carefully chapters xviii. to xxiv.

FOCAL POINT OF LEVITICUS
(PART II: XVIII.–XXVII.)

"Here (in the words 'I am the Lord your God') we have the founda-tion of the entire superstructure of moral conduct which these chapters present. Israel's actings were to take their character from the fact that Jehovah was *their* God. They were called to comport themselves in a manner worthy of so high and holy a position. It was God's prerogative to set forth the special character and line of conduct becoming a people with whom He was pleased to associate His name. The moment He entered into a relationship with a people their ethics were to assume a character and tone worthy of Him. This is the true principle of holiness for the people of God in all ages. They are to be governed and characterised by the revelation which He has made of Himself. Their conduct is to be founded upon what He is, not upon what they are in themselves. The whole of Leviticus finds its focal point in the words: 'Ye shall be holy; for I, JEHOVAH YOUR GOD, am holy'" (xix. 2).

C. H. MACKINTOSH.

THE BOOK OF LEVITICUS (3)
PART II (xviii.–xxvii.)

THE SECOND part of Leviticus, as we have noted, is concerned with the *walk* of God's people—with their morals and conduct. Mere *positional* sanctification (as in part one) is not enough: there must be *practical* sanctification (which is the purpose in part two). The new chapters are introduced with this weighty charge:

"And the Lord spake unto Moses, saying: Speak unto the children of Israel, and say unto them: I am the Lord your God. After the doings of the land of Egypt wherein ye dwelt, shall ye not do; and after the doings of the land of Canaan, whither I bring you, shall ye not do; neither shall ye walk in their ordinances. Ye shall do My judgments, and keep Mine ordinances, to walk therein: I am the Lord your God. Ye shall therefore keep My statutes, and My judgments, which, if a man do, he shall live in them. I am the Lord" (xviii. 1–5).

These words—"I AM JEHOVAH YOUR GOD," express at once and forever the basic reason for God's insistence on the holiness of His people. They are to be holy because of what He Himself is. Nearly fifty times in these later chapters of Leviticus the words occur, like the reiterated keynote in a piece of music— "I AM JEHOVAH."

The four sections in this second part of Leviticus are as follows.

(1) The People (xviii.-xx.)

This section covers chapters xviii.–xx., and consists of moral regulations for the whole of the people. These three chapters, marked off, as they are, by a formal introduction (xviii. 1–5) and a formal closing (xx. 22–6), are quite clearly a distinct section. First, in chapter xviii., we have *sex prohibitions*; next, in chapter xix., *general admonitions*; then, in chapter xx., *penal sanctions* against offenders.

The prohibitions in chapter xviii. are not given as an exhaustive sex code, but are directed against those grosser violations of chastity which were shockingly prevalent among the idolatrous nations around Israel—yea, which always have been and still are prevalent amid idolatry and heathenism. The reasons for the interdicts on blood-affinities in marriage, let it be remembered, are as valid today as then. In contrast with the laxity of our own time, the prohibitions of this eighteenth chapter show us the estimate which *God* puts on chaste sex relationships. Nothing is more vital to any people than the adequate safeguarding of matrimonial and family relationships; and it has been well said that in these days when the laws covering marriage and divorce are decided by a "majority vote," regardless of the law of God, there is an urgent call for Christians to stand up for the sanctity of the marriage bond and family relationships!

Again in chapters xix. and xx., the longish lists of moral precepts and penal sanctions are not meant as exhaustive, but as covering matters outstandingly affecting Israel's well-being. We cannot go through them here. They should be carefully read with a good commentary at hand. Uprightness is demanded in all the relationships of life; and disobedience is to be punished with firmness and severity. No maudlin pity for the individual wrongdoer must be allowed to jeopardise the moral safe-guarding of the whole community. Here, too, is a lesson which many sentimental pitiers of criminals in our own day would do well to ponder.

(2) The Priests (xxi.-xxii.)

Chapters xxi. and xxii. specially concern the priests. If the people as a whole were to be sanctified unto the Lord, how much more the priests! As the Tabernacle was a three-fold structure —Outer Court, and Holy Place, and Holy of Holies, so the nation itself was arranged in a three-fold way which corresponded—the congregation, the priesthood, the High Priest. And as the three parts of the Tabernacle became successively holier, so was it to be with the nation—Israel's sanctification was to reach its culminating expression in the High Priest, who therefore wore the golden crown inscribed with the words "Holiness to the Lord."

Associated with the priesthood were the most exalted privileges. Jehovah had selected a certain tribe, and from that tribe a certain family, and from that family a certain man; and upon this man and his house He had conferred the exclusive privileges of drawing nigh unto Himself as His own appointed and anointed mediaries. The priests, therefore, must be marked by the utmost sanctity; and it is to ensure this that these further regulations are here communicated.

The section is in three parts: first, *prohibited practices* (xxi. 1–15), concerning the priest's social relationships; second, *prohibited persons* (xxi. 16–xxii. 16), concerning personal disqualifications from serving in or eating of the things of the Tabernacle; third, *prohibited sacrifices* (xxii. 17–33), concerning defective animals which must not be offered upon the Lord's altar. In other words, these chapters tell us what the priest must not *do*, must not *be*, must not *offer*. Above all men the priest of Jehovah must be separated from that which defiles, lest the Sanctuary of God be profaned. (No less than twelve times that word "profane" occurs in these two chapters!)

How forcibly does this section of Leviticus speak to the Lord's people today. What need there is for truer sanctity among us who have been constituted a spiritual priesthood in Christ! How clearly we need to grasp the difference—as illustrated in this section—between our *standing* and our *state* as the Lord's priests! *All* the sons of Aaron, whether young or old, defective or normal, were priests to Jehovah, by virtue of their birth and life-relationship with Aaron; and nothing could break that relationship: yet those among them who were physically defective were not allowed to officiate at the altar or to enter within the veil of the sanctuary (xxi. 21–3); and those who were in any way defiled were not allowed even to eat of the priests' portion (xxii. 6–7). Even so, every true believer is a priest by virtue of life-giving union with the Lord Jesus, and nothing can break that union where it really exists; but all Christians do not enjoy the same intimacy of fellowship, or exercise the same ministry within the veil! Union is one thing: communion is another. Life is one thing: ministry is another. Standing is one thing: state is another. Relationship is one thing: serving within the veil is another. What deformities and defilements debar many of us from that elevated walk and ministry which might be ours!—yes, which "*might*" be ours; for although there is no record of any provision for miraculously rectifying the physical deformities which may have incapacitated some of Aaron's sons, yet those spiritual defilements and defor-mities which disqualify many of ourselves from a God-glorifying, priestly ministry between the heavenly sanctuary and our fellow-men may be completely done away through the blood of the Lamb and the refining fire of the Holy Spirit.

(3) The Feasts (xxiii.)

Each new section of Leviticus seems to vie with its predecessors in interest. This catalogue of Israel's annual religious "feasts" well merits a far fuller treatment than we can spare in this short synopsis. Unfortunately, to most English readers that word "feast" is misleading, as here used, because (in the Authorised Version) the one word "feast" is used to translate two Hebrew words of different meaning from each other. There is the Hebrew word *chag* (plural *chaggim*), which rightly enough is translated by our English word "feast"; and there is the other Hebrew word, *mo'ed* (plural *mo'adim*), which means simply an appointed time or season. (The ending *im*, pronounced *eem*, is the common Hebrew plural ending—seen in such words as seraph*im* and cherub*im*, the plurals of seraph and cherub.)

For the guidance of English readers we may say that in each case where the *singular* form, "feast," occurs in this twenty-third chapter of Leviticus, the Hebrew word is *chag*; and in each case where the *plural* form, "feasts," occurs, the Hebrew word is *mo'adim* (plural of *mo'ed*).

Now the point is this—in this twenty-third chapter we have a list of *mo'adim* (= appointed seasons, or annual observances); but not all of these *mo'adim*, or appointed annual observances, were *chaggim* (actual "feasts"). As a matter of fact, only three of the *mo'adim* (annual observances) were *chaggim* ("feasts"), as we shall see: but because these three "feasts" (*chaggim*) were fixed annual observances like the others, they are here included in the fuller list of the annual set seasons (*mo'adim*).

What we have, then, in this twenty-third chapter, is a list of the "set seasons" which God appointed for Israel to observe; and it would have been better if, in our Authorised Version, they had been called by that name rather than by the word "feast," seeing that the three which *are* actually feasts are here *included* among the "set seasons," or *mo'adim*.

What then were these annual "set seasons"? They were five in number—

    1. The Feast of Passover (verses 5–14).
    2. The Feast of Pentecost (verses 15–22).
    3. The Blowing of Trumpets (verses 23–5).
    4. The Day of Atonement (verses 26–32).
    5. The Feast of Tabernacles (verses 33–44).

Of these, only three were really "feasts"; and these were (1) the feast of *Passover*—called the Feast of Unleavened Bread, in Exodus xxiii. 15; xxxiv. 18 and other places; (2) the feast of *Pentecost*—called the Feast of Weeks, and the Feast of Firstfruits, in Exodus xxxiv. 22 and other places; (3) the feast of *Tabernacles* —called the Feast of Ingathering, in Exodus xxiii. 16 and other places. The special character of these three is seen in the fact that twice in Exodus, and again in Deuteronomy, they are grouped together and emphatically enjoined as the three great annual national "feasts" of Israel, viz.—

"Three times thou shalt keep a feast unto Me in the year. Thou shalt keep the feast of unleavened bread; . . . and the feast of harvest, the firstfruits of thy labours which thou hast sown in the field; and the feast of ingathering, which is in the end of the year, when thou hast gathered in thy labours out of the field" (Exod. xxiii. 14–16).

"Three times in a year shall all thy males appear before the Lord thy God in the place which He shall choose; in the feast of unleavened bread, and in the feast of weeks and in the feast of tabernacles: and they shall not appear before the Lord empty" (Deut. xvi. 16).

All five of these *mo'adim*, or appointed seasons, however, have this in common, that they were occasions of special *sabbaths*, or rests; and they were all times of holy *convocation*, or assemblings together of the people for worship and joyous thanksgiving.

The "Scofield" Bible makes out that there are seven, instead of five, "set seasons" in this twenty-third chapter of Leviticus. This is done by dividing the Passover into three separate feasts, and calling them (1) Passover; (2) Unleavened Bread; and (3)

Firstfruits. But such a division is quite unwarranted by the text here, and is unsupported by any Scripture elsewhere. Look at verses 5 and 6, and see how obviously the Passover and the days of unleavened bread are one and the same observance—as in all other Scriptures where they are mentioned. And as for verses 9 to 14 denoting another separate feast, there is no such suggestion. What we have in these verses is simply a supplementary provision concerning future observances of the Passover when Israel has entered Canaan (verse 10). That the presenting of the first fruits of the barley harvest was included in the one Passover, or Unleavened Bread observance, is made clear from verse 11, where we are told that the sheaf was to be presented "on the morrow after the Sabbath"—that is the Sabbath during the Feast of Unleavened Bread. Moreover, to make this added provision a separate feast, and call it the Feast of Firstfruits, is to confuse it with the real Feast of Firstfruits (Pentecost) which is mentioned immediately afterwards (verses 15–22).

Others try to show that there are seven "set seasons" in this twenty-third chapter, by dividing the Passover into two feasts, and then adding, to the six thus made, the weekly Sabbath, which is mentioned in verse 3. But the weekly Sabbath is mentioned here, not to include it with these annual "set seasons," but to separate it from them; and if there were any possible doubt about that, verses 37 and 38 would surely do away with it, for we are there told that "These (five) are the feasts of the Lord . . . *beside* the sabbaths of the Lord." What is more, the seventh-day sabbath was a *weekly* observance, whereas all the "set seasons" were *annual*.

As a matter of fact, those who wish to make up the "set seasons" of Leviticus xxiii. into the symbolic number seven defeat their own purpose!—for, as we shall see, there are actually *two other* great national "set seasons" enjoined on Israel, besides these in Leviticus xxiii. These two are found in chapter xxv.; and they are the seventh-year Sabbath (or Sabbatic year), and the Jubilee year (which was to mark off each seven-times-seven of years). Thus, all told, there were seven great periodic national observances enjoined on Israel:

1. The Feast of Passover.
2. The Feast of Pentecost.

3. The Blowing of Trumpets.
4. The Day of Atonement.
5. The Feast of Tabernacles.
6. The Seventh-year Sabbath.
7. The Sabbath Year of Jubilee.

Thus, also, we see that, with the special Sabbath of the seventh month (the Blowing of Trumpets), the Sabbath system of Israel was meant to be a seven-fold revolving cycle of seventh day, seventh month, seventh year, and a seven-times-seven of years.

Associated with the *five* annual "set seasons" were Israel's special *Sabbaths*, or seasons of rest. Thus, including the weekly Sabbath, there seem to have been *ten* Sabbaths given, as follows:

1. The weekly Sabbath.
2. The first day of Unleavened Bread.
3. The seventh day of Unleavened Bread.
4. The Feast of Pentecost.
5. The first day of seventh month ("Trumpets").
6. The Day of Atonement (tenth day of seventh month).
7. The first day of Feast of Tabernacles.
8. The eighth day of Feast of Tabernacles.
9. The seventh-year Sabbath (xxv. 4).
10. The Jubilee Sabbath (xxv. 10, 11).

Besides these, the first day of each month, while not actually a Sabbath in itself, was signalised by a blowing of trumpets, and special offerings. These first days were called the "beginnings of months" (Num. x. 10; xxviii. 11, 28). They were also called the "new moons," because the Hebrew monthly calendar was lunar, and therefore the first day of the month always coincided with the "new moon" (see 2 Chron. ii. 4; Isa. lxvi. 23, etc. And for an enlightening article on the Hebrew lunar calendar see *Imperial Bible Dictionary*, article on the word "Month," by Dr. D. H. Weir). Although the Hebrew month was *lunar*, it seems equally clear that the Hebrew year was *solar*, otherwise the different months would have come at varying seasons as the years passed—the first month (corresponding roughly to our April) would sometimes have been in the spring and sometimes in the winter; whereas we know that the months were *fixed* according to the seasons, so that, for instance, the seventh month always corresponded with the harvest ingathering. The difference between the lunar year of 354 days (29½ x 12) and the solar year of 365¼ days was probably bridged every two or three years by an intercalary month.

The purpose of all these "set seasons" and monthly obser-vances was to acknowledge that all harvest and other blessings came from God; that each new year and each new month should be dedicated to God; that the land belonged to God, and was occupied only because of His kindness; to be a memorial of Israel before God; and to be a constant reminder to Israel of their special covenant relationship with Jehovah, their God. No doubt, also, they fostered the sense of national unity. In their symbolical and typical meanings they cover the whole ground of redemption truths, and much dispensational truth also. The unifying idea running through them is the recognition of Jehovah as the Source and Sustainer of His people's life. They are called "the feasts *of the Lord*"; but alas, in New Testament times they had deteriorated into "feasts *of the Jews*" (John v. 1; vi. 4). It has been observed only too truly that "Divine institutions are speedily marred in the hands of man."

But the special interest of these "set seasons" to *ourselves*, is their typical setting forth of great New Testament truths. Let us quickly run through the five in this twenty-third of Leviticus.

The Feast of Passover (read verses 5–14).

This celebration, which began at even on the fourteenth day of the first month, was commemorative of Israel's deliverance from Egypt. It comes first because it speaks of that which comes first in redemption—the slain Lamb, and the appropriating of the shed blood as a covering from judgment.

The Passover lamb was to be slain and eaten in the evening of the fourteenth day. The slaying speaks of salvation; the feasting speaks of fellowship. Then, beginning on the fifteenth day, there were the seven days of unleavened bread. Leaven is the symbol of moral corruption, of sin; and Israel's abstention from it for seven days (a symbolic number signifying completeness) was to teach that the redeemed must separate themselves from evil, and

THE TABERNACLE

Cloud of Glory

Coverings
Holy of Holies

Encampment

Veil
Boards
Holy Place
Door

Ark
Mercy Seat
{ Cherubim
Shekinah
{ Glory
Altar of Incense
Table of Shewbread
Candlestick

Gate
Court
Brasen Altar
Laver & Foot
Hangings

be a holy people. Paul applies the typical meaning of this in
I Corinthians v. 7, 8.

The first and last of these seven days were to be sabbaths in
which no "servile work" was to be done, but an "offering made
by fire" was to be offered each day to the Lord. See the picture
here—man "ceased from his own works" (Heb. iv. 10); and resting
in his acceptance with God through the ascending odour of the
burnt-offering.

Finally, "on the morrow after the Sabbath" (verse 11), they
were to bring "a sheaf of the firstfruits" of the harvest, to be presented to the Lord. There seems to be a triple significance here.
The nation Israel itself was a kind of firstfruits, or "first-born,"
to the Lord in His redemptive plan for the nations. Then, also,
Christian believers are spoken of as "a kind of firstfruits"
(Jas. i. 18). But supremely the reference is to the Lord Jesus,
who, on the first day of the week (="the morrow after the Sabbath"), rose from among the dead. "Now is Christ risen from
the dead, and become the firstfruits of them that are fallen
asleep" (I Cor. xv. 20).

The Feast of Pentecost (read verses 15–22).

This observance was fixed for "the morrow after the seventh
Sabbath," reckoning from the presenting of the Passover wave-
sheaf. It fell, therefore, just "fifty days" afterwards (verse 16);
hence its being named "Pentecost" in New Testament times
(from *pentekoste*, the feminine of *pentekostos*, the Greek ordinal for
fiftieth). The Passover barley-sheaf marked the *commencement* of the grain harvest. The Pentecost wave-loaves marked its
completion. The Passover wave-*sheaf* was the grain as direct
from God's harvest. The Pentecost wave-*loaves* were the grain
as ready for man's food.

Typically, this observance speaks of that great New Testament
Pentecost which took place exactly fifty days after the Lord's
resurrection, namely, the coming of the Holy Spirit upon the
redeemed in Christ (Acts ii.). It is "the type of God's people
gathered by the Holy Spirit and presented before Him in con-
nexion with all the preciousness of Christ."

Note the singular stipulation that the two wave-loaves must

be "baken *with* leaven" (verse 17). This is true to the design of the type here; for even in the spiritual wave-loaves of the New Testament, in that blood-bought people consecrated to God, in Christ, and fused into spiritual union by the Holy Spirit, the leaven of sin yet remains. It is comforting, therefore, to see that with the two leavened wave-loaves a *sin*-offering and *peace*-offerings were to be offered as well as the sweet-savour offerings, typifying that, despite the presence of evil in the nature, there is acceptance and communion through the Divinely provided sacrifice of Christ.

The Blowing of Trumpets.
The Day of Atonement. }(read verses 23–44).
The Feast of Tabernacles.

The Blowing of Trumpets came first in that trio of annual observances which fell in the seventh month. There are two things which it is important to note. First, they all came within a few days of each other. Second, they were separated by a wide gap from the earlier two feasts of the year. Between the feast of Pentecost and the Blowing of Trumpets on the first day of this seventh month three and a half months elapsed. Time yet to come will show how full of prophecy is this grouping of these types, with this gap between; for these observances of the seventh month look on to the time of Israel's regathering at the end of the present age.

This seventh month was pre-eminently the Sabbatic season of Israel's year. The blowing of the trumpets on the first day was Jehovah's call to Israel to regather in preparation for the two great events which followed in this seventh month, namely, the annual Day of Atonement (on the tenth day), the most august ceremony of the year, when the High Priest went into the Holy of Holies to make atonement for the whole nation (verses 26–32); and, second, the Feast of Tabernacles, the completion of the harvest ingathering, and the final religious convocation of the year (verses 33–44).

As we have seen, the full picture of the Day of Atonement is given in chapter xvi. We need not go back there except to note that the High Priest, having gone into the Holy of Holies to sprinkle the blood on and before the Mercy Seat, was to come forth again to the people, wearing his beautiful high-priestly garments. This latter part of the type has not yet been fulfilled. The Lord Jesus, Israel's true High Priest, has entered into the heavenly sanctuary, with the blood of the one perfect sacrifice, but He is yet to come forth again to His people (Heb. ix. 24–8). At that time, also, there shall be a penitent Israel; and it is significant that in this twenty-third chapter of Leviticus the emphasis is laid on that very thing. Three times are the people of Israel told that on this day they must "afflict" their souls (verses 27, 29, 32). Corresponding with this Day of Atonement, at the end of the summer and harvest season, there will come a time when the earthly Israel will say: "The harvest is past, the summer is ended, and we are not saved." Then shall they look, in believing contrition, on Him whom they pierced, and shall be saved.

It will be then, also, that the type-fulfilment of the Feast of Tabernacles (more strictly, the feast of "booths," from the Hebrew plural *succoth*) will take place, and the glory of Israel's final ingathering. This Feast of Tabernacles lasted longer than any other of the *mo'adim*, or "set seasons," of Israel's calendar; and the verses describing it show it to have been the year's supreme season of festive joy. It looked back to Israel's exodus from Egypt. "Ye shall dwell in booths seven days; all that are Israelites born shall dwell in booths: that your generations may know that I made the children of Israel to dwell in booths when I brought them out of the land of Egypt" (verses 42–3). It is of interest to note that the first pause of the Israelites on their outgoing from Egypt was at Succoth (Exod. xii. 37; xiii. 20), which name, as pointed out above, is the Hebrew plural for booths. But, in its typical significance, the Feast of Tabernacles also points us forward to that seventh millennium of history yet to be, when, in the words of Zechariah xiv., "It shall come to pass that every one that is left of all the nations which came against Jerusalem shall even go up from year to year to worship the King, Jehovah of hosts, and to keep the feast of Tabernacles. In that day shall there be upon the bells of the horses, *HOLINESS UNTO THE LORD*."

THE BOOK OF LEVITICUS (4)
Lesson Number 12

THE BOOK OF LEVITICUS (2)

Lesson Number 13

NOTE.—For this study read Leviticus xxv. to xxvii.

" One of the most characteristic and prominent features of the Bible, considered as a whole, which runs through it from beginning to end, and which distinguishes it at once from all other books, is that it subordinates everything to the idea of GOD. It is not without reason called the Book of God; and would be so, in a very intelligible sense, even if it were wholly false, or if there were no God at all. From the first sentence to the last, He is the great theme of it, the Alpha and Omega."

HENRY ROGERS.

THE BOOK OF LEVITICUS (4)

PART II—concluded

(4) The Land (xxv.-xxvii.)

THE FINAL section of Leviticus consists of chapters xxv. to xxvii., and deals distinctively with Israel's occupation of Canaan. Several times already, in Exodus and Leviticus, we have come across words such as, "When ye be come into the land . . ." and this, of course, is as one would expect, since the whole of the Law given through Moses was anticipative of Israel's settling in Canaan. These last three chapters of Leviticus, however, are concerned almost exclusively with the Land, and with the terms of Israel's occupation of it. No less than thirty times in these three chapters we find reference to "the land."

Chapter xxv. enjoins the observance of the two periodic "sabbaths of *rest unto the land*," namely, the seventh year (verses 1–7), and the fiftieth (verses 8–55). These sabbaths were to be an acknowledgment of the Divine proprietorship of the land, and of Israel's tenure on the ground of covenant relationship (verse 23). They were a wise measure for the land itself, as agricultural science would now recognise. They were a graciously provided opportunity of joyous leisure for the people—for although, strictly speaking, they were times of "rest unto the *land*," yet, as a foreseen by-product, the people themselves were to enjoy the respite thus occasioned. Then, too, these land-sabbaths were to serve as a check upon covetousness. Every seventh year the Hebrew must suspend effort after gain. He must even forego his right to the spontaneous produce of his own fields, so that all alike—rich and poor, cattle and beasts—might have their fill (verses 5–6); and in the case of the Jubilee, following, as it did, the seventh of these seventh-year rests, this check covered two years running together. And if we couple with this the strict ruling that no interest was to be charged on money or goods loaned to a fellow-Hebrew (verses 35–8), and the further regulation that in the Jubilee all must go out free, we see still more clearly this restraint on greed. Furthermore, these land-sabbaths were meant to develop the people's faith in God, and to cultivate a sense of trustful dependence upon Him (verses 20–2).

It may be, however, that the foremost purpose of the regulations in this twenty-fifth chapter was to secure as far as possible "the equal distribution of wealth, by preventing excessive accumulations either of land or of capital in the hands of a few while the mass should be in poverty." We cannot here examine these most interesting regulations in detail, but we would advise that they should be carefully read with the foregoing considerations in mind.

The key to the seventh-year sabbath is the word "rest" (verse 4). It was to be a rest in three ways—(1) for the land, (2) from manual toil, (3) from debt (see Deut. xv. 1–11).

The key to the year of Jubilee is the word "liberty" (verse 10). It brought liberty in three ways—(1) to the slave, (2) to property, (3) to the ground itself (see below).

Of course, as it was with the five "set seasons" in chapter xxiii., so here, there is a typical content. Both the Sabbatic Year and the year of Jubilee were to begin on the Day of Atonement (verse 9), in which, as we have seen, Israel was to evidence special penitence for national sin; and on that day both these Sabbath years were to begin when the High Priest made his advent to the people after having made atonement for the nation in the Holy of Holies. Both these years, being connected with the sabbatic idea, point onward to the yet final redemption and consummation.

The seventh year "sabbath of *rest*," following the six years of toil, speaks of that seventh great thousand-year period yet to be which will be brought in by the second coming of Christ, when, after the six thousand years from Adam, which are now nearing their end, the earth shall have rest under the benign rule of Israel's true King.

The Jubilee, which was to be the year *after* the seventh of these seventh-year sabbaths, and was therefore to be always in the eighth year of the sabbatic calendar, speaks of that glorious condition of things *following* the millennial reign of Christ. What our Sunday is—the *first* day of the new week, following upon and doing away with the seventh-day sabbath of the old week and the old dispensation, the day of resurrection, of the outpoured Spirit, of a new order of things, even a new creation in Christ

Jesus, so the Jubilee looks on to the new heaven and new earth yet to be (Rev. xxi.–xxii.), when, following the seventh great thousand-year day of history, during which all rule and authority shall have been brought beneath Christ's feet, and even death, the last enemy, shall have been done away, the voice of God shall be heard saying: "Behold, I make all things new!"

We have noted that the key to the Jubilee is the word "liberty." How thrillingly prophetic this Jubilee word is! As the slave was freed in the Jubilee, and returned to his forfeited inheritance, so shall it be in that consummating Jubilee of the future. Then shall we know the prophetic meaning of our Lord's word—"The meek shall inherit the earth." Then shall we know the meaning of 1 Peter i. 4–5, and Revelation xxi. 2–4. That inheritance of the earth which was forfeited through sin, this glorious Jubilee of the ages shall bring back to us. The New Jerusalem descends from heaven, and the redeemed and glorified assume the possession of the purchased inheritance.

In Genesis iii. 17–19 we are told of the curse that fell on the very ground itself because of man's sin. It is remarkable that during the sabbatic year and the year of Jubilee this curse was to be temporarily suspended, at least in appreciable measure (Lev. xxv. 20–2).

Here is liberty indeed!—for the slave, for the inheritance, for the earth itself. "The creation itself also shall be delivered from the *bondage* of corruption unto the glorious *liberty* of the children of God" (Rom. viii. 21). The sabbatic year and the year of Jubilee were to be ushered in by the blowing of the trumpet. Oh, for the time when the trumpet of God shall sound, and the universe's sabbath rest and Jubilee shall set in!

The Alternatives of the Covenant (chapter xxvi.).

We can speak but a word or two about chapter xxvi., although this is one of the most solemn and important chapters in the Bible. It sets before Israel the categoric conditions of possession and prosperity, the inexorable alternatives hinging on whether they would obey or disobey. What blessings are promised to obedience! What warnings are uttered to deter from disobedience! Truly, the higher the privilege, the deeper the responsibility!

The warnings in the second part of the chapter are an amazing epitome of Israel's later history, reaching on even to time yet to be. "So strictly true is this that we may accurately describe the history of that nation, from the days of Moses until now, as but the translation of this chapter from the language of prediction into that of history." "These facts make this chapter to be an apologetic of prime importance. It is this, because here we have evidence of foreknowledge, and therefore of the supernatural inspiration of the Holy Spirit of God in the prophecy here recorded. The facts cannot be adequately explained, either on the supposition of fortunate guessing or of accidental coincidence."

It will be noted that the final punishment is expulsion from the land, and dispersion among the nations. After the falling of the other judgments, this last one has only too patently come to pass, and the land itself, as forewarned, has lain derelict and depopulated for generations. Yet going with this warning was the Divine promise guaranteeing Israel's preservation and restoration; and the preservation of Israel is one of the uneclipsed marvels of history. Professor Christlieb says: "We point to the people of Israel as a perennial historical miracle. The continued existence of this nation up to the present day, the preservation of its national peculiarities throughout thousands of years, in spite of all dispersion and oppression, remains so unparalleled a phenomenon, that without the special providential preparation of God, and His constant interference and protection, it would be impossible for us to explain it. For where else is there a people over which such judgments have passed, and yet not ended in destruction?"

Moreover, in our days we are seeing the earlier phases of Israel's restoration in progress. The land itself, also, is being transformed in preparation for the regathering of the people; and the time seems to be rapidly nearing when these words shall be fulfilled: "And I will pour upon the house of David, and upon the inhabitants of Jerusalem, the spirit of grace and of supplications: and they shall look upon Me whom they have pierced; and they shall mourn for Him as one mourneth for his only son, and shall be in bitterness for Him as one that is in bitterness for his firstborn. . . . In that day there shall be a fountain opened to the house of David and to the inhabitants of Jerusalem for sin and for uncleanness" (Zech. xii. 10–xiii. 1). "And it shall come to pass in that day that the Lord shall set His hand again the second time to recover the remnant of His people which shall be left, from Assyria and from Egypt and from Pathros and from Cush and from Elam and from Shinar and from Hamath and from the islands of the sea: and He shall set up an ensign for the nations, and shall assemble the outcasts of Israel, and gather together the dispersed of Judah from the four corners of the earth" (Isa. xi. 11–12).

Chapter xxvii. deals with voluntary consecrations, and tithings in the land. It is a unique conclusion to Leviticus that, after all its chapters concerning *obligatory* regulations, the final chapter should concern itself with *non*-obligatory expressions of regard and love toward God. These three chapters in this final section of Leviticus are full of interest; but we cannot tarry at them here. Still, we are confident that we have said enough about these eight sections of Leviticus to indicate how full of fascination and instruction this third book of Scripture really is.

A word of caution is needed regarding the word "atonement" as it is used in Leviticus by our English version. In commonly accepted theological usage today, the word "atonement" distinctively denotes the redeeming sacrifice of Christ; but here in Leviticus it is used, somewhat misleadingly, to translate a Hebrew word which simply means *to cover*. The Levitical offerings certainly did not make atonement for sin in the theologically accepted sense of the word. They merely *covered*, or put away from judicial view, the sins of Old Testament believers, through the forbearance of God, until the one real atonement was effected on Calvary, which the Levitical sacrifices anticipated and prefigured (see Rom. iii. 25).

The central figure in Leviticus is the High Priest. The central chapter is xvi.—the annual Day of Atonement. The central theme is fellowship through sanctification. The central lesson is: "Ye shall be holy; for I the Lord your God am holy" (xix. 2). (The Hebrew word translated "holy" comes over eighty times in Leviticus.) These well deserve special study.

We may now set out a fuller analysis of Leviticus so as to see at a glance the beauty and order of its structure.

THE BOOK OF LEVITICUS

FELLOWSHIP THROUGH SANCTIFICATION

1. THE GROUND OF FELLOWSHIP—SACRIFICE

(i.–xvii.).

THE OFFERINGS (ABSOLUTION)—i.–vii.
The sweet-savour offerings—i.–iii.
The non-sweet-savour offerings—iv.–vi. 7.
The Laws of the offerings—vi. 8–vii. 38.

THE PRIESTHOOD (MEDIATION)—viii.–x.
Consecration—viii.
Ministration—ix.
Provocation—x.

THE PEOPLE (PURIFICATION)—xi.–xvi.
Clean foods—xi.
Clean ways—xii.–xv.
Clean nation—xvi.

THE ALTAR (RECONCILIATION)—xvii.
The one place shown—verses 1–9.
The one use of blood—verses 10–11.
Other uses forbidden—verses 12–16.

2. THE WALK OF FELLOWSHIP—SEPARATION

(xviii.–xxvii.).

REGULATIONS CONCERNING THE PEOPLE—xviii.–xx.
Sex prohibitions—xviii.
General admonitions—xix.
Penal sanctions—xx.

REGULATIONS CONCERNING THE PRIESTS—xxi.–xxii.
Prohibited practices—xxi. 1–15.
Prohibited persons—xxi. 16–xxii. 16.
Prohibited offerings—xxii. 17–33.

REGULATIONS CONCERNING FEASTS, etc.—xxiii.–xxiv.
The annual set seasons—xxiii.
The oil and shewbread—xxiv. 1–9.
The penalty of blasphemy—xxiv. 10–23.

REGULATIONS CONCERNING CANAAN—xxv.–xxvii.
Sabbatic Year and Jubilee—xxv.
Alternatives of the covenant.—xxvi.
Consecrations and tithings—xxvii.

SOME QUESTIONS ON LEVITICUS

1. In what three ways does Leviticus express the holiness of God?

2. What is the standpoint of the book?

3. Which are the two main parts of Leviticus, and how are they distinguished from each other?

4. What are the eight sub-divisions?

5. What is the central message of Leviticus?

6. Can you name and group the five offerings in the first seven chapters?

7. Can you explain why Aaron was anointed *before* his sons, and afterwards *with* them?

8. Can you classify the teachings concerning cleanness, in chapters xi. to xvi.?

9. Why the one altar? and why the sanctity of blood?

10. What is the basic reason for God's insistence on the holiness of His people?

11. What were the seven great periodic national observances, and what their type-meanings?

12. What is the final punishment threatened, and what the final promise given, in God's great warning to Israel?

THE BOOK OF NUMBERS (I)

Lesson Number 13

NOTE.—For this study read the whole Book of Numbers through, to get a general picture of its story.

THE BOOK OF NUMBERS

"THE GOODNESS AND SEVERITY OF GOD"		
THE OLD GENERATION (Sinai to Kadesh)	THE TRANSITION ERA (In the Wilderness)	THE NEW GENERATION (Kadesh to Moab)
I.–XIV.	XV.–XX.	XXI.–XXXVI.
THE NUMBERING (i.–iv.) THE INSTRUCTING (v.–ix.) THE JOURNEYING (x.–xiv.)	THE WANDERING	THE NEW JOURNEYING (xxi.–xxv.) THE NEW NUMBERING (xxvi.–xxvii.) THE NEW INSTRUCTING (xxviii.–xxxvi.)

THE BOOK OF NUMBERS (1)

WHO AMONG Bible readers has not fallen prey to the spell of this fourth writing from Moses' pen? Tragic record though it is, in many respects, it speaks with undying appeal to God's pilgrims in every age and clime.

How does it get its name? In an earlier study we have referred to the Septuagint Version of the Old Testament—the translation of the Old Testament Scriptures into Greek, made by seventy Alexandrian Jews in the third century B.C. It was these Septuagint translators who first gave to the Old Testament books the names under which they now appear (in their English equivalents) in our English version. Thus, although the Hebrew name for this fourth writing of Moses was *Be-midbar*, which means "in the wilderness" (from the words in the first verse of the first chapter), the Greek name given to it by the Septuagint translators was *Arithmoi* (origin of our English word "arithmetic"), which in Latin becomes *Numeri*, and in English *Numbers*—the book being so named because in it the Children of Israel are twice numbered, once at the beginning of the book, and again toward the end. The Hebrew and Greek names taken together certainly give the gist of the book—"in the wilderness" and "numbers," or "numberings."

Its Nature

Numbers resumes the narrative where Exodus left off. The last chapter of Exodus (xl. 17) tells us that "in the *first month*, in the second year, on the first day of the month, the tabernacle was reared up." Numbers i. 1 says: "And the Lord spake unto Moses in the wilderness of Sinai, in the tabernacle of the congregation, on the first day of the *second month*, in the second year after they were come out of the land of Egypt." So there is a break of just one month between the erecting of the Tabernacle, at the end of Exodus, and the command to number the people, at the beginning of Numbers—with the Leviticus instructions coming in between the two.

Numbers obviously does not intend to be a full or strictly continuous narrative. Very little, for instance, is told us about the thirty-eight years of the so-called "Wandering," while certain other happenings which must have occupied a very small space of time, comparatively, are most carefully described. In accord with the consistent practice of the Scriptures, Numbers puts the emphasis, not on mere extent of time, but on the significance of events. It covers the period of Israel's history from the second month of the second year after the Exodus (i. 1) to the tenth month of the fortieth year (see Deut. i. 3). Possibly, indeed, a few parts of Numbers overlap into Deuteronomy (xxxii. 39–42), so that we may speak of it as *the book of the forty years.*

The record is of gripping interest. First the census is taken, with the primary object of determining Israel's military strength. Then the camp is strategically distributed with a view to facilitating orderly mobility—an undertaking as vital as complex with a crowd of over two million! The services of the Levites in connection with the Tabernacle are appointed. All is made ready for the advance to Canaan's border. The march ensues, in Divinely determined stages. Jehovah Himself leads on the mighty host, by the pillar of cloud and fire. The ground is covered. Kadesh is reached. Canaan is in sight! Then comes tragic breakdown. Israel disbelieves and then rebels. Judgment falls. The forty years of the "Wandering" set in; and the many thousands who came up from Egypt, with gleam of expectation in their eyes, gradually die off, leaving a pathetic trail of carcases beneath the hard crust of the wilderness. Then, eventually, God takes up with the new generation which reassembles at Kadesh. The new numbering is negotiated. The fresh advance takes place, to the plain of Moab, on Canaan's margin; and final preparations begin, with a view to Israel's going up, at long last, to possess the land.

Its Importance

Is there any need to insist on the importance of all this? Again and again Numbers is referred to in the New Testament. Indeed, the Holy Spirit has called special attention to it in that classic statement concerning Israel's early history, 1 Corinthians x. 1–12, which please read in full—

"Moreover, brethren, I would not that ye should be ignorant, how that all our fathers were under the cloud, and all passed through the sea, and were all baptised unto Moses in the cloud and in the sea; and did all eat the same spiritual meat; and did all drink the same spiritual drink, for they drank of that spiritual rock which followed them, and that rock was Christ. But with many of them God was not well pleased; for they were over-thrown in the wilderness.

"Now these things were our examples, to the intent we should not lust after evil things as they also lusted. Neither be ye idolaters as were some of them—as it is written: The people sat down to eat and drink, and rose up to play. Neither let us commit fornication as some of them committed, and fell in one day three and twenty thousand. Neither let us tempt Christ, as some of them also tempted, and were destroyed of serpents. Neither murmur ye as some of them also murmured, and were destroyed of the destroyer.

"Now all these things happened unto them for ensamples; and they are written for our admonition upon whom the ends of the ages are come. Wherefore, let him that thinketh he standeth take heed lest he fall." (See also Rom. xv. 4; Heb. iii. 7–iv. 6.)

Note the words: "All these things happened unto them for ensamples." As we pointed out in an earlier study, the Greek word here translated as "ensamples" is *tupoi*, that is, "*types*." The things recorded in Numbers are made immortal by their having been Divinely resolved into types, for our own learning. Indeed, we think it is not too much to say with A. C. Gaebelein, that the faithless failure of Israel to enter Canaan may well fore-shadow—as it certainly illustrates—the failure of the organised Church today to possess the heavenly things in Christ. It is the presence of these typical meanings and representative lessons which gives the book its rich spiritual values for us today. He who knows Numbers well will be well admonished for the pilgrim journey to the heavenly Canaan, and will escape many a sad set-back. All who preach the Word will do well to be familiar with this book for it gives many illustrations of Gospel truth. It notably exemplifies the fact that the greatest illustrations of New Testament doctrine are found in Old Testament story.

Its Structure

The structure of Numbers is unique, and when once seen is difficult to forget. We need to remember that, unlike the Book of Leviticus, in which we are geographically stationary, Numbers is a book of *movements*; and it is these movements which mark the main divisions of the book.

But what is most vital of all is to realise that in Numbers we deal, in turn, with *two different generations of people*—first, with the generation that came up from Egypt but perished in the wilderness; and second, with the new generation that grew up in the wilderness and then entered Canaan. This at once gives the clue to the book. In the first group of chapters (i.–xiv.) we are dealing with the *old* generation. In the final group (xxi.–xxxvi.) we are dealing with the *new* generation. Coming between the two groups, and unmistakably marking them off, we have the wilderness "Wandering" (xv.–xx.)—the period of transition during which the old generation died off and the new generation grew up. This threefold grouping in Numbers is so clear that no careful reader can fail to see it.

The one query which may occur to the student's mind is: How do we *know* that chapter xx. marks the end of the "Wandering" and the taking up with the new generation? The answer to this is conclusive. That twentieth chapter records the death of Aaron. Now at what point of time did Aaron die? Chapter xxxiii. 38 tells us: "And Aaron the priest went up into Mount Hor at the commandment of the Lord, and died there, *in the fortieth year after the children of Israel were come out of the land of Egypt*, in the first day of the fifth month." If, then, Aaron's death was in the fortieth year after the Exodus, it follows that it was *thirty-eight* years after the Kadesh-barnea crisis of chapter xiv., which marked the beginning of the wilderness "Wandering," for the Kadesh-barnea crisis took place in the *second* year after Exodus. (This is clear from Numbers x. 11, which tells us that the Children of Israel started the brief journey from Sinai to Kadesh in the second month of the second year after the Exodus; and we are told in Deuteronomy i. 2 that "there are eleven days' journey from Horeb (Sinai) by the way of Mount Seir unto Kadesh-barnea," so that even allowing generously for the different halts and incidents *en route*, we may safely say that Kadesh-barnea was reached about the end of the second year.) Thus the death of Aaron marked the lapse of forty years from the Exodus, and thirty-eight years from the beginning of the "Wandering"; and we know that thirty-eight years *completed* the "Wandering," for Moses tells us so in Deuteronomy ii. 14—"The space in which we came from Kadesh-barnea until we were come over the brook Zered (see Num. xxi. 12, following on the death of Aaron) was *thirty-eight years*." So Aaron's death *must* have marked the end of the "Wandering," which means that the twentieth chapter of Numbers marks the taking up with the new generation. Aaron's death, we may add, is the most important time-mark in the whole book of Numbers.

This point being settled, the structural features of Numbers stand out sharply. We have—

      1. The old generation (i.–xiv.).

      2. The transition era (xv.–xx.).

      3. The new generation (xxi.–xxxvi.).

Thus, also, we see that the book of Numbers is in three movements, as follows:

      1. Sinai to Kadesh-barnea (i.–xiv.).

      2. The wilderness wandering (xv.–xx.).

      3. Kadesh to Plain of Moab (xxi.–xxxvi.).

In the first of these divisions, concerning the *old* generation, we have first the numbering, or *census*; then the Canaan-ward advance, or *progress*; and then the Kadesh *crisis*.

In the final chapters, concerning the *new* generation, we have first the new *crisis* at Kadesh; then the new *progress* from Kadesh to the Plain of Moab; and then the new numbering, or *census*.

We may put it that in Numbers we have—

      Two generations (i.–xiv. and xxi.–xxxvi.);

      Two numberings (i.–iv. and xxvi.–xxvii.);

      Two journeyings (x.–xiv. and xxi.–xxvii.);

      Two instructings (v.–ix. and xxviii.–xxxvi.).

F

Its Central Message

Seeing these things thrown into relief suggests at once the central message of the book. This may be expressed in words which occur in the New Testament, in Romans xi. 22—

"BEHOLD THEREFORE THE GOODNESS AND SEVERITY OF GOD."

In Numbers we see the *severity* of God, in the old generation which fell in the wilderness and never entered Canaan. We see the *goodness* of God, in the new generation which was protected, preserved, and provided for, until Canaan was possessed. In the one case we see the awful inflexibility of the Divine justice. In the other case we see the unfailing faithfulness of God to His promise, His purpose, His people.

Closely running up to this central message of the book are two other lessons—two warnings to ourselves; and these also may be expressed in words from the New Testament. The first is a warning against *presumption*. Turning again to the Corinthian passage which we have just quoted in full (1 Cor. x. 1–12), we find that this warning against presumption is the lesson which Paul himself sees in the book of Numbers. After telling us that "all these things happened unto them as types" for us, he says: "*Wherefore, let him that thinketh he standeth take heed lest he fall.*"

The second warning is against *unbelief*. In Hebrews iii. 19 we read: "They could not enter in (to Canaan) because of unbelief"; and then it is added—"*Let us therefore fear* lest, a promise being left us of entering into His rest, any of you should seem to come short of it." And again: "*Take heed, brethren*, lest there be in any of you an evil heart of unbelief" (iii. 12).

Thus the New Testament itself interprets the book of Numbers for us. This fourth writing of Moses says:

1. "Behold the goodness and severity of God."
2. "Let him that thinketh he standeth take heed . . ."
3. "Take heed lest there be in you—unbelief."

Perhaps it will be helping memory through "eye gate" if we now set down our findings in a flat analysis.

(See analysis at beginning of this study: page 156.)

THE BOOK OF NUMBERS (2)
Lesson Number 14

NOTE.—For this study read again carefully chapters i. to xiv.

DISTRIBUTION OF THE CAMP OF ISRAEL

North

It is well to keep in mind that here, in this quadrangular formation of the camp of Israel, some two million people were mobilised, and that the quadrangle was about twelve miles square!

It will be noted, also, that there are now twelve tribes *besides* the tribe of Levi, which was formerly counted as one of the twelve, but which was now reckoned as a tribe apart, in connection with the Tabernacle (Num. i. 49, 50; iii. 12, 13). There still remain twelve without the tribe of Levi, because the two great families sprung from Joseph's two sons, Ephraim and Manasseh, are now and henceforth counted as two separate tribes, instead of being reckoned as the one tribe of Joseph.

THE BOOK OF NUMBERS (2)

PART I. THE OLD GENERATION (i.–xiv.)

(*Sinai to Kadesh*)

As WE have seen, Numbers is in three main parts. The first of these consists of chapters i.–xiv., and concerns the *old* generation which came up from Egypt but died during the "Wandering." This first part now breaks into three sub-sections—the numbering (i.–iv.), the instructing (v.–x. 10), the journeying (x. 11–xiv.).

The Numbering (i.–iv.)

These four chapters go in two pairs, thus—

Chapter i.—Numeration of adult males.
„ ii.—Distribution of the tribes.
„ iii.—Numeration of Levite males.
„ iv.—Distribution of Levite duties.

First, then, in chapter i., Moses is commanded: "Take ye the sum of all the congregation of the children of Israel, after their families, by the house of their fathers, with the number of their names, every male by their polls; from twenty years old and upward, all that are able to go forth to war in Israel" (i. 2, 3). The wording here makes clear that the primary purpose of this numbering was a military one. It gives us the man-power of the newly-formed nation. The figures are of much interest.

Reuben	46,500	Manasseh	32,200
Simeon	59,300	Benjamin	35,400
Gad	45,650	Dan	62,700
Judah	74,600	Asher	41,500
Issachar	54,400	Naphtali	53,400
Zebulun	57,400		
Ephraim	40,500	TOTAL	603,550

It is on the basis of this adult male census that the sum of the whole nation is computed at between two and three million. We cannot here go into the calculations involved in the working out of this total; nor can we discuss (what has seemed a problem to some) Israel's growth from "seventy souls" (Gen. xlvi. 27) to a nation of over two millions during the sojourn in Egypt. These will be found discussed in good Bible commentaries. There is an able article by Dr. Thomas Whitelaw in the *Pulpit Commentary*.

In the census, Israel's grown sons were numbered "after their families, by the house of their fathers" (i. 2); and they were evidently to "*declare their pedigree*" (i. 18). Only true Israelites were allowed to fight Israel's battles. None of the "mixed multitude" which came from Egypt with Israel were eligible. What a lesson for us today, when all sorts of persons are allowed to serve in the organised Church who are without the Divinely required spiritual pedigree of the new birth! The first question in connection with Christian service should ever be that of spiritual pedigree. How many church workers today are far from being able to say, "The Spirit Himself beareth witness with our spirits that we are the children of God" (Rom. viii. 16)!

Next, in chapter ii., we have the distribution of the tribes and the mobilisation of the camp. The twelve tribes were each to pitch by their own standard, and were arranged in four groups of three tribes each, one group being north, another south, another east, and the other west, of the Tabernacle.

Then, in chapter iii., we have the census of the tribe of Levi, which had been exempted from the general census because God had chosen it for special service pertaining to the Tabernacle (i. 49, 50). This Levite census, unlike the other, was to include all Levite males from a *month* old (iii. 15). Along with this comes the explanation that thenceforth God would count all the Levites as peculiarly His own *instead of* the firstborn from all the other tribes (iii. 12, 13).

The Levites were in three families—Gershonites, Kohathites, Merarites; and these were located "round about the tabernacle," westward, southward, and northward respectively. As for the eastern side, where the entrance was, verse 38 says: "But those that encamp before the tabernacle toward the east . . . shall be Moses and Aaron and his sons, keeping charge of the sanctuary; and the stranger that cometh nigh shall be put to death." Here are facts of the Levite census, location, and service at a glance—

Family	Number	Location	Service
Gershonites	7,500	west of Tabernacle	external coverings
Kohathites	8,600	south of Tabernacle	internal equipment
Merarites	6,200	north of Tabernacle	structural components

A difficulty crops up as to the total of the Levite males. The above figures (from iii. 22, 28, 34) give 22,300; but verse 39 gives 22,000. For two suggested solutions see Ellicott's commentary, and Wordsworth's. It certainly seems that the level 22,000 is the right total, for verse 43 says that the number of the firstborn in *all* the tribes was 22,273, and verse 46 says that this was 273 more than the Levite males.

Finally, in chapter iv., we have a census of Levite males from thirty years old to fifty; for only these were eligible for Tabernacle duties. The total is 8,580. Mark clearly the difference between the ministry of the Levites and that of the priests. The priests had to do with the ceremonial, sacrificial, and spiritual ministries of the Tabernacle. The Levites had to do with the material of the Tabernacle itself—with its erection, transportation, preservation, and other services necessary to its maintenance, such as the driving of oxen, the tending of animals for the sacrifices, and the preparing of incense.

The twelve tribes, as we have noted, were arranged in four groups of three tribes each, one such group on each side of the Tabernacle. In these four groups the leading (and probably central) tribes were Judah, Ephraim, Reuben, Dan. Some Jewish expositors say that the device on the standard of Judah was a young lion, on that of Ephraim an ox, on that of Reuben a man, on that of Dan an eagle. If these were indeed their ensigns, we have the probable origin of the forms attributed to the four living beings in Ezekiel's vision. It may be, in fact, that these tribal ensigns were themselves taken from the symbolic forms of the cherubim in the Tabernacle.

In the Bible account of this vast camp rationalistic critics have found ample scope for scorn. Their chief objection is that such a host could not possibly have subsisted for any length of time on the scant produce of the Sinai peninsula. But recent research shows that the regions traversed by Israel were far more productive then than now. Moreover, Scripture does not say the people lived simply on natural produce. They were sustained by *supernatural supply!* The syllogisms of rationalism collapse every time because God is left out of the premises!

These first four chapters are rich with spiritual lessons. In them we have the soldier, the priest, the Levite—warrior, worshipper, worker; warfare, fellowship, service. Both warring and working are to centre in fellowship with God—in the Tabernacle at the heart of the camp. Take the first of these—warfare. Israel's grown sons were first to declare their *pedigree* ("after their families"), then rally to their tribal *standards* ("by their standards"), then all to unite in common *conquest* ("so they set forward").

The Instructing (v.-x. 10)

The first four chapters have given us the outward formation of the camp. The next five deal with the inward condition of it. The key is chapter v. 3—"That they defile not their camps, in the midst whereof I dwell." This is the foundation principle of discipline, that the Holy One Himself being in the camp, the camp must be holy. This principle applies to the Church today.

Chapter v. commands that lepers be quarantined outside the camp; that dishonest gain be confessed and recompensed; that suspected immorality be tested before God. There must be purity, honesty, and truth.

Chapter vi. gives the regulations concerning the *nazir* vow. Among the "many thousands of Israel" there were doubtless many godly souls who would feel the need not merely for the negative rulings of chapter v. but for guidance of a positive kind regarding special expressions of devotion to God. Vows of abstinence have been common among all religions. Certainly, in many cases they have been mingled with much superstition, self-will, and pride; yet in the main they have sprung from

noble impulses. This Hebrew *nazir* vow was outside the compulsory requirements of the Law; and in the provision here made
relating to it is the implied recognition of the free movement of
the Divine Spirit in individuals. Thus, while chapter v. concerns
general separation from defilement, chapter vi. concerns *individual
separation to God*.

Chapter vii. records the free-will offering of the princes. As
these leaders really represented the people as a whole, what we
have here is a national recognition of the claims of the Sanctuary.
Three things strike us about it—(1) the *spontaneity* of the offering; it was not commanded; (2) the *uniformity* of the gifts; each
prince brought the same; (3) the *particularity* of the record; each
gift is separately recorded although all the gifts were alike; for our
God, who is rich beyond needing aught that man can subscribe,
looks not merely at the monetary value of the total, but prizes
each separate gift for what it expresses of the offerer's love to
Him.

It may be asked: "*Why* was this offering brought by these
princes?" The following words of Professor W. Binnie will throw
light on this. "The Lord's tabernacle has been constructed,
furnished, anointed, and (what is best of all) occupied by the
King whose pavilion it was intended for. Yes; and the construction and furniture of this royal tent have been effected by the
voluntary gifts of a willing people. The tabernacle and its furniture
are completed according to the pattern shown to Moses on the
mount. No necessary part is wanting. Still, there is room for
some supplementary gifts. Take two examples. (1) When the
tabernacle was first dedicated there would no doubt be a golden
spoon for Aaron's use when he burned incense at the golden
altar. One such spoon was all that was strictly necessary. But
it would occasionally happen that there would be more than one
call to burn incense about the same time; and it was evidently
unbecoming that in the palace of the King any worshipper should
have to wait till the golden spoon was available. Hence the gift
of the twelve golden spoons now presented by the princes. (2) The
Levites have been appointed to bear the tabernacle and its furniture. They are able to do it, but not without difficulty, especially
during the sojourn in the wilderness, where it is to be emphatically a moving tent. There was room, therefore, for a present
of carriages and draught oxen. There are Christian congregations

to whom this chapter teaches a much-needed lesson. The roll
of their membership includes men of substance, yet they suffer
the sanctuary to wear an aspect of threadbare penury, and its
services to be hunger-bitten. This ought not so to be."

Chapter viii. describes the consecration of the Levites. First,
however, in the chapter, the following instruction is given to
Aaron: "When thou lightest the lamps, the seven lamps shall
give light over against the candlestick." Then, by way of
explanation, it is added: "And this work of the candlestick was
of beaten gold, unto the shaft thereof, unto the flowers thereof,
beaten work; according unto the pattern which the Lord had
showed Moses" (viii. 1–4). A. C. Gaebelein says: "The candlestick is the type of Christ as in the sanctuary. The seven lamps
were to illuminate the candlestick of beaten gold, so that the
gold and beautiful workmanship might be seen. The oil in the
seven lamps represents the Holy Spirit. Spiritually applied, we
have here the Spirit of God shedding light upon Christ. For
this He is given, to glorify Christ." As it was in Israel's old-time
tabernacle, and as it now is in the heavenly sanctuary, so in the
assemblies of the Lord's people on earth, God would have the
glorious perfections of Christ displayed before His people.

Following this, in this eighth chapter, comes the consecration
of the Levites. Note the salient lessons. (i) Before they could
serve they must be *cleansed* (verse 7); so must we. (ii) Their
cleansing was twofold, partly wrought *upon* them and partly
wrought *by* them (verse 7); even so, in our own cleansing, there
is the Divine side and also the human side. (iii) The cleansing
wrought *upon* them was the sprinkling of "water of purification"
(lit. "water of sin"—i.e., to cleanse away sin); even so do we
ourselves need that cleansing which only the blood of Christ and
the renewing of the Holy Spirit can give to us. (iv) The cleansing
wrought *by* them was to "shave all their flesh, and wash their
clothes" (verse 7); even so, on our own part, there must be a
detachment from all those habits and impurities of common life
which cling to us as closely and easily as our clothes, and which
seem as much a part of us as our very hair. Especially in our
Christian service there must be the application of death to that
which is merely natural and "of the flesh," by the bringing of
the word of God to bear on heart and conscience. It has been
discerningly said that "there never was a more fatal mistake

than to attempt to enlist nature in the service of God." There must be the "water"—daily cleansing of our conduct in the teaching of the word; and there must be the "razor"—daily self-judgment and uncompromising disallowance of that which grows "of the flesh." (v) The acceptance of the Levites was on the ground of the *sin*-offering and the *burnt*-offering (verses 8 and 12); and even so, our own acceptance with God is solely by the atoning self-sacrifice of Christ. (vi) The Levites must be presented before, and wholly given to, the Lord (verses 13–16); even so must we too "present our bodies a living sacrifice, holy, acceptable unto God, which is our reasonable service" (Rom. xii. 1).

Chapter ix. first shows us the people keeping the Passover, and then tells us of the pillar of cloud (by day) and fire (by night) which abode over the Tabernacle when the host were to rest still, and which moved onward when they were to journey. The Passover feast speaks of *fellowship*. The pillar of cloud and fire speaks of *guidance*. Thus, after the mobilisation of the people for war (i.–ii.), the appropriation of the Levites for service (iii.–iv.), and the instruction of the camp in holiness (v.–viii.), comes the crowning lesson of fellowship and guidance (ix.–x. 10).

Here, in Numbers ix., the people's pilgrimage Passover was, in a special way, both retrospective and prospective. It was the memorial of a past deliverance, and it was the pledge of a prospective inheritance. Similarly, to the Christian pilgrim today, the Lord's table is both a memorial and a pledge. It looks back to an accomplished redemption. It points onward to a glorious consummation. It looks backward inasmuch as we thereby "*shew the Lord's death.*" It looks onward "*until He come*" (1 Cor. xi. 26). "And now abideth faith, hope, love" (1 Cor. xiii. 13). At the Lord's table *Faith* looks *back* to the *Cross*, and is *strengthened*; *Hope* looks *on* to the *Coming*, and is *brightened*; *Love* looks *up* to the *Throne*, and is *deepened*.

Note that God made provision for *all* His people to share in the Passover feast. In the camp there were "certain men who were defiled by the dead body of a man, that they could not keep the Passover on that day" (verse 6). These enquired what they should do. The mind of the Lord was that these should keep the Passover one month later (verses 7–12). This provision also covered those who should ever be "in a journey afar off."

God would have none excluded from this "feast" of redemption; nor would He have any of His blood-bought people in Christ deny themselves this fellowship with Himself on the ground of redemption and through the "Spirit of adoption whereby we cry, Abba Father" (Rom. viii. 15).

And now read again, in verses 16 to 18, about that pillar of cloud and fire covering the Tabernacle.

Here was Divine guidance, direct, continuous, unmistakable, infallible. Israel's "many thousands" were spared the confusion of being left to search out by themselves a doubtful course which might have brought them to disaster. They were to make no plans of their own. They were not to know the route for even one day ahead. When they camped they could not say how long they would be staying. When they marched they could not say how long they would be moving. To watch that guiding pillar was all they were required to do. On that guidance they were absolutely dependent; and following that guidance they were absolutely safe.

"And does God do anything less for His people living in the present age?" asks one. Nay, "Every Christian knows that he is under His care and guidance. If He guided Israel thus, how much more will He guide us who are, through grace, members of His body, one spirit with the Lord! How often we frustrate the manifestations of His power and His love by choosing our own path! We are to follow Him. It is not acting according to the letter of certain rules and regulations: it is following a living Christ." He says, "I will guide thee with Mine eye" (Ps. xxxii. 8). *Our* eye must ever be toward *His* eye. There is guidance continuous and progressive for those who truly follow. Our lifelong motto must be: "The will of God, nothing more, nothing less, nothing else, always, everywhere, and at all costs." Our Lord's *work* for us is perfect; we must *rest* in it. Our Lord's *word* to us is perfect; we must *live* by it. Our Lord's *will* for us is perfect; we must *walk* in it.

Finally, in chapter x. 1–10, Moses is commanded—"*Make thee two trumpets of silver; of a whole piece shalt thou make them; that thou mayest use them for the calling of the assembly, and for the journeying of the camps*" (x. 2). These trumpets, like the pillar of cloud and fire, were for guidance. The pillar gave guidance

for the eye. The trumpets gave guidance for the ear. Four uses
are assigned to these silver trumpets. They were to be, first, a
rallying call to the people (verse 3); second, a signal for advance
(verses 5–6); third, a clarion in time of war (verse 9); fourth,
a memorial before God (verses 9–10). It was the *priests* who
were to blow the trumpet; for the silver trumpet was "the
trumpet of *God.*"

All these things may be related to ourselves. Does the trumpet
sound a *regathering*? That trumpet is yet to sound for the regathering of dispersed Israel! (See Isa. xxvii. 13; Zech. ix. 14.)
Besides this, when the Lord Jesus returns for His own, He shall
"descend from heaven with a shout, and *with the trumpet of
God*"—to gather together His redeemed to Himself (1 Thess iv. 16).
"*The trumpet* shall sound, and the dead shall be raised incor-
ruptible, and we shall be changed" (1 Cor. xv. 52). Does the
trumpet speak of *war* and *conquest*? Turn to Joel ii. 1: "Blow
ye the *trumpet* in Zion, and sound an alarm in My holy mountain:
let all the inhabitants of the land tremble: for the day of the
LORD cometh." Turn to Revelation viii. and ix. and see the
angels with their trumpets sounding the Armageddon conquest
of Christ. Oh for the trumpet that proclaims His coming!

The Journeying (x. 11–xiv.)

Here, then, in the first ten chapters of Numbers, we have seen
the camp of Israel at Sinai, marked by every preparation and
provision for advance, for conquest and possession. Get the
picture of that camp well in mind. There is that mighty host, the
twelve tribes lying in vast foursquare formation "far off about
the tabernacle," the Levite groups encamped round about the
outer court of the Tabernacle, with Moses and Aaron and the
priests on the east, guarding the entrance to the sacred enclosure; while there, at the very heart, giving unity, strength,
and glory to the camp, is the sanctuary, speaking of God as the
centre of His chosen people, even as Christ is now the centre and
life and glory of His Church.

All is now ready for advance; and "on the twentieth day of
the second month, in the second year," the guiding pillar lifts
from the Tabernacle (x. 11). The moment the pillar lifts, the
silver trumpets sound, and the whole camp is in motion.

First come the tribes of Judah, Issachar, and Zebulun; followed by two of the Levite groups—the Gershonites, with the coverings and the curtains of the Tabernacle, and the Merarites, with the golden boards and silver sockets and other structural parts of the Tabernacle. (To help them in transporting these, the Gershonites and Merarites would use the waggons and oxen given to them in the offering of the princes—see chapter vii.) Next come the tribes of Reuben, Simeon, and Gad; with the Kohathites following, and bearing the ark, the golden altar, the golden candelabrum, and the other precious internal appointments of the Tabernacle. Next come Ephraim, Manasseh, and Benjamin; and lastly Dan, Asher, and Naphtali (x. 14–27). There have been many wonderful things in history; but has there ever been anything to eclipse the marvel of this vast national transplantation, this orderly-moving multitude of between two and three million people, with all their children, their tents, their beasts, and personal equipment?—and the ark of God leading them on? We can understand the earnestness with which Moses would pray for this great multitude the two prayers recorded at the end of chapter x.—"And it came to pass, when the ark set forward, that Moses said: Rise up, Lord, and let Thine enemies be scattered; and let them that hate Thee flee before Thee. And when it rested, he said: Return, O Lord, unto the many thousands of Israel."

Chapters x. to xiv. (the journey from Sinai to Kadesh) make sad reading. See x. 29–32. How strange to find Moses saying to Hobab, his Midianite relative, "Leave us not, I pray thee, forasmuch as thou knowest how we are to encamp in the wilderness, and thou mayest be to us instead of eyes!" How soon the temptation comes to look away from the guiding pillar of cloud and fire! Such is the weakness of the human heart. We profess to trust God, and then look to man. We find it easier to lean on a puny mortal whom we can see, than on the almighty Lord Himself whom we cannot see.

See chapter xi. 1–3. After only three days' journey the people are complaining. The ark has sought out for them a resting place. Their comfort has been provided for. Canaan is just ahead. They carry with them the pledge of victory. They should be singing songs of rejoicing. Yet they are murmuring. The fire of judgment breaks out but is mercifully stayed at the prayer of Moses. The place was thus named *Taberah*, which means a burning. Murmuring never makes the way easier. It usually brings added trouble. Those who murmur without cause are soon given cause to murmur. Murmuring against God's providences leads on, bit by bit, to open rebellion and pitiable collapse, as we see in these chapters. Let us guard against it.

See chapter xi. 4-35. The "mixed multitude" lust for the savouries of Egypt. Then the rest join them,—"Who shall give us flesh to eat?" The fire at Taberah has not chastened them! Having murmured at the way by which God led them, they murmur now at the food by which God fed them. Yet this miracle-bread from heaven (a beautiful type of Christ), and called "angels' food" in Psalm lxxviii. 25, was the perfect diet for their (intendedly brief) journeying to Canaan. Moses himself becomes discouraged (verses 10–15)—"I am not able to bear all this people alone." Seventy elders are chosen to share the burden with him; and upon these comes the Spirit of God, so that they prophesy, presumably exhorting the people to faith and obedience. Note that prophecy, which is a gift of the Spirit, has a special place in time of apostasy and failure. The craved-for flesh is miraculously provided in the form of quails; yet even as the people greedily devour the flesh, judgment falls in a plague which devours the eaters,—judgment because they greedily fall on the provision merely for the gratifying of their own fleshly lust, without repentance and without recognition of the Giver behind the gift. The plague spot became named Kibroth-hattaavah, which means "graves of lust."

See chapter xii. The murmuring has now got to Israel's highest leaders. Moses' own brother and sister contentiously question his leadership. Aaron was already High Priest. Miriam was Israel's prophetess. Jealous pride now seeks higher position still. Their reference to Moses' Gentile wife was a mere pretext. See Moses' greatness. There is no self-vindication, and no trace even of resentment (see verse 13). His gentleness makes him great. His meekness is his majesty. God vindicates him (verses 4–10). "Wherefore were ye not afraid to speak against My servant Moses?" Judgment falls on the rebels. Miriam, the obvious instigator, becomes a leper. Note, it is grave sin to speak against a true servant of God. The Christian's real safety is to leave God to vindicate him. God guards the man He calls to service. Observe Moses' forgiving spirit. He prays for Miriam, and she is healed.

This brings us to chapters xiii. and xiv., to the Kadesh crisis; and the preceding chapters have prepared us to see why the fateful failure came about. The people had been failing bit by bit before. "How often we look upon grumbling as a little sin," says one expositor; "and not until we try to check ourselves in it do we find how complete is its possession of us, and how it is ready to spring upon us at all hours of the day under the slightest provocation. The weather is bad, the tea is too sweet, the chops are half cold, the potatoes are not done, the maid is unpunctual or careless, the parcel we expected is not delivered, and we are vexed and complain. It was a secret heart-grumble that led to Eve's disobedience. Trace Israel's downward course in Numbers, from discontent to lust, despising the Lord, speaking against His servants, provoking, tempting, doubting God, rebellion, presumption, discouragement, striving with, and speaking against God, and at last gross whoredom and idolatry. Beware! To be saved from this evil thing is one step towards perfection; see Philippians ii. 14."

The details of Israel's breakdown at Kadesh are well known. The twelve spies search the land for forty days. In their report all concur that Canaan is indeed a goodly land (xiii. 27); but ten bring back the doleful advice that its conquest is impossible. The other two, Caleb and Joshua, still the people, saying, "Let us go up at once and possess it." "The Lord is with us; fear them not." The ten put the difficulty between themselves and God. The two put God between themselves and the difficulty. The ten saw with the eye of the flesh. The two saw with the eye of faith.

We know the outcome. Israel disbelieved, then rebelled, even bidding that Caleb and Joshua be stoned (xiv. 10), and suggesting the appointment of a new leader who should take them all back to Egypt (xiv. 4)! The cutting irony is that Israel was but a stone's throw from the prize. Israel disobeyed. Judgment fell. Moses' touching intercession is heard for the nation (xiv. 11–20); but the judgment of the forty years' "wandering" is imposed (xiv. 29–30). Oh, the tragedy—a whole generation must now die off in the wilderness, and forty years be spent moving about without really getting anywhere! Certainly, although human unbelief cannot finally frustrate the purposes of God, it can hold back their gracious fulfilment. But the most pronounced lesson here is surely this, that *unbelief defeats the unbeliever*!

THE BOOK OF NUMBERS (3)

Lesson Number 15

NOTE.—For this study read once or twice again chapters xv. to xx.

Ten men who failed to see God
Saw cities impregnably high;
    Two men, "looking off" unto God,
Saw doom for those cities draw nigh.

Ten men who failed to see God
Saw giants affrightingly tall;
    Two men, "looking off" unto God,
Saw giants as grasshoppers small.

Ten men who failed to see God,
Reported, "We're certain to fail";
    Two men, "looking off" unto God,
Cried, "Up! for with God we prevail."

Ten men who failed to see God
Discouraged their brother men;
    Two men perceived *God everywhere*;
Are you of the two—or the ten?

"One bold push forward, and their feet would tread on their inheritance. But, as is so often the case, courage oozed out at the decisive moment, and cowardice, disguised as prudence, called for 'further information,' that cuckoo-cry of the faint-hearted"

—ALEXANDER MACLAREN.

(Don McFarland spoke on this recently)

THE BOOK OF NUMBERS (3)

Part II. THE WILDERNESS WANDERING (xv.–xx.)

WE ARE now at the central section of Numbers—chapters xv. to xx., the chapters which cover the thirty-eight years of the so-called "Wandering." This delay-period marks the transition from the old generation to the new. It sets in immediately after the Kadesh crisis, and terminates in the year of Aaron's death (xx.), as we have already shown.

Both at the beginning and at the end of Numbers we see an Israel carefully prepared, so far as organisation is concerned, for immediate conquest and possession: but this needless, tragic delay of thirty-eight years intervenes; and Numbers thus becomes distinguishingly *the book of arrested progress.* As such it speaks to us today regarding arrested progress in the Christian Church as a whole, and in the lives of individual Christians. It took only forty hours to get Israel out of Egypt; but it took forty years to get Egypt out of Israel! Within two years the people of Israel were at Kadesh-barnea, the gate of Canaan. Thirty-eight years later, there they were again, at the very same spot. Why? Well, there was that "mixed multitude" of pseudo-Israelites who were allowed to travel with the congregation, and who were not really one at heart either with the people or with the project. That "mixed multitude" lusted, and set the others lusting too, for the flesh-pots and cheap tasties of Egypt, the fish, the cucumbers, the melons, the leeks and onions and garlic. Very soon, besides the "mixed multitude," there were mixed motives! Oh, what a curse is the "mixed multitude" in the Church of today!—and how prevalent, in consequence, are the mixed motives!—and how obvious is the arresting and thwarting of real progress! We need never wonder at God's insistence on separation. It is vital to spiritual progress and effectiveness.

The following quotation is abundantly true. "In our churches are thousands of cases of arrested development. In the case

of many the arrest, as in the case of Israel, is the direct consequence of disobedience. They heard the Divine call, they experienced the Divine deliverance, they passed from death unto life,
and they began the new life well. As young Christians they were
full of zeal, full of love: they cried in their confidence, 'All that
the Lord commanded us we will do.' They seemed ready to possess
their possessions, and to enter spiritually into all the blessed
experiences God has for those who follow Him fully. But there
was a day when the call came definitely to enter the land, definitely
to yield themselves into the hand of God for a deeper, richer
life than they had ever known. They saw the land, they confessed that it was a good land; but they saw the giants and the
walled cities; they saw the persecution, the scoffing, the isolation,
the difficult service to which full consecration would lead; and
they said, 'We could not face it; we will not go up'; and immediately an arrest was put on their progress, their religion lost
its freshness, and its power; and the truest hymn they can now
sing is that most mournful one to be found on a Christian's lips
—'What peaceful hours I once enjoyed; how sweet their memory
still! But they have left an aching void the world can never
fill.' If there be any of you whose experience this is, remember
that the cure for it is the return to Kadesh. Go back to the place
where you disobeyed God; confess your sin; take up the life
of obedience once more; and the old joy, power, and progress
will be yours again. And to those who have not put back the
purposes of God for them by wicked wilfulness, beware of the
initial sins which end in such catastrophe, the sins that lie at
the base of all backsliding—dissatisfaction and discontent. How
little Israel realised the danger of their first yielding to discontent!
Probably not one of them had any idea to what an abyss of sin
those first murmurs would lead."

This solemn lesson of the "Wandering" should not be lost on
any reader of this Book of Numbers. Let us now briefly but
thoughtfully look again through the chapters which tell about it.

The so-called "Wandering" must be distinguished, first of all,
from the journeyings which preceded it and those which followed
it. At the Kadesh mutiny there was a collapse of organisation.
The people ceased to be pilgrims, and became nomads. We need
also to have clear views as to what the "Wandering" really was.
Most Bible readers seem to think that during those years the

whole camp of Israel moved from place to place, with the pillar of cloud and fire directing their movements, and the Levites setting up and taking down the Tabernacle at each place. Yet there is no record of any such concerted movings during this time. It would rather seem that the Tabernacle abode throughout at Kadesh, and that roving, break-away bands dispersed more or less widely into the surrounding region, recognising Kadesh as a centre, and regathering there toward the end of the long delay. We shall touch on this again at chapter xx. The earlier name of Kadesh was En-mishpat (Gen. xiv. 7). Its later name of Kadesh, which is equivalent to "the sanctuary," may possibly have been given to it because of the long stay of the Tabernacle there.

Israel was in the wilderness all this time. Kadesh itself was in the wilderness or open country, being in (or between) the wilderness of Paran (xiii. 26) and the wilderness of Zin (xx. 1; xxvii. 14; xxxiii. 36).

Further, it is well to be clear about that word "wandering." In chapter xiv. 33, where God imposes the judgment of the "wandering," the Hebrew word translated as "shall wander" is literally "shall *pasture*"—"Your children shall pasture the wilderness (or open country) forty years." Going with the judgment is an implicit assurance that the Lord will shepherd them and provide for their needs. Here is goodness as well as severity!

An Historical Suspension.

These thirty-eight years simply mark time without making history. There is an almost complete submergence of the chosen people from view. During these years the real history of Israel was actually in abeyance; for that history is the history of a theocracy, and is therefore, in the highest sense, the history of God's dealings with His own people as He leads them onward to the fulfilment of His great purposes. The thirty-eight years are a hold-up of the purposes, and therefore a gap in the history. The generation which excommunicated itself at Kadesh had henceforth no heritage in Israel. Their lives were spared at the time, but their own professed wish that they had died in the wilderness was turned back upon them (xiv. 2, 28); they must now die out, and another generation take their place before the

history of the theocracy could be resumed. The Kadesh breakdown and the thirty-eight years' suspension may well speak to
us of that still graver breakdown at Calvary and the present long
suspense-period in Israel's history, during which God is calling
out for Himself a spiritual people in Christ, irrespective of nation-
ality (see Rom. ix.–xi. with Eph. ii.–iii.).

Let us note the following facts about the so-called "Wandering." First, God did not wholly abandon the rebellious people.
He continued to communicate with them through Moses (xv. 1,
17, 35, etc.); and He gave the manna and supplied water and
provided raiment and shoes (Deut. viii. 2–6; xxix. 5, 6).

Second, the rite of circumcision was discontinued (Joshua v.
4–8). It seems also as though the Passover was omitted throughout. Perhaps we can understand this. The rebellious generation
knew that they were never to enter Canaan, and therefore it is
unlikely that they could have found much heart to celebrate
the memory (now made so bitter to them) of that fruitless deliverance. Indeed it seems probable that during these years the
sacrificial system as a whole fell largely into disuse.

Third, from Ezekiel xx. 10–26 and Amos v. 25, 26, we learn
that during this time the Law was badly disobeyed, the Sabbaths
were profaned, idolatrous practices persisted, and the people
even caused their firstborn to "pass through the fire" to Moloch!

Fourth—and in the words of an Old Testament scholar—
"We have no authority for supposing that the host held together
during these years of wandering which had no aim but waste
of time, and no end but death. The presumption is that they
scattered themselves far and wide over the wilderness (itself of
no great extent), just as present convenience dictated. Disease
and death, and all those other incidents revived in full force
which make the simultaneous march in close array of two million
people an impossibility. No doubt the headquarters of the host
and nation, Moses and Aaron, and the Levites generally, remained
with the ark, and formed the visible and representative centre
of the national life and worship."

Turning now to the chapters themselves (xv.–xx.), let us quickly
pick out the main things.

Chapter xv. begins—"And the Lord spake . . . When ye be
come into the land. . . ." We do not know how soon or how

long after the Kadesh revolt these words were spoken, but it is striking that the first recorded word of God after Israel's turning from the land is a reference to their eventual entering it. Man's delay does not mean God's defeat. Greater than man's failure is God's faithfulness.

Verse 17 introduces another speaking of God, concerning sacrifices for sins of error, and punishment for sins of presumption. Since Israel's law is given by God, and not by any merely human authority, to disobey wilfully is to reproach Jehovah Himself, and to merit severest penalty (verses 30, 31).

Verses 32-6 give illustration of such presumption and its punishment—the "man that gathered sticks upon the Sabbath day." What may seem a trivial thing at a superficial glance was in reality a wilful scorning of God Himself.

The chapter closes with the "ribband of blue" which the Israelites were to wear. They were to make fringes (or possibly the meaning is tassels) to the borders (lit. wings) of their garments, and were to attach to the fringe or tassel a "ribband" or cord of blue. Thus did God design a mark of distinction when many other distinctions had fallen into abeyance. Blue is the heavenly colour. It was to remind them of their heavenly calling, and cause them to "remember all the commandments of the Lord, and do them" (verse 39). It was to remind them also of their separation unto God—"holy unto your God" (verse 40). It was to be in the borders of their garments, so that the reminder might be with them everywhere and all the time, and so that every time they looked selfward and earthward their thoughts might be directed heavenward. There should be that ribband of blue— that distinguishing mark of God's Spirit—about every Christian today, too.

The "Gainsaying of Korah" (Jude 11).

Chapters xvi. to xviii. really belong together. In xvi. comes the "gainsaying of Korah" which was really an attack on the Aaronic priesthood. Over fifteen thousand die in the retribution of earthquake, fire, and plague. Then, in xvii., comes the budding of Aaron's rod, the new Divine attestation of the Aaronic priesthood. Then, in xviii., we have the Divine reaffirmation of the Aaronic priesthood, spoken to Aaron himself. Thus, in these three chapters we have the Aaronic priesthood defended, attested, confirmed.

Note, in xvi., that rebel Korah was son of Kohath. The Kohathites had the choicest services among the Levites. They bore the most sacred things of the Tabernacle. Apostasy often comes from the very leaders of religion. Their censers were kept as a warning (verse 38).

Note, in xvii., that Aaron's rod, in its budding and blossoming is a beautiful miracle-type of Christ's resurrection. The founders of the non-Christian religions were dead rods, and so are the systems they originated. Christ is the rod which has budded and blossomed in resurrection life and glory; and His resurrection is the Divine attestation that He is the one true Saviour-Priest of men.

The Red Heifer (xix.).

The ordinance of the red heifer, in chapter xix., probably follows as a consequence of the Korah revolt. Besides dying at the ordinary rate, the people had been carried off in thousands by the plague. Means were required for the cleansing of the very many who became defiled by contact with the dead. The ashes of the red heifer were used for this purpose, in the way described, and probably as an emergency measure, for no such ordinance is anywhere prescribed in Leviticus.

Hebrews ix. 13–14 suggests that here we have a type of our Lord's saving death for ourselves. The red heifer was to be without blemish, even as was the character of Christ. It must be a heifer on which no yoke had come (the yoke being that which is put upon an animal to subdue its wild nature and compel subjection), even as our Lord was without any need of such a yoke, but came saying "Lo, I come to do Thy will." The heifer must be red,—and since this is the only place where the colour of a sacrificial animal is stipulated does it specially speak of our Lord's obedience even to the death of the Cross? The heifer must be slain without the camp; and so was our Lord (Heb. xiii. 12). The blood must be sprinkled seven times toward the Sanctuary, speaking of perfect atonement; and the ashes of the heifer, with water of cleansing, must be sprinkled on the defiled people, to provide cleansing. Unlike the other offerings, this one was never to be repeated. In other cases, if a man sinned, fresh blood must be spilt; but here the virtue of what had been already offered and accepted remained. Even so, the sacrifice of Christ has made provision for our complete and continuous cleansing from all the defilement of our hearts which may be contracted as we pass through "this present evil world" which, in a spiritual sense, is stamped with death everywhere. See 1 John i. 7.

End of the "Wandering" (xx.).

We are now at chapter xx., the end of which coincides with the end of the "Wandering." The first verse of this twentieth chapter is of special importance in its bearing upon the "Wandering," and it is important to understand it correctly. Rather than lengthen this present study, however, with the somewhat close reasoning involved in that connection, we deal with it in the Addenda to our studies in this Book of Numbers (at the end of the next lesson) where it can be looked up afterwards.

Meanwhile, in this twentieth chapter, we find significantly grouped together the death of Miriam, the sin of Moses, and the death of Aaron. It was because of Moses' lapse here at Meribah that he was denied leading the nation into Canaan (verse 12); yet even this, pathetic as it is, becomes overruled to teach us, typically, that the Law, which Moses represents, can never lead us into that rest of which Canaan is a type. The account of Aaron's death is touching; and, as we have already pointed out, it is this event which (by comparison with xxxiii. 38) marks the end of the "Wandering." Thus, Aaron, representative of the priesthood, could not lead Israel into the promised rest; nor could Miriam, representative of the prophets; nor could Moses, representative of the Law. This was reserved for Joshua, who in a unique way was a type of our heavenly Saviour and Captain, the Lord Jesus Christ.

The Meribah rock-smiting incident is stamped with strong type-teaching. Moses was told simply to speak to the rock; but he exasperatedly struck it twice with the rod. The rock (Christ: 1 Cor. x. 4), having been once smitten (Exod. xvii. 5), need not be smitten again. The striking of it again would imply, in type, that the one sacrifice was inadequate, thereby contradicting the finality and abiding efficacy of Calvary. However, despite Moses' action, the water gushed from the rock; for despite the misunderstandings and wrong reactions of men in relation to the Cross, the "living water" still flows "more abundantly" from the cleft Rock of Ages, to bless the souls of tens of thousands in every generation.

THE BOOK OF NUMBERS (4)

Lesson Number 16

NOTE.—For this study read again chapters xxi. to xxxvi.

"A cynical man of science long ago sneered at the Bible as 'a collection of rude imaginings of Syria,' as 'the worn-out old bottle of Judaism into which the generous new wine of science is being poured.' The cynical savant is dead, but the Bible is still alive, for it is the Book of Books. The old wines of science grow sour in their cellars, and its new vintages have their day. But the Bible shows no signs of senility. Its youth is eternal. When our men of science and their theories are forgotten, the Bible will remain what it has been for mankind for two thousand years, the one universal book of wisdom, of truth, of sublimity, and of consolation."

JAMES DOUGLAS.

THE BOOK OF NUMBERS (4)

Part III. THE NEW GENERATION (xxi.–xxxvi.)

(*Kadesh to Plains of Moab*)

THE DREARY delay is over. A new morning breaks. The old generation is no more. A new generation has arisen. Aaron is gone, and Eleazar is appointed the new high priest. Moses is soon to go, and Joshua is to be appointed the new leader. The hour has struck for a new departure. Israel is to move over to the plains of Moab, and to prepare again for entering the promised land. In this final division of Numbers we have—

> The new Journeying (xxi.–xxv.),
> The new Numbering (xxvi.–xxvii.),
> The new Instructing (xxviii.–xxxvi.).

The New Journeying (xxi.–xxv.)

The new journeying, to the plains of Moab, would take about four to five months. We gather this from the fact that the people left Mount Hor about one month after Aaron's death (xx. 29), which took place in the *fifth* month of the fortieth year (xxxiii. 38) ; and it was in the *eleventh* month of that same year, on their having reached the plains of Moab, that Moses commenced his great charge to Israel which constitutes the book of Deuteronomy (Deut. i. 3, 5). The journey was made much longer because Edom refused Israel the shorter way through Edomite territory (xx. 14–22; xxi. 4).

The chief halts and incidents are given in chapter xxi., which chapter opens with two significant facts. First, there is *Jehovah's new response to Israel*—"the Lord hearkened to the voice of Israel and delivered up the Canaanites" (verse 3). During the Wandering, while Israel has been out of line with the directive will of God, there has been no such response. Turn to Deuteronomy i. 44. Looking back on the beginning of the Wandering,

189

Moses says: "And the Amorites which dwelt in that mountain came out against you, and chased you as bees do, and destroyed you in Seir, even unto Hormah: and ye returned and wept before the Lord; *but the Lord would not hearken to your voice, nor give ear unto you.*" Now, however, with the taking up again of Israel's true history, the covenant privileges again become operative. Israel calls and Jehovah hearkens. Mark the great lesson here. When we get out of the purposive will of God for us, the real power of prayer is suspended; but if we continue in the line of that will, none can effectually stand against us. Outside that will we are misguided wanderers. Inside it we are militant pilgrims with a clear objective.

Second, here is *Israel's new victory*—"The Lord . . . delivered up the Canaanites; and they (Israel) utterly destroyed them and their cities: and he called the name of the place (lit.—the name of the place was called) Hormah" (verse 3). Hormah was the place of humiliating defeat at the *beginning* of the Wandering (see xiv. 45). Now, at the *end* of the Wandering, as Israel re-emerges into the light of the Divine purpose and favour, there is victory in the place of the old defeat. How true it is that when we turn away from the Canaan into which God would lead us we cannot stand before our *spiritual* foes! To keep in the will of God is the secret of triumphant progress.

Next, in verses 4 to 9, we have the episode connected with the lifting up of *the brazen serpent*. We shall refer to the type-teaching here later. What we would note here is Israel's discouragement (see verse 4). The people had been refused permission to go *through* the land of Edom, and were having to go *round* it. This not only made the way longer, it gave a sense of grievance which made the way seem *much* longer. Israel falls into the old sin of murmuring (verse 5), and suffers again (verse 6). This, after their recent victory! We need to be watchful in times of victory, lest we suffer depressing reactions. Note also, the brazen serpent, being in appearance like the destroying serpents which infested the camp, served both to remind the people of their wrong and at the same time to provide healing. Similarly, at Calvary we see, as nowhere else, the awfulness of our sin, and at the same time our salvation from it.

We move on now, through several stages, to *the well of singing* (verses 16–18)—"That is the well whereof the Lord spake unto

Moses: Gather the people together, and I will give them water. Then sang Israel this song:

> '*Spring up, O well; sing ye unto it;*
> *The well which the princes digged,*
> *Which the nobles of the people delved,*
> *With the ruler's staff and their staves.'*"

Thank God for song! What sighing could not do, in verse 5, singing does, in verse 17. It began to look as though Israel had forgotten how to sing. There is no record of any singing between this well of song and that which Israel had sung at the Red Sea.

Why did Israel sing at this well? Had the people at last discovered that the water from the smitten Rock was following them through all their journeyings, and that even amid the most arid stretch of desert all they had to do was to sing the song of faith, and dig through the hard crust to find the supply there, at the very point of their need? Had they now learned that besides its being unnecessary for the Rock to be *struck* more than the once, it was also unnecessary to provide *another* rock for each new need? We do not know. But have we ourselves learned not only the finality of the once-smiting on Calvary, but the continuity of supply from that once-smitten Rock ("and that rock was Christ"—1 Cor. x. 4)? Are *we* living by the continuous flow of that "living water," the Holy Spirit? Have *we* found that just beneath the hard surface of life's most arid stretches there is that crystal stream following us from the Rock, and ready to gush forth at the voice of prayer and the song of faith? Are *we* with joy drawing from the wells of salvation? Such songs and fountains transform the drabbest wilderness! In the remainder of this chapter there is nothing but victory. Had Israel sung the song of faith at Kadesh, thirty-eight years before, instead of venting the dirges of unbelief, what conquests might have taken the place of the Wandering!

And now, in chapters xxii. to xxiv., one of the strangest characters in the Bible appears on the scene—Balaam. On the problems and special features pertaining to him see our Addenda at the end of this study. These three chapters really lie athwart the narrative, as is seen by the fact that the end of chapter xxi. links right over to xxv. The great point to note here is that even the subtlest stratagems of evil against Israel are overridden now that Israel once more marches in Jehovah's will. Balaam, who tries to curse, is forced to bless.

But alas, the people themselves now turn aside and do the accursed thing. Chapter xxv.—an awful chapter—begins: "And Israel abode in Shittim, and the people began to commit whoredom with the daughters of Moab. And they called the people unto the sacrifices of their gods; and the people did eat, and bowed down to their gods: and Israel joined himself unto Baal-peor. And the anger of the Lord was kindled against Israel." From chapter xxxi. 16 we learn that Balaam, although unable to curse the sons of Israel, had evidently counselled that the women of Moab and Midian should solicit them. The sons of Israel became a foolish prey. The remainder of this twenty-fifth chapter of Numbers makes sorry reading. Twenty-four thousand die in the plague which breaks forth in judgment. What a tragedy after the recent record of victories! What a tragedy, this idolatry and obscenity in the people blessed with such high teaching and such a high calling! Of a truth, these chapters of Numbers teach us that it is not enough for us to have an outward law or ideal, however high and pure it may be. What we need is an inward change to strike down the inbred perversity of our fallen nature!

The New Numbering (xxvi.-xxvii.)

Chapters xxvi. and xxvii. give us the new military census of Israel, and certain matters consequent upon it. It is interesting to see the figures side by side with those of the earlier count.

Tribe	Old Census	New Census	Decrease	Increase
Reuben	46,500	43,730	6 per cent	
Simeon	59,300	22,200	63　,,　,,	
Gad	45,650	40,500	11　,,　,,	
Judah	74,600	76,500		2½ per cent
Issachar	54,400	64,300		18　,,　,,
Zebulun	57,400	60,500		5½　,,　,,
Ephraim	40,500	32,500	20　,,　,,	
Manasseh	32,200	52,700		63　,,　,,
Benjamin	35,400	45,600		29　,,　,,
Dan	62,700	64,400		2½　,,　,,
Asher	41,500	53,400		28　,,　,,
Naphtali	53,400	45,400	15　,,　,,	
	603,550	601,730		

The new numbering was evidently taken in hundreds, as the one before. The slight decrease in the new total, and the strange increases and decreases in certain of the tribes, suggest at once the genuineness of these figures. An artificial record would have avoided such difficult variations.

The new total pathetically harmonises with the whole story of Numbers. At the beginning of the forty years the number is roughly 600,000; and again at the end of the forty years the number is 600,000. They are no further forward for the whole period. There is arrested progress even numerically. The strange drop in some of the tribes may be accounted for by the plagues which fell in judgment. We gather that Simeon figured prominently in the Baal-peor sin and plague (see xxv. 14). The principle on which the land is to be apportioned is given in verses 53 to 56; and the new total of the Levites, in verses 57 to 62.

Arising in connection with this new numbering is the plea of Zelophehad's daughters respecting their family inheritance (xxvii. 1–11). It is self-explanatory and requires no comment here. Also, after the new numbering Moses receives intimation of his own impending departure (verses 12–14). Touching indeed is Moses' acknowledgment of this—

"Let the Lord, the God of the spirits of all flesh, set a man over the congregation, which may go out before them, and which may go in before them, and which may lead them out, and which may bring them in; that the congregation of the Lord be not as sheep which have no shepherd" (verses 16–17).

There is no thought of self here. It is the people and the Lord's own cause which are upon his heart. If their well-being is assured he is content. May there breathe such a spirit in our own hearts! Following Moses' prayer, he is instructed publicly to induct Joshua into office as new leader, the account of which induction closes the chapter (verses 18–23). Here, then, is newly numbered Israel's fighting strength at the change-over to Joshua's command and the going up to possess the land.

"And Moses laid his hands upon him
(Joshua), and gave him a charge, as
Jehovah had commanded" (v. 23).

G

The New Instructing (xxviii.–xxxvi.)

This final section of Numbers need not detain us long. Chapters xxviii. and xxix. go together. They deal with the subject of the Lord's offerings, specifying their constituents and routine, and thus amplifying the instructions already given in Leviticus xxiii. First come the daily offerings (xxviii. 3–8), then the Sabbath offerings (verses 9–10), then the new month offerings (verses 11–15), and then the offerings going with the "feasts" of the Lord (xxviii. 16–xxix. 40). For the typical aspects of these offerings and feasts look back over our study of Leviticus.

We ought just to note that the special offering for the *Sabbath* is here ordered for the first time, as also is that for the *new month*, or new moon. The *daily* offering, which was prescribed in Exodus xxix. 38–42, and which, we presume, had subsequently continued uninterruptedly, is again specified here because it was the foundation of the whole sacrificial system. Whatever else was offered was in addition to it, not in lieu of it.

Typically, all the offerings speak of Christ, and it is therefore significant that God speaks here of them as "My bread" (xxviii. 2). In Christ God has found His delight. The heart of God feeds, as it were, on Him, and is perfectly satisfied.

Chapter xxx. concerns vows—of men (verses 1, 2), of maidens (verses 3–5), of maidens betrothed (verses 6–8), of widows (verse 9), of wives (verses 10–15). On the Divine recognition of the place of vows see our note on chapter vi. The purpose of the new instructions here is to *safeguard* vows from being lightly regarded—from being either easily made or easily broken. They are to be made only to God Himself (verses 2, 3). They must not be broken (verses 2, 9, 15). In the case of maidens they must be parentally controlled (verses 3–5). In the case of the betrothed (the words of verse 6, literally translated, indicate betrothal) there must be care not to make *rash* vows (the words "uttered ought out of her lips" should rather be translated "the rash utterance of her lips"). In the case of the married woman there must be concurrence by the husband.

We may learn much from all this. There is a place for special covenanting with God, whether it be for self-denial, seasons of prayer, gifts of money, fasting, or other things; and these may provide a blessed release for the urgent love of the heart toward

God; but we should ever hold such vows or covenantings as the most inviolably sacred of all contracts. Moreover, let us say it thoughtfully, does not the old-time Hebrew vow suggest to ourselves, the redeemed at costliest price, that with utter earnestness we should vow our very selves away in life-long yieldedness to the will and service of our adorable Redeemer?

Retribution against Midian (xxxi.).

Chapter xxxi. brings the command to war on Midian. There is enough in the account to revolt the mind. The moral difficulty involved in Israel's Divinely sanctioned assault on the Canaanites here appears in its gravest form. What shall we say about it?

We suggest that the key to it is in that word "avenge." God's command is: "Avenge *the children of Israel* of the Midianites" (verse 2). Moses' transmission of the command is: "Avenge *the Lord* of Midian." If, therefore, we are dealing with honest language this war on Midian was certainly Divinely authorised and fulfilled a Divine purpose. Not that this in itself either involves or excuses the behaviour associated with the carrying out of it; but it gives the basis for a true consideration. The war on Midian was not merely a human retaliation: it was a Divine retribution. It was to "avenge *the children of Israel*" because Midian had deliberately, craftily, and gravely injured Israel, without provocation. It was to "avenge *the Lord*" because, in seducing Israel into licentious idolatries, they had knowingly (through the counsel of Balaam) been striking at Israel's holy God. Let us then be clear about this, that Midian justly merited retribution.

As to the *fact* of God's commanding Israel to destroy the Midianites, this falls in with God's command to destroy the Canaanite nations generally (Exod. xxiii. 24; Deut. vii. 1–6, etc.). There are those whose sentimental sympathies are so drawn out in commiseration for the foul-living Canaanites as to find it professedly impossible to believe that God could give such a command or sanction any such war; and on this account they reject the claim of the record to be inspired. But when we read of the utterly vile enormities of the Canaanites, in passages like Leviticus xviii. (noting specially verses 24, 27, 30), are we not driven to ask (if we are really honest) how a righteous Governor among the nations could do anything other—either in justice to these filthy-living people themselves or in consideration towards those corrupted by their influence—than effect their extermination in one way or another?

As for the *method* by which this should be effected, God has sovereign right to decide: and He commits the imperative surgery to a living nation called out to holiness and to the execution of the Divine purpose both in its necessary severity and its beneficence, so that the race as a whole might learn and heed. Now had God chosen, instead, to use pestilence, earthquake, famine, those who profess to find God's command to Israel unthinkable would make no charge of injustice; yet by these dumb agencies the lessons God wished to teach could never have been taught; and the physical suffering inflicted would have been much greater. Let us clearly and honestly face up to this, that if we believe in an overruling Providence, we must also believe that in one way or another God has provided that great wickedness in a nation shall be greatly punished; and God has the absolute right to decide the means to this end.

As for the vengeance on *Midian*, that which seems the most brutal, namely, the slaying of the women and male children (verse 17), is seen to have reason enough behind it, when we consider it in the light of all we are told. The men of Israel had spared Midian's women and children from the sword, and had brought them back prisoners. Moses' anger, coupled with words like those of Deuteronomy vii. 2, indicates that in this they had failed of full obedience. Moreover, the context suggests that the motive may have been as much sexual as benevolent. Now it was these very women who had earlier seduced the men of Israel, bringing death to twenty-four thousand (xxv. 9). What now was to be done with them? It seems an awful thing to kill a woman; yet it was the women, far more than the men, of Midian of whom there was reason to be afraid, for they would have spread physical and moral contagion through the camp. In justice to the men, and still more for the sake of Israel's own wives and mothers and maidens, it was unthinkable to let loose this host of strange women; and this appears the more forcibly when we consider the general immorality of these women, and the venereal disease certain to be rife among them. There is surely a swift recognition of this in Moses' distinction of verse 17 (and even after this, there were thirty-two thousand of the more harmless younger women left!—see verse 35).

Again, it seems a dastardly thing to slay a child; yet to suffer a whole generation of Midianites to grow up beneath the very roofs of Israel, so to speak, would have been madness; for it would have been to invite fatal national disaster. Must then these captives be driven back to their desolated hamlets to perish of hunger and disease? There was merciful perception in Moses' seemingly harsh intolerance, even though for the specific command of verse 17 he does not seem to have sought special Divine direction. Moses realised what many of his unsympathetic critics today will not allow inside the Bible but will allow outside it—that a severe evil often necessitates severe action. When mercy means compromise it is false kindness to the wrong-doer, and cruelty to the wronged.

In fairness to the men of Israel, it is well to add that throughout the account there is no trace of savagery, of torture, or of violence to the women—all of which things were the ordinary customs of war in those days.

Three remarkable things stand out about this anti-Midian action—first, the easiness of the victory; second, the largeness of the spoil (verses 25–47); third, that not one Hebrew life was lost (verse 49). Had Israel remained true to the Law of the Covenant, how quickly would the necessary dealing against the Canaanite nations have been over, and how different might have been the subsequent history of the human race!

Final Chapters (xxxii.–xxxvi.).

In chapter xxxii. we have the request of Reuben, Gad, and Manasseh, for permission to settle in the territory recently captured on the east of the Jordan. The ground of the appeal was the evident suitability of the area for their "very great multitude of cattle" (verse 1). Their request was reasonable-sounding—like most of the arguments which excuse compromise; but it was one of compromise none the less. Israel's place was inside Canaan, not just outside. Choosing by the sight of their eyes ("when they saw", verse 1), even as Lot had done, long before (Gen. xiii. 10–11), instead of in faith and according to the will of God, and being content with their portion just outside the place of promised blessing, they become types of so-called "worldly" Christians today. We see the result of their choice in 1 Chronicles v. 18–26, and 2 Kings xv. 29. They quickly bowed to the gods of the nearby peoples, and were first to go into captivity. The condition of their descendants at the time of Christ's first coming is found in Mark v. 1–17.

In chapter xxxiii. we have the summary of Israel's journeyings from Egypt to the Jordan, over which we need not tarry. Nor need we stay at chapter xxxiv., except to point out that the boundaries of the land here described mark out a considerably less area for occupation than that covenanted to Abraham (Gen. xv. 18), to which fact we shall refer again later. The full inheritance reaches eastward right to the Euphrates.

The cities of refuge, in chapter xxxv., should be studied; their number (verses 6–8), their purpose (verses 9–12), their distribution (verses 13–14), their regulations (verses 15–34), and their typical lessons (along with passages elsewhere concerning them). The *final* chapter fittingly deals with the security of inheritance in the land; and it may well speak to us of the eternal security of the believer's inheritance in Christ. Thus ends this wonderful fourth book of the Pentateuch. How it invites our further and fuller study!

ADDENDA TO THE BOOK OF NUMBERS

The Hireling Prophet Balaam (xxii.–xxiv.)

Chapters xxii. to xxiv. go together. The strange wizard-prophet, Balaam, here moves before us. This section of Numbers is complete in itself. It lies athwart the Israel narrative rather than forming an ordinary continuation of it—as may easily be seen in the fact that chapter xxv. 1 continues the narrative from where the last verse of chapter xxi. left it. But this section is also strikingly marked off from the rest of Numbers by its literary form. Its form is that of a drama, in which characters and happenings of highest interest are handled with consummate art. Three problems present themselves in the person of this mongrel prophet—his knowledge of the true God, his enigmatical character, his strange prophetic gift.

How shall we account for *his knowledge of the true God* ? We believe that he is one of the many evidences of an original pure revelation of God which became perverted and obscured as time elapsed and the human race dispersed throughout the earth. Numbers xxii. 5 tells us that Balaam was of *Pethor*; and Deuteronomy xxiii. 4 tells us that Pethor was in *Mesopotamia*. Balaam himself, also, speaks of being "brought from Aram out of the mountains of the *East*" (Num. xxiii. 7). Balaam, therefore, came from the very cradle of the race; so that the natural and adequate explanation of his knowledge of the true God is that such knowledge had far from disappeared at this time from that region. The following quotation from an Old Testament scholar confirms this. "Every glimpse which is afforded us of the descendants of Nahor in their Mesopotamian home confirms the belief that they were substantially at one with the chosen family in religious feeling and religious speech. Bethuel and Laban acknowledged the same God, and called Him by the same name as Isaac and Jacob (Gen. xxiv. 50; xxxi. 49). No doubt idolatrous practices prevailed in their household (Gen. xxxi. 19; xxxv. 2; Joshua xxiv. 2), but that, however dangerous, was not fatal to the existence of the true faith amongst them, any more than is the existence of a similar cultus amongst Christians. Centuries had indeed passed away since the days of Laban; and during those centuries we may well conclude that the common people had developed the idolatrous practices of their fathers, until they wholly obscured the worship of the one true God. But the lapse of years and the change of popular belief make little difference to the secret and higher teaching of countries like the Mesopotamia of that age, which is intensely conservative both for good and evil. Men like Balaam, who probably had an hereditary claim to his position as seer, remained purely monotheistic in creed, and in their hearts called only upon the God of all the earth, the God of Abraham and of Nahor, of Melchizedec and of Job, of Laban and of Jacob. If we knew enough of the religious history of that land, it is possible that we might be able to point to a tolerably complete succession of gifted (in many cases Divinely-gifted) men, servants and worshippers of the one true God, down to the Magi who first hailed the rising of the bright and morning Star."

But what of Balaam's *character*? He is a walking paradox—a true prophet and a false prophet both in one. He is a true prophet in that he knows the true God, has a real faith in Him, has real dealings with Him, receives real communications from Him, conveys real messages from Him. Yet he is a false prophet in that he also resorts to the use of magical arts, is called a soothsayer (Joshua xiii. 22), and prostitutes his strange prophetic gift for base gain. How shall we explain such an unhallowed blend of contradictions? The writer quoted above says: "This is undeniably one of the instances (not perhaps very numerous) in which the more trained and educated intelligence of modern days has a distinct advantage over the simpler faith and intenser piety of the first ages. The conflict, or rather the compromise, in Balaam, between true religion and superstitious imposture, between an actual Divine inspiration and the practice of heathen sorceries, between devotion to God and devotion to money, was an unintelligible puzzle to men of old. To those who have grasped the character of a Louise XI, of a Luther, or of an Oliver Cromwell, or have gauged the mixture of highest and lowest in the religious movements of modern history, the wonder is not that such a one should have been, but that such a one should have been so simply and yet so skilfully depicted." Truly, Balaam is a study, drawn by an inspired hand, of a "strangely but most naturally mixed character the broad features of which are constantly being reproduced."

What now of Balaam's *prophecies*? We believe that although Balaam's other recorded speakings and doings were far from inspired, his prophecies about Israel were Divinely inspired utterances. In xxiii. 5 we read: "And the Lord put a word in Balaam's mouth, and said: Return unto Balak, and thus thou shalt speak." Again, in xxiii. 16, we read: "And the Lord met Balaam, and put a word in his mouth, and said: Go again unto Balak, and say thus." Yet again, in xxiv. 2, we read: "The Spirit of God came upon him." If we take these words in their plain meaning, we are left in no doubt.

But how could the Holy Spirit come upon such a man as this double-minded Balaam? That is the problem felt by many. Yet once we grant the *fact* of inspiration, is not the problem with Balaam more seeming than real? The Spirit of Jehovah, whom Balaam is double-mindedly invoking, comes upon this man not because he is a worthy vehicle, but despite him, crushing his secret thought to curse Israel, and sovereignly overriding the stratagems of hypocrisy, so that he who in his heart would fain curse Israel for reward is actually made the mouthpiece of marvellous benedictions. Balaam himself seems to have been driven eventually to realise the futility of any endeavouring to circumvent the will of God, for in chapter xxiv. 1 we are told that "when Balaam saw that it pleased the Lord to bless Israel, *he went not, as at other times, to seek for enchantments.*"

As for the prophecies themselves, their language is sublime and their content is profound. See chapter xxiv. 5–9 and 17–19. The following sayings are memorable, also,—chapter xxiii. 10, 19, 21, 23. To go into an interpretation of these Balaam prophecies would be a "launching out into the deep" which is beyond our present scope.

We ought just to note, however, the three New Testament references to Balaam. In 2 Peter ii. 15 we read of "the *way* of Balaam." In Jude 11 we read of "the *error* of Balaam." In Revelation ii. 14 we read of "the *doctrine* of Balaam." The *way* of Balaam is the prostitution of a spiritual gift for base gain. The *error* of Balaam is the secret idea that the will of God may be circumvented under cover of an outward respect for His word. The *doctrine* of Balaam is the counsel to ruin by seduction the people who cannot be cursed by permission (see Num. xxxi. 16).

The Brazen Serpent—a Type (xxi. 4–9)

The three main types in the Book of Numbers are, the Smitten Rock (xx. 7–11), the Brazen Serpent (xxi. 4–9), the Cities of Refuge (xxxv.). These connect up, in the New Testament, with 1 Corinthians x. 4, John iii. 14, Hebrews vi. 18. They are wonderful types. As an example, we set out here the main analogies in the Brazen Serpent. Note, in the narrative,—sin (verse 5), suffering (verse 6), supplication (verse 7), salvation (verses 8–9). This order is ever true to experience. Note further, the murmuring was twofold—about the way and the manna. Its direction was twofold—"against God and against Moses." Its punishment was twofold—pain and death. The supplication was twofold—"we have sinned" (confession), and "pray unto the Lord" (entreaty). The salvation was twofold—in the serpent, and by a look. Even so today men complain against God's way and against the living Bread He has provided in Christ. And today it is because men are not right with God that they are against Moses their fellow-man. And today sin fills the world with pain and death. And today salvation is in Christ, and by the look of faith.

Now note further—salvation by this serpent of brass was outside the Tabernacle, and apart from all ordinances, sacrifices, and priestly ministrations. So today, salvation is not by priests, confessionals, communions, or any church ceremonials. It was not Aaron the priest who had to erect the brass serpent, but Moses the layman. The Lord Jesus, according to Jewish law, was a layman, for He was neither of the family of Aaron nor of the tribe of Levi. He preached in the Temple court, but never ministered at the brazen altar. The apostles, also, were laymen. The Lord Jesus and His apostles never pointed men to the Temple or the sacrifices or the ordinances for their salvation, but to Calvary. But were not the Tabernacle and the ordinances and the priesthood of Divine origin and authority? Yes, they were, but they had not power to deal with serpent-bitten men and women. Many of the priests and Levites themselves were bitten and dying and dead, as well as other people. The point is that the Tabernacle was the appointed means of access for those who were already in covenant relationship with God, and who were healed of the serpent venom.

So, the "means of grace" today are for those who have been healed, saved, made meet for communion, through Christ the Saviour. Sinners must come to Calvary before they become true worshippers in the Sanctuary. Note the main type-aspects in the Brazen Serpent.

1. ITS APPOINTMENT

(a) It was prescribed by *God*. So the Cross of Christ is the Divinely appointed means of salvation.

(b) It was *informing*. Brass a type of judgment; the serpent, of sin. Both together show sin judged.

(c) It was the *only* Divinely appointed remedy. So the Christ of the Cross is the only way (Acts iv. 12).

(d) It was *enduring*. It was of brass. It was only destroyed long after, because superstitiously regarded.

(e) It was *conspicuous*. It was erected high in the centre of the camp. Even so is Christ uplifted.

2. ITS ALL-SUFFICIENCY

(a) It availed wherever a man was bitten. So there is provision in the Cross of Christ for all manner of sin.

(b) It availed however serious a man's condition. So the Cross saves the worst of sinners.

(c) It availed however many times a man might be bitten. So there is no limit in the Cross.

(d) It availed whoever the bitten person was,—young, old, priest, slave. So is the one Cross for all.

(e) It was infallible. There is no hint of any case in which it failed. So the Cross never fails.

3. ITS APPROPRIATION

(a) It was very *easy*. Life came simply by a look. So salvation is by the look of faith today.

(b) It may have seemed *improbable*. What connection between it and the wound? So do men speak of the Cross.

(c) It was intended as a *lesson*. They must look to a serpent, the very thing causing pain. So the Cross charges home sin even as it saves.

(d) It was *individual*. Each must look for himself. So the Cross must be individually appropriated.

(e) It brought cure *instantaneously*. No hint of any gradual or delayed cure. So it is with the Cross. It brings immediate pardon and justification.

Chapter xx. 1, and the " Wandering "

The usual idea of Israel's so-called " Wandering " in the wilderness, after the Kadesh breakdown, is that the whole camp, tabernacle and people, moved in futile procession from one place to another in the wilderness, making moves and halts, but no progress toward Canaan. The purpose of our Addendum is to show how wrong that idea is. There were not *two* comings to Kadesh-barnea—one at the beginning of the thirty-eight years of "wandering" and the other at the end. There was only the one coming. The Tabernacle and all connected therewith stayed at Kadesh-barnea throughout the thirty-eight years, while the people spread in roving bands pasturising in the open country.

The first verse of this twentieth chapter is of special importance in its bearing on the Wandering. It claims the more careful considera-tion because most Bible readers misunderstand it. *"Then came the children of Israel, even the whole congregation, into the desert of Zin in the first month; and the people abode in Kadesh; and Miriam died there, and was buried there."*

These words seem to teach a second coming to Kadesh toward the end of the Wandering ; and on the strength of this it is usually assumed that there were two comings to Kadesh—the first in chapter xiii., when the breakdown occurred, and the second here in chapter xx. 1, —with the thirty-eight years of the Wandering intervening.

Now we reject that assumption for certain good reasons. First, in the summary of Israel's movements given in Numbers xxxiii. only the one coming to Kadesh is recorded, with not a hint of any thirty-eight years of moving around elapsing and then another coming to Kadesh before the going to Mount Hor where Aaron died. Nay, the implication is that they stayed all the while in the vicinity of Kadesh (see xxxiii. 36–8). Similarly, in the review of the journeyings given in Deuter-onomy i. and ii., there is but the one coming (see i. 19, 46; ii. 14). If there *was* a second coming it should be recorded between the last verse of Deuteronomy i. and the first verse of chapter ii., for it is quite clear that the compassing of Mount Seir (Edom) in the first verse of the second chapter corresponds with the compassing of Edom in Numbers xx. 14 and xxi. 4, at the *end* of the thirty-eight years. That the first verse of Deuteronomy ii. refers to the end of the thirty-eight years is made clear by verse 7. If, then, there was a second coming to Kadesh, it should appear between the last verse of chapter i. and the first verse of chapter ii. But there is no such hint. Surely it is no mere "argument from silence" to say that had there been such an important second coming to Kadesh, marking the death of Miriam and Aaron, and terminating the Wandering, it would certainly have found a place in both these summaries!

Second, this first verse of Numbers xx. says that Israel came to Kadesh "*in the first month.*" But which first month was this? Those who hold that this was a new and second coming to Kadesh can only connect this first month with the end of the chapter where we are told of Aaron's death. They say that the first month in verse 1 must be the first month of the year that Aaron died. Yet it surely seems strange that this "first month" should be mentioned without any connection to explain it except one which comes later,—all the more so because although Aaron's death is described in this chapter we are not told here what year or month he died,—not until away on in chapter xxxiii. 38! Surely this reference to Israel's having come to Kadesh in the first month is such as to suggest that the writer intends us to connect it with a time-mark which has gone shortly before.

That this is what he *did* intend is made clear by Bishop Ellicott's translation of the Hebrew—"Now the children of Israel *had come* . . . in the first month." The "had come" makes clear that the writer is connecting up this coming to Kadesh with that which is recorded in xiii. and xiv. when the breakdown occurred. Between that Kadesh breakdown and this twentieth chapter he has told us certain things which followed the breakdown, and now he wishes to connect back before telling us of Israel's new advance toward the plain of Moab. This is a procedure which is adopted not only in the Scriptures but in all historical writings.

This first verse of chapter xx., therefore, now becomes clear. The children of Israel had come to Kadesh (as in chapters xiii. and xiv.) in the first month of the third year after the Exodus. We know this because chapter x. 11 tells us they left Sinai in the second month of the *second* year, which gives eleven months between their leaving Sinai and their reaching Kadesh. Is it likely, then, that the journey from Sinai to Kadesh would take eleven months? It is. Deuteronomy i. 2 says: "There are eleven days' journey from Horeb (i.e. Sinai) by the way of Mount Seir unto Kadesh-barnea." Allowing for the travel difficulties arising from the hugeness of the host, with all its equipment, the necessary slowness and haltings because of babes and young children, and cattle, and belongings, beside the normally allotted rest intervals, and incidents which delayed the journeying, such as Miriam's leprosy and exclusion from the camp, when the journeying was suspended seven days,—allowing for all these things, we say, it is reasonable to suppose that the journey would take some eleven months.

That there was just this one coming to Kadesh is well supported, too, by incidental considerations. Our verse says that the people "*abode*" in Kadesh, suggesting a long stay there. The same thing is suggested by Deuteronomy i. 46. We have already shown that between this last verse of Deuteronomy i. and the first verse of chapter ii. there is no hint of a second coming to Kadesh; but now we would point out that what the last verse of chapter i. *does* say is that the people "abode in Kadesh many days." Both these verses indicate that at the one coming to Kadesh and vicinity there was a remaining there.

Again, if we say that our verse (xx. 1) indicates a *second* coming to Kadesh, at the end of the thirty-eight years, what of Miriam's age? The verse says: ". . . the people abode in Kadesh: and Miriam died there, and was buried there." Now Miriam was probably about fifteen years older than Moses (as we judge from Exod. ii. 4), which means that she was about one hundred and thirty-five, if still alive, at the end of the Wandering,—a remarkably greater age than either Moses or Aaron was allowed to reach. Yet our verse gives no hint that she was this great age, though we may reasonably have expected some such notice if she had died at that great age at the end of the Wandering. If, on the other hand, we take our verse as linking back to Israel's one coming to Kadesh, in chapter xiii., and understand that the people thereafter stayed in the Kadesh vicinity, and that Miriam's death occurred sometime *during* that period, then this note of her death, in chapter xx. 1, becomes at once quite normal. As in chapters xv.–xix., the writer is simply picking out things of special note which happened during the thirty-eight years, without concern for their exact chronological location.

Another argument in favour of the foregoing is the weakness of the objections to it. It is objected that if chapter xx. 1 links back with chapter xiii., making just the one coming to Kadesh, then all the twenty-one stopping stations given in chapter xxxiii. 16–36 must have occurred in the one short journey from Sinai to Kadesh, whereas Deuteronomy i. 2 says it was but an eleven-day journey. Going with this, it is also objected that an eleven-day journey would not take Israel eleven months. Now these objections are really confirmations. The distance would be between one hundred and fifty and two hundred miles. Divide this by twenty-one, and what could be more natural than that Israel's halts should have been at intervals of seven to ten miles, as the division indicates? As for the journey's taking eleven months, we have already pointed out the necessary slowness of so great a multitude; and when we add yet further the necessary time taken in dispensing legislation, and that the host moved or stayed simply at the guidance of the pillar, without there being the slightest suggestion that speed was in any way considered important, we see at once that the eleven months is a quite likely time for such a journey.

It is also pointed out that God's command in chapter xiv. 25 is "Tomorrow turn you, and get you into the wilderness by the way of the Red Sea." This, however, does not express a leaving of the Kadesh vicinity, but simply a turning from the danger-spot where enemies were ambushed. Read the whole verse—"Now the Amalekites and the Canaanites dwelt (lit.—are abiding, i.e. are ambushed) in the valley; tomorrow turn you (from there) and get you into the wilderness (nearby Kadesh)."

No more need be said here about this question. We are confident that further enquiry by any interested student will confirm that there was indeed but the one coming to Kadesh, and that this twentieth chapter links back thereto. This twentieth chapter, therefore, is of special importance. It not only groups the death of Miriam, the sin of Moses, and the death of Aaron; its first verse takes us back to the beginning of the Wandering, while its last verse marks the end of it.

TWELVE QUESTIONS ON NUMBERS

1. At what date and in what place does the book of Numbers commence?

2. Wherein lies its importance for ourselves? Answer by reference to the New Testament.

3. What are the structural features of the book of Numbers?

4. Which is the most important time-mark in Numbers and why?

5. How are parts 1 and 3 of the book sub-divided?

6. Why were the whole of the Levite males taken for Jehovah instead of just the firstborn?

7. What were the three families of the Levites, and what were their respective Tabernacle duties?

8. Give a diagram of the distribution of the Camp.

9. Where do we read of the silver trumpets, and what were their uses?

10. What are the main happenings recorded during the years of the Wandering?

11. Where do we read of the brazen serpent, and in what way was it typical?

12. Where do we read of Balaam, and how would you explain his knowledge of the true God?

THE BOOK OF DEUTERONOMY (1)

Lesson Number 17

NOTE.—For this first study in Deuteronomy read the first eleven chapters through twice.

" Human literature requires a lexicon and often a library of reference books to disclose its meaning. For the most part the Word of God is its own dictionary and library of reference. Within its own compass may be found either the direct or indirect definition of its own terms, making the careful student in a large measure independent of outside help, and so enabling even the poor and simple to learn its meaning, and bringing it within universal reach."

A. T. PIERSON, D.D.

THE BOOK OF DEUTERONOMY (1)

AFTER the fiery testing to which the Pentateuch has been subjected by the merciless Biblical criticism of recent years, there can remain little if any doubt that the first five books of our Bible—substantially as we now have them—are from the pen of Moses.

It is equally clear that these writings of Moses fall into the five natural divisions indicated in our Bible under the titles, Genesis, Exodus, Leviticus, Numbers, Deuteronomy. Each of the five is, in a real sense, complete in itself. Each has its distinctive subject, emphasis and message. Yet the five obviously cohere; and together they constitute one of the grand divisions of the Scriptures.

Indeed, as we have pointed out in an earlier study, the ruling messages of these five writings of Moses, when taken together, make the Pentateuch a kind of Bible in miniature. In Genesis we have *ruin* through man's sin; in Exodus *redemption* by "blood" and "power"; in Leviticus *communion* on the ground of atonement; in Numbers *direction* by the guiding will of God; in Deuteronomy *destination* through the faithfulness of God. These five books also give us a progressive revelation of God. In Genesis we see the Divine *sovereignty*, in creation and election; in Exodus the Divine *power*, in redemption and emancipation; in Leviticus the Divine *holiness*, in the insistence on separation and sanctification; in Numbers the Divine *"goodness and severity,"* in judging the old generation and preserving the new; in Deuteronomy the Divine *faithfulness*, in discipline and destination. We see, therefore, that Deuteronomy, the last of the five, which we are now to consider, is not *merely* the last in order, but the natural and beautiful *completion* of the Pentateuch.

The Hebrew name for this fifth writing of Moses was *Haddebharim*, that is, "The Words"—this name being taken from the opening verse of the book: "These be the words which Moses spake unto all Israel on this side Jordan in the wilderness. . . ." This name sufficiently marks off its special character from the more definitely historical and legislative books which have preceded it. The history and legislation of the earlier books are *reviewed* in Deuteronomy, but only as the basis for the words of admonition which are now recorded. In the truest, deepest, and profoundest sense, Deuteronomy is a book of words; for never were wiser or weightier words uttered.

Our own title, "Deuteronomy," is taken from the Greek *deuteros* (second) and *nomos* (law)—the title which the Septuagint translators gave to the book when they translated the Old Testament into Greek, somewhere about the third century B.C. In Deuteronomy we have a second giving of the Law, or, rather, a new expounding of it to the new generation of Israel who had grown up in the wilderness and were needing to have the Law repeated and expounded to them before their entering into Canaan. Deuteronomy is not the giving of a new Law, but an explication of that which was already given.

A Book of Transition

Deuteronomy is a book of *transition*. It marks a transition in a fourfold way. First, it marks the transition to a new *generation*; for with the exception of Caleb and Joshua, and Moses himself, the old generation which came up from Egypt and was numbered at Sinai, had passed away, and a new generation had grown up. Second, it marks the transition to a new *possession*. The wilderness pilgrimage was to give place to the national occupancy of Canaan. Third, it marks the transition to a new *experience*, to a new life—houses instead of tents, settled habitation instead of wandering, and, instead of the wilderness diet, the milk and honey and corn and wine of Canaan. Fourth, it marks the transition to a new *revelation* of God—the revelation of His *love*. From Genesis to Numbers the love of God is never spoken of; but here, in Deuteronomy, we have the wonderful words: "Because He *loved* thy fathers, therefore He chose their seed" (iv. 37); "The Lord did not set His *love* upon you, nor choose you because ye were more in number than any people, for ye were the fewest of all people; but because the Lord *loved* you" (vii. 7–8); "The Lord had a delight in thy fathers to *love* them" (x. 15); "The Lord thy God turned the curse into a blessing unto thee, because the Lord thy God *loved* thee" (xxiii. 5).

While speaking of the transitionary nature of Deuteronomy, it is interesting to mention that just as the Old Testament begins with five historical books—Genesis to Deuteronomy, so the New Testament begins with five historical books—Matthew to Acts; and there is a striking parallel between the Acts of the Apostles, the fifth book of the New Testament, and Deuteronomy, the fifth book of the Old. The Acts, like Deuteronomy, marks a great transition. It marks the transition from the distinctive message of the "Gospels" to that of the epistles. Like Deuteronomy, it marks the transition to a new *generation*—a *re*-generation in Christ. Like Deuteronomy, it marks the transition to a new *possession*—a *spiritual* Canaan with "all blessings in the heavenlies, in Christ." Like Deuteronomy, it marks the transition to a new *experience*—a new birth, a new life, a new dynamic, in the Holy Spirit. Like Deuteronomy, it marks the transition to a new *revelation* of God—the revelation given in the Church epistles of "the mystery which from the beginning of the world hath been hid in God," namely, the *Church*; so that now "there might be known, by the *Church*, the manifold wisdom of God" (Eph. iii. 10).

But what is equally striking is that both Deuteronomy, the fifth book of the one group, and Acts, the fifth book of the other group, are books in which God gives His people a *second chance*. What is Deuteronomy? It is *deuteros nomos*, the second giving of the Law. Before the new generation is committed to Joshua's charge, Moses, at God's command, rehearses the Law to them. What is the book of the Acts? It is the second offer of the Kingdom of Heaven to the Jews, first at the capital, to the Jews of the homeland, and then through the empire, to the Jews of the dispersion. Of this we shall say more later; but it is well to have it in mind even now.

Its Structure

The structure of Deuteronomy is simple, clear, and impressive. The first eleven chapters are all *retro*spective. The remaining chapters are all *pro*spective. In view of the transition now upon them, the people are to look backward and then forward, and to ponder both, as in the sight of God. They are to *recall*, and to *reflect*, and to *resolve*. Thus, in the first part (i.–xi.), which looks backward, we have *retrospection and reflection*; and in the second part (xii.–xxxiv.), we have *anticipation and admonition*.

Of course, in the retrospective part of the book (i.–xi.), there are passing references to the future, and in the prospective part (xii.–xxxiv.) there are references to the past; but no careful reading is required to see that in both parts such references are merely incidental to the main course of the lawgiver's dissertation. We may therefore now set forth the broad outline of Deuteronomy. It is as follows:

THE BOOK OF DEUTERONOMY

THE DIVINE FAITHFULNESS

I. LOOKING BACKWARD (i.–xi.).

REVIEW OF THE WAY SINCE SINAI (i.–iii.).
REVIEW OF THE LAW FROM SINAI (iv.–xi.).

II. LOOKING FORWARD (xii.–xxxiv.).

FINAL RULES AND WARNINGS TO ISRAEL, *before entering the earthly inheritance (xii.–xxx.).*
FINAL WORDS AND ACTIONS OF MOSES, *before entering the heavenly inheritance (xxxi.–xxxiv.).*

The Central Message

The central message of Deuteronomy, as we have already intimated, is *the Divine faithfulness.* In both parts of the book this is brought out—in God's gracious, wise, and righteous dealings with the nation in the past, and in His renewed pledges to the nation concerning the future. Despite the heart-rending perversities of Israel in the past, Jehovah has been, and ever will be, faithful to His promises, His purposes, and His people.

This is the central message of Deuteronomy: and what a source of comfort it is to us in days like our own, when things sometimes seem to have run completely out of control!

> God is still on the throne;
> And He will take care of His Own.
> His promise is true;
> He will see us right through;
> God is still on the throne.

We can never read Deuteronomy without thinking of Paul's words in I Corinthians i. 8–9. "God is *faithful*, by whom ye were called into the fellowship of His Son Jesus Christ our Lord: who shall also confirm you unto the end, that ye may be blameless in the day of our Lord Jesus Christ."

THE BASIC THINGS OF DEUTERONOMY

Deuteronomy being practically throughout a *discourse*, it is quite out of question for us here to think of going through it chapter by chapter, even in the brief way in which we have done so with Exodus, Leviticus and Numbers. Nor, however, is this needful to our present purpose; for as we stated at the outset, what we are specially concerned with in this present course of study is the getting hold of the broad outlines and principal significances of things. As for Deuteronomy, we shall best get the gist and drive of the book by picking out and clearly noting the several *basic* pronouncements in it, upon which all the other teachings are built.

(1) The Basic Fact

The basic *fact* beneath all else (and with which goes the basic command of the Law), is that which is declared in chapter vi. 4, 5—

"HEAR, O ISRAEL: THE LORD OUR GOD IS ONE LORD; AND
   THOU SHALT LOVE THE LORD THY GOD WITH ALL THINE
   HEART, AND WITH ALL THY SOUL, AND WITH ALL THY MIGHT."

Our Lord Jesus Himself has told us that this is the foundational pronouncement and "first commandment" of the Law (Mark xii. 29, 30).

It is well to be precise about the wording of this bedrock statement, since Unitarians have seized upon it as their prime argument against the orthodox doctrine that God is triune. "There now," they say, "nothing could be plainer: God is a unity, not a plurality; He is one, not three; for Deuteronomy vi. 4 says: 'Hear, O Israel: the Lord our God is *one* Lord.'"

Alas, for their argument, a closer examination of this verse shows that, far from supporting them, it actually refutes what they say it teaches; for the Hebrew original here is nothing short of a solemn declaration that Jehovah is a plurality in unity. The word translated "our God" is *elohenu*, which is the plural *elohim* (gods), with the first personal possessive plural suffix appended to it, causing it to become *elohenu*, that is, "our gods." This, then, is what the great publication to Israel says: "*Hear, O Israel: Jehovah our Gods, Jehovah is one.*"

But to make the matter clearer still, the Hebrew word translated as "one" (*echad*) is a word which, strictly taken, expresses "one" in the *collective* sense. That is, it signifies, not an absolute unity, but a *compound* unity, such as is indicated in the expression "one cluster of grapes." The Hebrew word for "one" in the sense of *absolute* unity is the word *yacheed*; and this word is never used to express the unity of the Godhead. May it not also have a significance that in this solemn and basic declaration of Deuteronomy vi. 4, 5, the name Jehovah occurs just the three times? Certainly the declaration clearly conveys that God is a plurality in unity; and it possibly suggests the Divine triunity in the threefold occurrence of the name Jehovah.

This was the basic fact of Divine revelation to Israel; and this was to be the first article of Israel's religion. This is also the basic fact on which Christianity is built, even the solitariness and triunity of God. Israel's God is *our* God: there is no other. Israel's Messiah is *our* Saviour: there is no other. Christianity is Monotheistic and Christocentric.

Here, then, we have an affirmation not so much of the moneity as of the unity and simplicity of Jehovah, Israel's God, the one true God; and this affirmation of the unity of God is equally opposed to Unitarianism, Polytheism, and Pantheism. Israel's God, the alone true God, is one, indivisible, and incommunicable, the absolute and infinite One, on whom all depend, whom all must ultimately obey, and who alone is the true Object of the creature's worship. To Jehovah, therefore, Israel's undivided devotion and love are due; so that the natural accompaniment of the basic affirmation is the "first and greatest commandment"— "*Thou shalt love the Lord thy God with all thine heart, and with all thy soul, and with all thy might.*" Oh that Israel had hearkened!— for then would her peace have been as a river, and her prosperity as the immovable mountains. Oh that we ourselves, God's people by a dearer covenant than that in Abraham, may truly love this glorious and gracious God with all *our* heart and mind and soul and strength!

THE BOOK OF DEUTERONOMY (2)

Lesson Number 18

NOTE.—With this study read Deuteronomy chapters xii. to xxxiv.

"He brought us out from thence, that He might bring us in, to give us the land which He sware unto our fathers"—Deuteronomy vi. 23.

He brought them out!
He brought them out!
Well now may Israel sing and shout!
  Their enemies, God came to view them;
  Their enemies, God overthrew them;
  They said: "Arise, let us pursue them";
  Jehovah came; He drowned and slew them;
But Israel, He brought them out!

He brought *me* out!
He brought *me* out!
Well may my own heart sing and shout!
  From out of deepest condemnation;
  From Conscience's grim accusation;
  From inbred, Godward alienation;
  From sin, with all its implication;
Oh, praise His grace, He brought *me* out!

THE BOOK OF DEUTERONOMY (2)

(2) The Basic Truth

THE BASIC *truth* laid down in Deuteronomy is that which is expressed in chapter vi. 23—

"AND HE BROUGHT US OUT FROM THENCE, THAT HE MIGHT BRING US IN, TO GIVE US THE LAND WHICH HE SWARE UNTO OUR FATHERS."

Here is a threefold statement of truth. First, here is a *fact*—"He brought us out." Second, here is the *purpose* behind the fact—"that He might bring us in." Third, here is the *reason* behind both the fact and the purpose—"He sware unto our fathers." As for the fact—"He brought us out," we see here the *power* of God; for He brought them out with "a mighty hand." As for the purpose—"that He might bring us in," we see here the *grace* of God; for it was to bring them into a land "flowing with milk and honey." As for the reason—"He sware unto our fathers," we see here the *faithfulness* of God: He was true to His covenant.

This threefold statement is both basic and summary. It is the whole story in one sentence. What wealth of meaning did the words hold for Israel! "He brought us out from thence." No more the crack of the slave-driver's whip! No more the cruel threat of the heartless task-master! No more the blinding dust and sickening heat of the overworked brick kilns! No more the grovelling on hands and knees after straw for the tale of bricks demanded by the royal monster! No more the rigorous servitude, the iron heel, the bitter bondage, the downtrodden condition, and the shame of Egypt! It was gone! Israel was "brought out," with "not a hoof left behind"!

Yet the words assume a still greater significance when applied to Christian believers. From what an Egypt has God delivered *us*, in Christ! He has brought us out from the *condemnation* of sin; for "there is therefore now no condemnation to them which are in Christ Jesus" (Rom. viii. 1). He has delivered us from the *bondage* of sin; for "the law of the Spirit of life in Christ Jesus hath made me free from the law of sin and death" (Rom. viii. 2). And what more shall we say? He has saved us from the accusations of our awakened consciences, from Godward alienation of heart, from spiritual darkness and death, from paralysing fear of the future. In a word, God has provided for us, in Christ, a full salvation from *sin*. "He brought us out from thence."

But "He brought us out from thence *that He might bring us in*." Besides an Egypt left behind there is a Canaan on before, with its vines and fig trees, its grapes and pomegranates, its hills and streams, its olives and cedars, its milk and honey and corn and wine—a fertile, fragrant, fruitful, sun-bathed Canaan! And can we think of the earthly Canaan without thinking of the *spiritual* Canaan which is ours in Christ? In the type-teaching of Scripture, Canaan stands not so much for heaven (as many of our hymns would imply), but for an experience of holiness and spiritual fulness realisable by Christians here and now, in this present life. We think of passages and promises, like 1 Thessalonians v. 23; Galatians ii. 20; Ephesians i. 4; iii. 19; iv. 23; v. 18; John iv. 18; Colossians i. 9–11; and a score of other, similar glorious expressions of the New Testament ideal for the Christian life. The tragedy is that most of the Lord's spiritual Israel live far below their redemption rights and revealed privileges. We do not possess our possessions. We live in the wilderness when we might be enjoying the Canaan of "all spiritual blessings in heavenly places in Christ" (Eph. i. 3).

"*He sware unto our fathers*"—here we are at the heart of things. God never goes back on His word. Despite wilderness rebellings and Kadesh breakdown, God remains true to His gracious covenant. "If we believe not, yet He abideth faithful: He cannot deny Himself" (2 Tim. ii. 13). Let us gather the honey from this flower as we pass. Is the Canaan to which God calls us, in Christ, the seemingly impossible one set forth in 1 Thessalonians v. 23—"The very God of peace sanctify you wholly; and your whole spirit and soul and body be preserved blameless unto the coming of our Lord Jesus Christ"? Entire sanctification—does it seem too much to "go up at once and possess" this land? Then read the next verse—"*Faithful* is He that calleth you, who also will do it"! What we cannot attain by self-effort we may *ob*tain in Christ.

(3) The Basic Requirement

The basic requirement which God makes of Israel, in Deuteronomy, is that which is found in chapter x. 12, 13:

"AND NOW, ISRAEL, WHAT DOTH THE LORD THY GOD REQUIRE
OF THEE, BUT TO FEAR THE LORD THY GOD, TO WALK IN ALL
HIS WAYS, AND TO LOVE HIM, AND TO SERVE THE LORD
THY GOD WITH ALL THY HEART AND WITH ALL THY SOUL;
TO KEEP THE COMMANDMENTS OF THE LORD, AND HIS
STATUTES, WHICH I COMMAND THEE THIS DAY FOR THY
GOOD."

"And now, Israel . . ." Those two little words, "and now," really gather up into a focal expression the significance of Deuteronomy. This is distinguishingly the "and now" book. The people have reviewed the faithfulness of God, in His wonderful dealings with Israel right down from the time when He entered into covenant with Abraham. They have seen how He watched over Israel during the predicted bondage in Egypt, how He brought them out with "great signs and wonders," how He constituted them an elect nation at Sinai, guarded and guided them to the borders of Canaan, suffered their many murmurings and their rebellion at Kadesh, protected, provided, preserved them through the thirty-eight years delay, bringing them again, at length, to the gateway of the promised inheritance—they have reviewed all this, *"AND NOW"* . . . what about it? What is it that is required of them as they now enter the promised Canaan? Simply this—*"to fear the Lord thy God, to walk in all His ways, and to love Him, and to serve the Lord thy God with all thy heart and with all thy soul."*

This is the basic requirement, the obligation which comprehends all others—obedience, *loving* obedience, flowing from the grateful consciousness of covenant relationship and fellowship with this glorious and faithful God. "Obedience is the key-note of almost every chapter." It has been pointed out that the word "do" occurs over fifty times. This is the outstanding lesson of the book; and a careful examination shows that the obedience which is required has a threefold reason behind it. Jehovah it to be obeyed because of (1) what He has done for them; (2) what He is in Himself; (3) the perfection of His Law (iv. 7, 8, etc.).

This, we say, is the basic requirement found here: and is anything less required of ourselves today? Nay, because of our exalted privileges in Christ, privileges which the earthly Israel never knew, we are the more under obligation to obey, in the spirit of love and godly fear. Hear what our Lord Himself says —"He that hath My commandments, and keepeth them, he it is that loveth Me." "If a man love Me, he will keep My words" (John xiv. 21-3). May it ever be to us our supreme delight to hear His dictates, and obey!

(4) The Basic Pledge

It is important to understand that Israel entered Canaan under the conditions set forth in the Sinai covenant, the precepts, terms, and issues of which are rehearsed to the new generation of Israel in this book of Deuteronomy. The privileges and corresponding responsibilities of the Sinai covenant were such that the most solemn sanctions were attached to it and the most serious penalties were contingent upon Israel's violation of it through disobedience. We have already seen these penalties warningly set before Israel, in Leviticus xxvi., at the end of the *first* declaration of the covenant law, to the old generation, at Sinai. We now have these penalties set forth again before Israel, in Deuteronomy xxviii., at the end of the *second* declaration of the covenant law, to the new generation, at Moab. The extreme penalty threatened, both in Leviticus xxvi. and Deuteronomy xxviii., is the dispersion of Israel and the desolation of Canaan (see Lev. xxvi. 32, 33; Deut. xxviii. 63-8); and we know, alas, that Israel *did* foul the covenant, that the threatened penalties have been effected, that both the dispersion of the people and the desolation of the land have ensued. All this was pre-envisaged in the Sinai Covenant.

But the thing to grasp here is this, that the Sinai covenant is not the last word between God and Israel: it is not the end of God's dealings in covenant relationship with His chosen people. No; there is another covenant relationship between God and Israel which *stands outside* and goes *beyond* the Sinai covenant, a covenant to the force of which there is no end: that is the *Abrahamic* covenant. Nothing can destroy *this* covenant between God and Israel, which was not only sealed with blood, but confirmed with a Divine oath. No, not even can Israel's unfaithfulness nullify it! It is an unconditional and everlasting covenant to Abraham and his posterity.

Now Israel has never yet possessed Canaan under the unconditional *Abrahamic* covenant. As we have said, the nation entered Canaan under the terms of the *Sinai* covenant; and we know the result. Nor has Israel ever possessed the *whole* land as it was given to Abraham (see Gen. xv. 18), but only the portion assigned in connection with the Mosaic covenant (see Num. xxxiv. 1–12).

What we wish to stress here, however, is that the Abrahamic covenant lies *behind*, and stands *outside*, and goes *beyond* the Sinai or Mosaic covenant; and this is why, despite Israel's failure, God's covenant relationship with Israel continues. It is highly significant that in each case where the extreme penalty for violating the Sinai covenant is mentioned, namely, the dispersion of Israel and the desolation of Canaan, there is an immediate follow-up reference to the *Abrahamic* covenant, showing that even when the Sinai covenant has exhausted itself in its final penal infliction on Israel, God can (and will) still be gracious to Israel on the ground of the earlier and greater Abrahamic covenant. Take Leviticus xxvi. 33, etc.—

"*And I will scatter you among the heathen, and will draw out a sword after you; and your land shall be desolate, and your cities waste. . . . Then . . . MY COVENANT WITH ABRAHAM WILL I REMEMBER; and I will remember the land.*"

Take Deuteronomy iv. 27–31—

"*And the Lord shall scatter you among the nations, and ye shall be left few in number among the heathen, whither the Lord shall lead you. . . . When thou art in tribulation and all these things are come upon thee, even in the latter days, if thou turn to the Lord thy God, and shalt be obedient unto His voice (for the Lord thy God is a merciful God), He will not forsake thee, neither destroy thee, nor forget THE COVENANT OF THY FATHERS WHICH HE SWARE UNTO THEM.*"

And when we come right to the end of the Deuteronomy

reiteration of the Sinai covenant, the very last words of all are (xxx. 20)—

> "*That thou mayest dwell in the land which THE LORD SWARE UNTO THY FATHERS, TO ABRAHAM, TO ISAAC, AND TO JACOB, TO GIVE THEM."*

Nothing can nullify the Abrahamic covenant; for Jehovah Himself accepts responsibility for the fulfilment of the whole. He undertakes for the people's part of the covenant as well as His own; for here in Deuteronomy xxx. 6, in connection with the regathering of Israel yet to be, we read: "*And the Lord thy God will circumcise thine heart, and the heart of thy seed, to love the Lord thy God with all thine heart and with all thy soul, that thou mayest live.*" God Himself will do for them and in them, by His Spirit, what they themselves have pitifully failed to do under the Sinaitic covenant! It is on the ground of this Abrahamic covenant that Jeremiah looks on to the glorious time of Israel's regeneration, and sings:

> "*Behold, the days come, saith the Lord, that I will make a new covenant with the house of Israel, and with the house of Judah:*
>
> "*Not according to the covenant that I made with their fathers in the day that I took them by the hand to bring them out of the land of Egypt; which my covenant they brake, although I was an husband unto them, saith the Lord:*
>
> "*But this shall be the covenant that I will make with the house of Israel; After those days, saith the Lord, I will put my law in their inward parts, and write it in their hearts; and will be their God, and they shall be my people.*
>
> "*And they shall teach no more every man his neighbour, and every man his brother, saying, Know the Lord; for they shall all know me, from the least of them unto the greatest of them, saith the Lord: for I will forgive their iniquity, and I will remember their sin no more.*" (Jer. xxxi. 31–4.)

It is on the basis of the Abrahamic covenant, we repeat, that such prospects are held in view; and it is in connection with this basic Abrahamic pledge that we have the crowning demonstration of the Divine faithfulness to Israel.

The so-called "Palestinian" Covenant.

We have said that Israel entered Canaan under the conditions of the *Sinai* covenant. Perhaps while we are speaking of this we ought to mention that there are certain Bible expositors who hold that in Deuteronomy xxix. and xxx. *another* covenant is set forth which is additional to the Sinai covenant, and that it was under *this* covenant that Israel entered Canaan. The Scofield Bible teaches this, and calls the supposed extra covenant the "Palestinian" covenant. We refer our student to the Scofield footnote going with chapter xxx. In our own judgment, to see in these chapters a new and different covenant is to see what is not there. Why should it be thought that we here have a further covenant, different from that at Sinai?

The argument seems to be that the *wording* of chapter xxix. indicates this. The chapter begins thus: "These are the words of the covenant which the Lord commanded Moses to make with the children of Israel *in the land of Moab, beside the covenant which He made with them at Horeb* (i.e., *Sinai*)." Then again in verse 12—"That thou shouldest *enter into* covenant with the Lord thy God, and into His oath, which the Lord thy God *maketh with thee this day*." See also verses 9 and 14. To our own mind the objections to this are conclusive. When the covenant was made at Sinai, the covenant *sacrifices* were offered, and the people were *sprinkled* with the blood whereby the covenant was ratified; but here, in Deuteronomy xxix. and xxx., no such sacrifices or sprinkling mark off the new contract as a separate covenant. (If it be said that an altar is mentioned in chapter xxvii. 5, etc., then a mere glance at the context will show that this altar had to do with "all the words of this law" in the *Sinai* covenant: and if it be claimed that in xxix. 1, where it says, God commanded Moses to "*make*" the covenant, the Hebrew word is *lichroth*, meaning literally "to cut," and alluding to the cutting or dividing of covenant *sacrifices*, then the only possible connection is with the altar in chapter xxvii. 5, etc., which, as we have shown, has to do with the *Sinai* covenant.)

But the thing that most really reveals the artificiality of finding a separate covenant in Deuteronomy xxix. and xxx., is that even those who profess to find it cannot find anything in it but what is already included in the Sinai covenant. Scofield, in his footnote, says: "The Palestinian Covenant is in seven parts," and then lists the seven; but when we examine the seven we find that they are none other than the things contained in the *Sinai* covenant, in such passages as Leviticus xxvi.!

As for the wording in chapter xxix., which speaks of the contract here made as a covenant "*beside* the covenant which He made with them at Horeb," and speaks of the people as *then* "entering into covenant" with God, the simple answer is that God is now renewing the Sinai covenant with *the new generation* of Israel, consisting of those who were either unborn or under eighteen at the time of the Exodus. The old generation have now perished in the wilderness, through their own sin; yet the covenant with the nation, as such, holds good; and the new generation, having heard the Sinai covenant rehearsed, through the chapters of Deuteronomy, are now for themselves to "enter into" the covenant. In this sense, also (and *only* in this sense), the further contract was "*beside* the covenant which He (God) made with them (the children of Israel) at Horeb." It was a new covenant only in the sense that it was the same covenant now made with the new generation.

Moreover, God's covenant with the nation is mentioned again and again in the chapters of Deuteronomy, both before and after chapters xxix. and xxx., and the reference throughout is to the Sinai covenant. Why then try to find a different covenant inserted here, in chapters xxix. and xxx. which is never once mentioned elsewhere, either in Deuteronomy or in the rest of Scripture? It was under the *Sinai* covenant that Israel entered Canaan. Alas, the tragic story which followed we know well enough! Yet behind and beyond the Sinai covenant is the covenant with Israel through Abraham which is yet going to bear fruition in glorious consummations for God's long-scattered people.

The signs are now present in the earth that this consummation is near. After an interval of over 2,000 years Israel is once again an independent state. There is no king; and Israel will not be a *kingdom* until Christ returns; but Israel is once again an independent *state*, which fact, plus other present-day happenings, is indeed a significant sign.

THE BOOK OF DEUTERONOMY (3)

Lesson Number 19

NOTE.—For this final study in Deuteronomy read chapter xii., and then chapters xxvii. to the end.

" All our hopes for eternity, the very foundation of our faith, our nearest and dearest consolations, are taken from us, *if one line of that Sacred Book be declared unfaithful or untrustworthy.*"

—From a united protest by the Archbishops and Bishops of the Church of England, made to Bishop Colenso in 1863.

THE BOOK OF DEUTERONOMY (3)

(5) Basic Differences

WE HAVE been considering the basic facts and truths enunciated through the lips of Moses in this venerable Book of Deuteronomy. We do well to ponder them most carefully, and to fix them thoroughly in our memory. Would that the people of Israel had meditated day and night in the solemn yet gracious counsels of this book! Would that they had never turned their backs upon these wise and weighty words; for then would their peace have been as a river, and their prosperity as continuing as the hills. And, as we have seen, these parting counsels of Moses speak a living message to ourselves today. It is the same God with whom we have to do today. It is *He* who has brought *us* out from Satanic bondage, that He might bring us into a wonderful inheritance in Christ. He asks no less of us today than He asked of Israel through the lips of Moses long ago, in this Book of Deuteronomy, namely, that we should love Him with all our heart and soul, and walk "in all His ways." God give us hearing ears and responsive hearts!

But now, with this Book of Deuteronomy still before us, we ought to note certain *basic differences* which it emphasises, between the old dispensation and the new, between the Old Testament and the New Testament.

Place versus Person.

One of the great differences between the Old Testament and the New is that in the one the emphasis is upon a *place*, whereas in the other all the emphasis is upon a *Person*. Under the old dispensation there was one special place of sacrifice, of worship, of the Divine presence. For instance, we read in Deuteronomy xii. 10–14:

"When ye go over Jordan, and dwell in the land which the Lord your God giveth you to inherit . . . there shall be a place which the Lord your God shall choose to cause His name to dwell there. Thither shall ye bring all that I command you, your burnt-offerings and your sacrifices, your tithes, and the heave-offerings of your hand, and all your choice vows which ye vow unto the Lord. Take heed to thyself that thou offer not thy burnt-offerings in every place that thou seest; but in the place which the Lord shall choose in one of thy tribes, there shalt thou offer thy burnt-offerings, and there shalt thou do all that I command thee."

This emphasis on a place gave focus to the religious life of the nation of Israel; it fostered the sense of national unity; it was suited to the nature of the old dispensation; and, without doubt, it took a deep hold on the thought of the people. To the old-time Hebrew, nearness to Jerusalem and to the Temple came to mean nearness to the special presence of God. The Gentiles, living in the lands beyond, were the "far off ones." It is this thought which lies behind such verses as Isaiah xlix. 1; lvii. 19; Acts ii. 39; and Ephesians ii. 17.

In the New Testament, this localisation of the Divine presence and of worship is gently but completely superseded. The emphasis is transferred from a *place* to a *Person*. It is no longer a material temple and a locality, but a spiritual Presence having the attribute of universality. This transference of emphasis may be seen in our Lord's dealing with the Samaritan woman at the well of Sychar. The woman said to Him: "Our fathers worshipped in this mountain, and ye say that in Jerusalem is the place where men ought to worship." The Lord said: "Woman, believe Me, the hour cometh when ye shall *neither in this mountain nor yet at Jerusalem* worship the Father: but the hour cometh, *and now is*, when the true worshippers shall worship the Father in spirit and in truth, for the Father seeketh such to worship Him. God is a Spirit, and they that worship Him must worship Him in spirit and in truth." Then the woman said: "I know that Messias cometh, which is called Christ: when He is come He will tell us all things." The woman herself thus looked off from place to Person; and her words evoked the wonder-inspiring reply, "I that speak unto thee am He." The Greek, literally translated, is: "*I AM who am speaking to thee.*" It is no longer God in a temple merely, but in the Person of the Lord Jesus Christ.

The same transition from place to Person is seen in Acts viii., in the account of the Ethiopian eunuch. The man had been to the right *place*—"Jerusalem." He had been for the right *purpose*—"worship." He was reading the right *book*—"the Scripture" (verses 27 and 32); but he was "returning" unsatisfied. He needed the new emphasis—on the *Person*. God sent Philip for this very purpose. "Then Philip opened his mouth, and began at the same scripture, and preached unto him *JESUS*." The Ethiopian learned the secret of salvation and satisfaction that day, and "went on his way rejoicing."

The last utterance of our Lord before His ascension is a finally renewed emphasis on this change from place to Person: "Lo, I am with you alway, even unto the end of the age." The emphasis here upon the Person is *the strongest possible*. There are two words used in the Greek, the one emphasising the "I" the other emphasising the "am." Taken together, what do they involve? It is the God-Man speaking. "*I AM*"—with you. See here His Divine *omnipresence*—He is with us always and everywhere. See here His Divine *omnipotence*—"all power, in heaven and on earth." See here His Divine *omniscience*—seeing the end from the beginning, and speaking of the "consummation of the age." It is *He* who is with us through all the days. What a Saviour! What a glorious Presence! The omnipresent Christ is with each of His blood-bought people. He delights to be with the poorest and humblest of us; and He will never leave us or forsake us, for He is with us "to the end."

Note the striking order of the words. Literally, it is "I with you *AM*." The "with you" is sandwiched in between the "I" and the "*AM*." Our Jehovah-Jesus is not only "with" us, He is *all round us*, to protect, preserve, provide, by His mighty, tender, personal presence! How safe are we in His blest keeping!

(6) Basic Choices

In our study of Leviticus we saw that the first giving of the Law wound up with a solemn warning of the punishments which would follow Israel's infidelity to the Covenant (see Lev. xxvi.). The same kind of ending marks the second giving of the Law in Deuteronomy. A glance back at our broad outline of Deuteronomy will remind us that the second of the two main parts (xii.–xxxiv.)

is itself in two parts. In chapters xii. to xxx. we have the main rehearsing of the Law, while in the remaining chapters (xxxi.–xxxiv.) we have, in a more personal sense, the last words and acts of Moses before his passing from the earthly scene. Now this second giving of the Law, running through chapters xii. to xxx., winds up, in chapters xxvii. to xxx., with renewed and most solemn warnings regarding the alternatives before the nation. The nation is called upon to make basic choices.

Chapter xxvii., the first of these four chapters, claims special note here, however, because it exposes in a striking way the true (and tragic) ministry of the Law. It was a ministration of condemnation and death (2 Cor. iii. 7, 9). The Law, although in itself holy, can only administer a curse upon such as Adam's fallen sons, if they are placed under it, because of the perversity of their nature. See how this is shown in Deuteronomy xxvii.

After his long and moving rehearsal of the Law and the Covenant, Moses tells Israel that when they cross Jordan and enter Canaan they are to set up "great stones" inscribed with the words of the Law (verses 2, 3, 8). These stones were to be erected on Mount Ebal (verse 4). Then Israel is to proclaim (as already commanded in xi. 29) the blessing and the curse of the Law. For this purpose six of the tribes are to station themselves on Mount Gerizim, and six on Mount Ebal. The six on Mount Gerizim are to proclaim the blessings of the Law: the six on Mount Ebal the curse.

Now two things are at once noticeable. First, on Mount Gerizim, the mount of blessing, no stones with the Law written on them are to be erected. Why? The mount could not have been the mount of blessing had the Law spoken from it; for the Law is an ethic without a dynamic, a precept without power, an outward rule without an inward renewal; and it can therefore only pronounce a curse upon such as Adam's sons, who are now, by nature, sinful.

Second, although blessings were to be proclaimed from Mount Gerizim, where are they? The chapter gives no record of any such proclamation. Twelve times the curse is solemnly uttered from Ebal (verses 15–26), yet not a word of blessing from Gerizim. How strikingly this again preaches the inability of a law system to confer blessing on such as ourselves! Well says Paul: "For as many as are of the works of the law are under the curse; for it is written: Cursed is every one that continueth not in all things which are written in the book of the law to do them."

There is a mercifully relieving feature, however, about this twenty-seventh chapter of Deuteronomy. Look again at Mount Ebal. Not only are there the great memorial stones of the Law erected on it; there is also *an altar*. See verses 5 to 7—"And there shalt thou build an altar unto the Lord thy God, an altar of stones: thou shalt not lift up any iron tool upon them. Thou shalt build the altar of the Lord thy God of whole stones; and thou shalt offer burnt-offerings thereon unto the Lord thy God: and thou shalt offer peace-offerings, and shalt eat there, and rejoice before the Lord thy God." There can be no rejoicing in the curse of the Law; but we may well rejoice at the altar which sets us free from the curse! That altar speaks of Calvary. "Christ hath redeemed us from the curse of the law, being made a curse for us" (Gal. iii. 13). As the Law testified to sin, so the sacrifices on that Mount Ebal altar testified to grace—to the provision of mercy, which lay within the Covenant, for the covering of guilt. Without this provision of grace Israel's position under the Law would obviously have been a mockery. When Israel later fouled the Covenant, she not only disobeyed the writing on Ebal's memorial pillars, she forsook the Lord's altar also, and offered to strange gods. Moreover, the approach to the Lord's own altar was often insincere or unintelligent, as the Lord Himself testifies against Israel through His prophets. Yet that altar spoke with comforting eloquence of grace to cover man's failure, if only faith and sincerity came thither. The peace-offerings and burnt-offerings speak of peace made for us with God, through Christ, and of God's perfect delight in the sacrifice of His Son, whereby we become fully accepted with Him. Oh, well may we "rejoice before the Lord our God" at that altar! The old dispensation pronounces curse, yet is made to point to the new dispensation in Christ, which administers blessing. Under the old—curse. Under the new—blessing. Thank God, the old has given place to the new!

> Free from the Law, oh, happy condition!
> Jesus hath bled, and there is remission!
> Cursed by the Law, and bruised by the Fall,
> Grace hath redeemed us, once for all!

Moses

We must not leave this parting book of the Pentateuch without taking a steady look of admiration at Moses himself. In these sunset chapters of Deuteronomy his noble character expresses itself with the richness and fulness of a maturity reached through the bearing of heavy burdens, the weathering of trying experiences, the discipline of big responsibilities, the disillusionment which comes with increasing knowledge of the human heart, and most of all by a broadening understanding of the profound majesty and patience of God. There is a ripeness, tenderness, mellowness, and a godly sagacity about Moses' deliverances in Deuteronomy which make this book—to quote G. H. C. Macgregor—"in many ways the most intensely interesting and impressive of the Pentateuch."

We cull an anonymous quotation from an article by the late Joseph W. Kemp—"Moses never appears quite so fine, noble, and practical as in Deuteronomy. His personal history comes out in great prominence, and with a solid grandeur, a calm earnestness, and affectionate persuasiveness, and unflinching fidelity to truth, a singleness of aim and unselfishness of purpose, which command the most reverent attention, bespeak the most intense sympathy, and endorse to the fullest extent the statement of Divine inspiration: 'There arose not a prophet since in Israel like unto Moses, whom the Lord knew face to face.'"

As a character-study Moses has few peers. He is one of the greatest figures in the Bible, and in all history. His life falls into three clearly marked periods of forty years each. During the first forty years he is the prince in Egypt; during the second forty the shepherd in Midian; during the final forty the leader of Israel. The time-marks indicating these three forties are Exodus ii. 11 with Acts vii. 23; Exodus vii. 7 with Acts vii. 29, 30; and Deuteronomy xxxi. 2.

Moses is an outstanding type of Christ; and the points of analogy should be traced: but what we would stress here is that quite apart from type interests Moses is a richly rewarding biographical study. Here, in Deuteronomy, is the completing of the picture; and here, in these last four chapters of Deuteronomy, we have the final words and acts of this great man, and the yielding up of his life, on Mount Nebo. The four chapters fall thus—

Here, then, we must leave Moses; and we cannot do so with a worthier tribute than that of the late Dr. John Kitto. "As the mind tries to rest upon the prominent points of the character which his career evinces, we find ourselves unexpectedly baffled. All the great men of sacred, as well as of profane history, possessed some prominent virtue or quality, which stood out in bolder relief than their other excellences. We think of the faith of Abraham, of the conscientiousness of Joseph, of the contrition of David, of the generosity of Jonathan, of the zeal of Elijah—but what do we regard as the dominant quality of Moses? It is not to be found. The mind is perplexed in the attempt to fix on any. It is not firmness, it is not perseverance, it is not disinterestedness, it is not patriotism, it is not confidence in God, it is not meekness, it is not humility, it is not forgetfulness of self, that forms his distinguishing characteristic. It is not any *one* of these. It is *all* of them. His virtues, his graces, were all equal to each other; and it was their beautifully harmonious operation and development which constituted his noble and all but perfect character. This was the greatness of Moses—this was the glory of his character. It is a kind of character rare in any man—and in no man historically known has it been so completely manifested. When we reflect that Moses possessed all the learning of his age, and that he wanted none of the talents which constituted human greatness, we honour his humility more than his glory; and, above all, we venerate that Divine wisdom which raised up this extraordinary man, and called him forth at the moment when the world had need of him."

Moses was 120 years when he died (xxxiv. 7). He is the only man whom God himself buried. God laid His servant's body to rest in "a valley in the land of Moab," but "no man knoweth" the grave (6). The body was not left there long, however, for despite a contention of Satan (Jude 9), it was raised and glorified; and Moses reappeared in it on the Mount of Transfiguration (Luke ix. 30, 31).

CAN YOU ANSWER THESE?

1. How does Deuteronomy get its name?

2. How does Deuteronomy mark a transition?

3. What book in the New Testament parallels with Deuteronomy, and how?

4. Give the broad outline of Deuteronomy.

5. What is the basic fact and command in this book?

6. What is the basic requirement made of Israel in the book?

7. Since Israel broke the Sinai Covenant, on what basis does God continue special relationship with Israel?

8. Mention two basic differences between the old dispensation and the new.

9. What four final things of Moses do we get in the last four chapters of Deuteronomy?

10. Can you give the three verses in Deuteronomy which our Lord quoted when tempted of Satan?

THE BOOK OF JOSHUA (1)

Lesson Number 20

NOTE.—For this first study in the book of Joshua read the book right through.

"He who has once got fairly into the Scriptures can never leave them The book holds you as a magnet holds a needle, or as a flower holds a bee. If you want great thoughts, read your Bible. If you want something simple, read your Bible. If you want the deepest and highest truth that ever was, read your Bible. The book talks to us in our own mother tongue. Why should I have to ask another what my Father says? . . . The Bible to many is a dull book, as dry as an old will. But when you hear your own name read out in a will, you prick up your ears. What if there should be something in the Testament of our Lord Jesus for *you*. When I found my own name there my heart danced for joy. It was in these lines: 'God so loved the world that He gave His only begotten Son, that whosoever believeth in Him should not perish, but have everlasting life' . . . Get your legacy at once!"

C. H. SPURGEON.

THE BOOK OF JOSHUA (I)

IN A LETTER to a certain Miss Chalmers, Scotland's Robbie Burns wrote:

> "*I have taken tooth and nail to the Bible, and am got through the five books of Moses, and half-way in Joshua. It is really a glorious book. I sent for my bookbinder today, and ordered him to get me an octavo Bible in sheets, the best paper and print in town, and bind it with all the elegance of his craft.*"

In our present course of study we, too, have now got through the books of Moses, and they have given us good reason to press on with Burns-like zest to the book of Joshua.

Joshua is complementary to the five books of Moses, and introductory to the new historical group of twelve (Joshua to Esther). The five books of Moses lead Israel *up to* Canaan; and Joshua complements these by leading Israel *into* Canaan. The further twelve books cover Israel's history inside Canaan; and Joshua introduces these by describing the Israelite *settlement* in Canaan. It is thus the link book between the two historical groups in the Old Testament. It covers a period of about twenty-five years, and describes one of the most memorable conquests in history. "The occupation of this small strip of territory scarcely larger than Wales, though it led to no further results in the way of conquest, has nevertheless to a great extent moulded the moral and religious history of the world."

Authorship

It would seem that the book of Joshua is so named because Joshua is its focal figure, and not necessarily as implying that Joshua himself was its author. Jewish tradition does indeed ascribe the authorship to him, and certainly, despite the dexterous theories of some recent scholars, there is no solid reason for categorically rejecting it. There are evidences of other hands than Joshua's, however, in the work as it has come to us. Possibly these may be simply of an interpolative nature; but the probability is that while Joshua himself supplied the materials, these were arranged and supplemented by some scribe a little later. Or it may be that Joshua contributed the substance of the work, while certain of the elders completed it. The really important thing to maintain is that the editor-author was a contemporary, or practically so, having first-hand knowledge, or authentic documents, so that the work is really a product of the period which it records. Such hectic higher critical arguments as that which attributes the book to some fictitious author in Manasseh's reign have been so effectively demolished by orthodox scholars that there is no need to burden our minds with them here.

Structure

Joshua is a book of graphic movement, of campaign, and conquest and subjugation. We see Israel going up, winning through, and settling in. The account is distributed in three phases, thus:

1. ENTERING THE LAND (i.–v.).

2. OVERCOMING THE LAND (vi.–xii.).

3. OCCUPYING THE LAND (xiii.–xxiv.).

Key Thought

Entering, overcoming, occupying!—if these are the three movements recorded in Joshua, then there can be no doubt as to what is its key thought, or central message. Clearly, it is *the victory of faith.* In this, the Book of Joshua stands in sharp contrast to the Book of Numbers where we see the failure of unbelief—failure to enter (xiv. 2–4), failure to overcome (xiv. 44, 45), failure to occupy (xiv. 28–34). Spiritually interpreted, the exploits of Israel under Joshua proclaim the great New Testament truth—"This is the victory that overcometh the world, even our faith" (1 John v. 4). Each of the victories in the programme of conquest was ordered so as to exhibit that victory was due to faith in God, not to the arm of man. To quailing unbelief, the overthrow of giants and great cities was an *impasse*, but to the eye of faith it was a *fait accompli*.

Typical Significance

Already, in the five books of Moses, we have found the presence of types in the Old Testament Scriptures—typical persons, events, and objects, such as Joseph, the Exodus, and the Tabernacle. Now in the case of Joshua, the whole story is one grand type. It is the Old Testament type-picture of a great spiritual reality revealed in the New Testament, as we shall shortly see. What then *is* the main typical significance of Joshua? The answer to that question depends upon the answer to the further question as to what *Canaan* typifies.

In some of our hymns, the river Jordan is taken as representing death, and the land of Canaan as representing heaven. This, however, is surely a misinterpretation of these types. If Jordan is death and Canaan heaven, then it follows that the whole of the Christian life, right till the hour of death, corresponds to the wilderness through which the Hebrews tramped—not exactly an enamouring picture—and we might feel a spark of sympathy with the argument that a death-bed conversion is preferable so as to cut the wilderness as short as possible!

Moreover, Canaan cannot very well be a type of heaven for two or three other reasons. Canaan was a place of conquest through *conflict*. There had been little fighting during the wilderness years, but as soon as Canaan was entered Israel must draw the sword. Enemies must be destroyed. Israel must fight. How then can Canaan typify the calm restfulness of the ultimate inheritance in heaven?

Moreover, it was possible for Israel to be ejected from Canaan by powerful foes; and eventually they actually *were* ejected, as we know. How then can this typify that heaven of uninterrupted felicity which is pledged to the justified in Christ?

But, to settle the question conclusively, we are expressly taught, in Hebrews iii. and iv., what the typical meaning of Canaan really is. Those two chapters should be read carefully, and they will then fix this Canaan type once for all in our intelligent understanding. They make it quite clear that Canaan pictures the believer's *present* position and possession in Christ. It was ordained to pre-figure that spiritual Sabbath-keeping into which we may enter here and now. A few verses from one of those Hebrews chapters will be enough to certify this—"For if

Joshua had given them rest He (God) would not have spoken afterward of another day (of rest). There *remaineth* therefore a rest for the people of God. For he that is entered into His rest hath himself also rested from his works as God did from His. Let us therefore *give diligence to enter* into that rest" (Heb. iv. 8–11 R.V.). The same chapter tells us that "we which have believed *do* enter into that rest" (verse 3).

The meaning of Canaan, then, as a type, is fixed, both by circumstance and New Testament explanation. Jordan does not typify death of the body and departure into the beyond, but that deeper union of our hearts with Christ in *His* death whereby we become completely separated unto Him, and introduced into "the *fulness* of the blessing of the Gospel of Christ." That New Testament phrase, "The fulness of the blessing of the Gospel of Christ," more aptly than any other sums up the type-meaning of Canaan. Certainly, as the writer of the epistle to the Hebrews says, it is the believer's "rest"; but the rest is part of the *fulness*. Canaan is that "breadth and length and depth and height" of spiritual life in which we really "possess our possessions" in Christ. The tragedy is that the majority of Christians live far below their revealed privileges and redemption rights in Christ. The Christian life is no more meant to be a wilderness than a wedding feast is meant to be a time for sackcloth and ashes. God has opened up to us in Christ a present experience of sanctification comparable to a fertile, fragrant, fruitful, sunbathed Canaan—a "land of corn and wine," a land "flowing with milk and honey."

Canaan in Christian Experience

C. H. Spurgeon says: "There is a point of grace as much above the ordinary Christian as the ordinary Christian is above the world." Speaking of those who live this higher life, he continues —"Their place is with the eagle in his eyrie high aloft. They are rejoicing Christians, holy and devout men doing service for the Master all over the world, and everywhere conquerors through Him that loved them." The experience here referred to has been called by various names—"Christian Perfection," "Entire Sanctification," "The Higher Life," "The Rest of Faith," "The Life More Abundant," "Perfect Love"; but all these are simply different names for different aspects of the one spiritual reality.

Both Scripture and the experience of many of Christ's people seem to confirm that there is a work of Divine grace in the believer, quite distinct from that which we commonly call conversion, and usually, though not necessarily, subsequent to it, in which the soul is brought into an experience of inwrought holiness and fellowship with God never known by conversion alone. "The law of the Spirit of life in Christ Jesus" makes gloriously free from "the law of sin and death" (Rom. viii. 2). There is complete renewal in the very "spirit of the mind" (Eph. iv. 23). There is effected such a love-blend of the believer's life and will with the life and will of Christ that, instead of being egocentric, the believer becomes Christocentric. Self-consciousness is sublimated in Christ-consciousness, so that the experience now is, "I live, yet not I; Christ liveth in me" (Gal. ii. 20); and "To me to live is Christ" (Phil. i. 21). The personality becomes monopolised and suffused by the Holy Spirit (Eph. v. 18). Perfect love fills the heart and casts out fear (1 John iv. 18). The soul is in Beulah Land (Isa. lxii. 4). "The winter is past and gone; the flowers appear on the earth, and the time of the singing of birds is come" (Song of Sol. ii. 11–12). There is a "walking in the light" of a cloudless "fellowship" with Heaven, while "the blood of Jesus Christ, God's Son, cleanseth from all sin" (1 John i. 7); and the believer now reads his experience in such words as these—"The sun shall be no more thy light by day, neither for brightness shall the moon give light unto thee; but the Lord shall be unto thee an everlasting light, and thy God thy glory. Thy sun shall no more go down, neither shall thy moon withdraw itself; for the Lord shall be thine everlasting light, and the days of thy mourning shall be ended" (Isa. lx. 19–20).

Characteristics of Canaan

Now this is the experience to which Canaan and the book of Joshua point in a typical way. It is therefore of the highest interest to observe what we are told about Canaan; and there are three things which are outstandingly characteristic.

First, Canaan was Israel's promised *REST*. Itineracy was to give place to settled dwelling. Instead of the inhospitable wilderness there was to be a home where they should sit down, every man "under his vine and under his fig tree." The tired hands

I

and blistered feet were to find refreshing contrast in the responsive yields of Canaan's fertile plains and valleys. The promised rest had been wonderfully prepared for their coming. They should not need even to build the cities and houses which they would need to live in, for they were to possess "great and goodly cities which thou buildedst not, and houses full of all good things which thou filledst not, and wells digged which thou diggedst not, and vineyards and olive trees which thou plantedst not" (Deut. vi. 10–11): and here they should lie down in safety, none making them afraid (Lev. xxvi. 6).

Second, Canaan was the place of *BOUNTY*. This was the land "flowing with milk and honey," a "good land and a large" (Exod. iii. 8), a "land of corn and wine" and kissed with the dews of heaven (Deut. xxxiii. 28), a land of olives and vines, of firs and cedars, of rich fruits and harvests where an obedient people should "eat to the full," where the threshing should reach unto the vintage and the vintage unto the sowing time (Lev. xxvi. 5); a place of which God had said: "The land whither thou goest in to possess it is not as the land of Egypt from whence ye came out, where thou sowedst thy seed and wateredst it with thy foot as a garden of herbs: but the land whither ye go to possess it is a land of hills and valleys, and drinketh water of the rain of heaven: a land which the Lord thy God careth for; the eyes of the Lord thy God are always upon it, from the beginning of the year even unto the end of the year" (Deut. xi. 10–12). Yes, Canaan was the place of bounty!

Third, Canaan was the place of *TRIUMPH*. Were there enemies in Canaan? Yes: but they were a defeated foe before ever Israel struck the first blow, for God had said: "The Lord thy God shall . . . cast out many nations before thee, the Hittites, and the Girgashites, and the Amorites, and the Canaanites, and the Perizzites, and the Hivites, and the Jebusites, seven nations greater and mightier than thou" (Deut. vii. 1). Israel was to remember what Jehovah had done "unto Pharaoh and unto all Egypt" and not be afraid. Five of them should chase a hundred, and none of their enemies should be able to stand before them. God was calling Israel not merely to conflict but to an assured *victory*. Yes, to a faithful Israel Canaan was to be the place of triumph.

In all this the Spirit of God is pictorially exhibiting to us that life in the "heavenly places" (Eph. i. 3) which is our present privilege in Christ; and our conception of New Testament truth is thus vivified by Old Testament type.

Resting, abounding, triumphing!—this is our rich inheritance in Christ; and it may be ours in actual experience—

A rest where all our soul's desire
   Is fixed on things above;
Where doubt and sin and fear expire,
   Cast out by perfect love.

Fair fields where peace and love abound,
   And purest joys excel,
And heavenly fellowship is found,
   A lovely place to dwell.

Holiness is not something to be *attained* by self-effort; but it may be *ob*tained in Christ. Consecration and appropriation are the two hinges on which the gate to Canaan swings. If we really yield, and then plant our feet on the promises, the delectable land is ours. God will not fail us. Let us go up and possess! "Faithful is He that calleth you, who also will do it" (1 Thess. v. 24).

Sanctify me wholly,
   Sovereign Saviour mine;
Spirit, soul and body
   Now make fully Thine.
Make my motives blameless,
   Purify my heart;
Set me now entirely
   For Thyself apart.

Thou to this dost call me,
   In Thy written word;
Thou Thyself wilt do it,
   If I trust Thee, Lord.
Faithful is Thy calling
   And Thy promise, too;
Give me now to trust Thee,
   And to prove Thee true.

THE BOOK OF JOSHUA (2)

Lesson Number 21

NOTE.—For this second study in the book of Joshua read the whole book through again, checking off what we have said about the three main divisions of the book, and its three main characteristics typically.

There is a Canaan rich and blest,
    Which all in Christ may know,
By consecrated saints possessed
    While here on earth below.

There is a vict'ry over sin,
    A rest from inward strife,
A richer sense of Christ within,
    A more abundant life.

'Tis here that peace and love abound,
    And purest joys excel,
And heavenly fellowship is found—
    A lovely place to dwell!

Oh, this is Beulah Land indeed,
    Where heaven itself is nigh;
Where all our emptiness and need
    Is lost in full supply!

Lord slay all subtle love of sin,
    Our doubt and fear remove;
Oh help us now to enter in,
    And all Thy blessing prove!

J.S.B.

THE BOOK OF JOSHUA (2)

JOSHUA AND EPHESIANS

ALREADY, in our study of the Pentateuch, we have noted the correspondence between Deuteronomy and the Acts of the Apostles, and the connection between Leviticus and Hebrews. There is also a remarkable parallel between the Book of Joshua and the epistle to the Ephesians. The epistle to the Ephesians is distinctively the epistle of the "heavenly places in Christ" (i. 3). The book of Joshua, as we have pointed out, is in type that fuller Christian life in which we really "possess our possessions" in Christ, enter into heart-rest, and experience fulness of "joy and peace in believing." That Ephesian phrase, "heavenly places," or more literally, "the heavenlies," denotes the *sphere* of this higher and fuller life. It indicates a union of life and mind and will with the risen Christ, a union with Him in nature, relationships, and purposes, a union with Him in death to sin and to the flesh and to the world, a union with Him in service and suffering and desire, a union with Him in His resurrection and ascension, which lifts the believer to a level where there is a fulness of light and love and power and spiritual understanding unknown to others. This is life on the highest plane. This is the true place of the believer's present life in Christ. Seldom is it entered right away at conversion. Alas, how many believers seem never to enter it at all! Yet this indeed is God's provision; this is our inheritance in Christ Jesus; and young Christians should early be pointed to it.

Now in Joshua we see Israel entering and possessing the earthly inheritance given in Abraham. In Ephesians we see the Church entering and possessing the heavenly inheritance given in Christ.

The correspondence, however, is not merely general. There is a five-fold parallel, marked by the five occurrences of that expression, "the heavenlies," in Ephesians. The five references are Ephesians i. 3; i. 20; ii. 6; iii. 10; vi. 12. Trace the parallel briefly then between the land of Canaan in the book of Joshua, and "the heavenlies" in the epistle to the Ephesians.

1. *Each was the predestined inheritance of a chosen people.* Away back, five hundred years before Joshua led the people over Jordan, God had said to Abram: "Lift up now thine eyes, and look from the place where thou art, northward and southward and eastward and westward, for all the land which thou seest, to thee will I give it, and to thy seed for ever" (Gen. xiii. 14, 15). And when at length He brought Israel up from Egypt He said: "The Lord shall bring thee into the land . . . which He sware unto thy fathers to give thee" (Exod. xiii. 5).

Even so, turning to the first occurrence of that phrase, "the heavenlies," in Ephesians, we find that here we have the predestined inheritance of the Church, in Christ.

"Blessed be the God and Father of our Lord Jesus Christ, who hath blessed us with all spiritual blessings IN THE HEAVEN-LIES in Christ, according as He hath CHOSEN US IN HIM before the foundation of the world, that we should be holy and without blame before Him in love" (Eph. i. 3, 4).

With our eye on these two verses from Ephesians, let us note the contrastive parallel. Israel was blessed with all *material* blessings in *earthly* places in *Abraham.* The Church is "blessed with all *spiritual* blessings in *heavenly* places, in *Christ.*" Note also, that to enjoy this fulness of material blessings Israel must be *in the land.* Similarly, to enjoy the fulness of spiritual blessings in Christ we must be *"in the heavenlies."* The reason why we miss them is because we are not in the place where God bestows them.

2. *Each was opened up by a Divinely ordained leader.* In the case of Israel all was put into the hands of Joshua. It was said to him: "Unto this people shalt *thou* divide for an inheritance the land which I sware unto their fathers to give them" (Joshua i. 6); and, *"Thou* shalt cause them to inherit it" (Deut. xxxi. 7). Joshua was thus the appointed administrator of the Israelite settlement in Canaan; and we are told that at the end of the seven-years' war "Joshua took the whole land . . . and gave it for an inheritance unto Israel according to their divisions by their tribes" (Joshua xi. 23).

Even so, turning to the second occurrence of that phrase, "the heavenlies," in Ephesians, we find that the Church's inheritance is opened up by the Lord Jesus.

"That ye may know . . . what is the exceeding greatness of His power to usward who believe, according to the working of His mighty power which He wrought in Christ when He raised Him from the dead, and set Him at His own right hand IN THE HEAVENLIES . . . and gave Him to be the HEAD OVER ALL THINGS TO THE CHURCH" (Eph. i. 18–22).

Thus is Joshua a beautiful type of Christ as the trustee and representative of His people. It is the ascended Saviour who divides the goodly inheritance, and allots it to His believing people as by faith they plant their feet upon the promises.

3. *Each was a gift of grace to be received by faith.* Canaan was given to Israel in Abraham, not in Moses the man of the Law. By the Law Israel could never have become entitled to Canaan. Moses was not privileged even to lead the people in. Nor can the Law ever lead *us* into God's promised rest for our souls in Christ. Hence, Moses must die, and Joshua must take his place; and Joshua must open up the inheritance. The very first words of this book of Joshua are significantly in harmony with this— "Now after the death of Moses, the servant of the Lord, it came to pass that the Lord spake unto Joshua, the son of Nun, Moses' minister, saying: Moses my servant is dead; now *THEREFORE* arise, and go over this Jordan, thou and all this people, unto the land which I do give them, even to the children of Israel" (i. 1, 2).

So is it with the spiritual Canaan which is ours in Christ, as the third occurrence of the expression, "the heavenlies," in Ephesians, shows.

"Even when we were dead in sins (God) hath quickened us together with Christ (by GRACE are ye saved); and hath raised us up together, and made us sit together IN THE HEAVEN- LIES in Christ Jesus: that in the ages to come He might show the exceeding riches of His GRACE in His kindness toward us through Christ Jesus. For by GRACE are ye saved, through FAITH; and that not of yourselves; it is the gift of God" (Eph. ii. 5–8).

F. B. Meyer aptly says: "The law of God can never bring the soul of man into the land of Promise, not because there is any defect in it, but because of human infirmity and sin. It is the presence of this evil law in our members which makes obedience to the law of God impossible, filling us with disappointment and unrest, ceaseless striving and perpetual failure. We must therefore leave the Law, as an outward rule of life, behind us, in that lonely valley over against Bethpeor, that the Divine Joshua may lead us into the land of Promise. Not by vows or resolution or covenants of consecration signed by blood fresh-drawn from the veins; not by external rites or by ascetic abstinence from good and healthy things; not by days of fasting and nights of prayer; not even by obedience to the voice of conscience or the inner light, though attention to these is of prime importance—by none of these shall we enter the land of blessedness. They all become forms of legalism, when practised with a view to obtaining the full rest and victory of Christian experience. Valuable many of them unquestionably are, when the river is crossed and the land is entered; but they will not of themselves unlock its gates or roll back its guardian river." No; in the words of Ephesians ii. 8, it must be "by grace, through faith."

The Old Covenant rest-day was the *seventh*. The New Covenant rest-day is the *first*. Under the Old Covenant we must work the six days *up to* the rest. Under the New Covenant we work *down from* it—from a perpetual rest already possessed in Christ.

4. *Each is the sphere of a striking Divine revelation.* Israel's entering and possessing of Canaan was intended to be a revelation of the true God to the nations of that day—"That all the people of the earth might know the hand of the Lord, that it is mighty: that ye might fear the Lord your God forever" (Joshua iv. 24). "All people of the earth shall see that thou art called by the name of the Lord; and they shall be afraid of thee" (Deut. xxviii. 10). Israel's yet future regathering to Canaan will consummate that revelation. See Isaiah xi. 11, 12, Jeremiah xxiii. 5–8, and other passages in the Old Testament prophets.

Parallel with this, we find the fourth Ephesian reference to "the heavenlies" telling us that the Church is a wonderful revelation of God to the powers of the spirit-realm. Paul goes on to say, in chapter iii:—

"Unto me who am less than the least of all saints is this grace given, that I should preach among the Gentiles the unsearchable riches of Christ; and to make all men see what is the fellowship of the mystery which from the beginning of the world hath been hid in God, Who created all things by Jesus Christ: to the intent that now UNTO THE PRINCIPALITIES AND POWERS IN THE HEAVENLIES MIGHT BE KNOWN BY THE CHURCH THE MANIFOLD WISDOM OF GOD" (Eph. iii. 8–10).

The crowning revelation of the Divine wisdom and power through Israel in Canaan, as we have said, will be in the restoration yet to be. Even so the consummating display of the Divine wisdom and purpose through the Church, to the spirit-powers in "the heavenlies," will be effected by the second coming of Christ, when the completed Church will be manifested with Christ in His glory.

5. *Each is described as a scene of conflict.* In the earthly Canaan there were the giant sons of Anak, and cities "walled up to heaven." There were the Hittites and Girgashites and Amorites and Canaanites and Perizzites, and Hivites and Jebusites, who held the land with strongholds and iron chariots—seven nations "greater and mightier" than Israel. They were exceedingly *evil* nations, and they had to be dispossessed and destroyed. Therefore must Israel wield the sword against them, though not with any doubt as to the final issue, for God was with Israel; and if they would but remain true to Him none should be able to stand against them. Conflict was inevitable, but defeat was impossible, for there was an alliance invincible.

So is it with that spiritual Canaan which is ours in "the heavenlies." We turn to Ephesians again and find these words in the last occurrence of that phrase "the heavenlies"—

"We wrestle not against flesh and blood, but against principalities, against powers, against the rulers of the darkness of this world, against spiritual wickedness IN THE HEAVENLIES" (Eph. vi. 12).

Thank God, as no power could withstand Joshua and Israel, so no power in the spirit-realm can withstand the power of

Christ, for He has defeated Satan, and is now "far above all principality and power and might and dominion" (Eph. i. 21). In Him victory is ours. In Him our prayer-life may become a victorious spiritual warfare which shall be effectual to the pulling down of Satanic strongholds, the casting down of imaginations which oppose themselves to God, and the releasing of regenerating forces among men. When we are truly abiding in Him, and are "reigning in life by One, Jesus Christ" (Rom. v. 17) in "the heavenlies," all foes are beneath our feet, and we enter into the meaning of that word in Psalm ii. 4, "He that sitteth in the heavens shall laugh."

These, then, are the five points of parallel between the earthly inheritance opened up through Joshua, and the spiritual inheritance opened up to us Christian believers in Christ. Perhaps a recapitulation will help to fix them in memory.

1. Each was the predestined inheritance of a chosen people.
2. Each was opened up by a Divinely ordained leader.
3. Each was a gift of Divine grace to be received by faith.
4. Each is the sphere of a striking Divine revelation.
5. Each is described as a scene of conflict.

This parallel between Canaan, in Joshua, and "the heavenlies," in Ephesians, is as instructive as it is striking, and well merits a fuller consideration than we can give to it here. God grant that we ourselves may live in the goodly land, and "possess our possessions," to the joy of our own hearts and the glory of God!

THE BOOK OF JOSHUA (3)

Lesson Number 22

NOTE.—For this third study in the book of Joshua re-read the first twelve chapters.

They on the heights are not the souls
   Who never erred nor went astray,
Who trod unswerving to their goals
   Along a smooth, rose-bordered way.
Nay, those who stand where first comes dawn,
   Are those who stumbled—but went on.

THE BOOK OF JOSHUA (3)

THE PARTS

WE OUGHT now to glance over the three main parts of the book. Even in their broad features we shall find much to profit us. First we see Israel *entering* (i.-v.), then *overcoming* (vi.-xii.), and then *occupying* (xiii.-xxiv.).

PART I. ENTERING THE LAND (i.-v.)

The five chapters of part one run in an orderly sequence thus—

Chapter i.—Joshua charged.

,,   ii.—Jericho spied.

,,   iii.—Jordan crossed.

,,   iv.—Memorials raised.

,,   v.—Gilgal occupied.

If we bear in mind that the key idea in Joshua is *the victory of faith*, we shall quickly see how eloquent these chapters are.

Chapter i.—Joshua charged.

The emphasis in this chapter is upon the fact that Joshua's assumption of leadership originated in a commission from God Himself. It was grounded in the word of God (see verse 9). The going up into Canaan, also, was based upon a clear Divine authorisation (verses 2-5). This is ever the beginning of things where faith is concerned—that God has spoken. True faith is therefore far removed from mere credulousness. It refuses to act on the basis of mere human reasoning : but once it is satisfied that God has spoken, it asks nothing more, for there can be no higher authority than that, and no higher reason than to obey. Here then, in chapter i., we have the *warrant* of faith, namely, the word of God. True faith always works on the principle denoted in Hebrews xiii. 5, 6—"HE hath said . . . so *we* may say."

Chapter ii.—Jericho spied.

Having received such Divine assurance of invincibility (as in i. 5–6), Joshua might easily have felt it needless to exercise cautiousness or to resort to military strategy. But this second chapter shows us that the reaction of true faith is in fact the opposite of any such carelessness. Joshua sends the two spies to Jericho; and there was good reason for his doing so, as we shall see later, for Jericho was a key city. True faith does not despise the use of means. There is a wide difference between believing and presuming. To make the promises of God an excuse for not taking reasonable precaution is to tempt God, as our Lord Jesus Himself has taught us. When the deceiver urged the Master to cast Himself from the temple tower because God had promised supernatural preservation, the Master replied: "It is written again: Thou shalt not tempt the Lord thy God." In this second chapter of Joshua we have the *prudence* of faith.

Chapter iii.—Jordan crossed.

The crossing of "this Jordan" was a major crisis of faith. The same crisis had come to the former generation of Israel some forty years earlier under somewhat different circumstances, and they had failed in their reaction to it. It was bound to repeat itself to the new generation. To be "brought out" of Egypt was one thing; but it was another thing altogether to "go over this Jordon" and thus become committed, without possibility of retreat, to the struggle against the powers of Canaan in their seemingly impregnable fastnesses, with their chariots of iron, and their large armies among which were the renowned giants. To do this was to commit themselves to a course which had been condemned by ten out of the twelve spies who had reported on the land forty years before! To the natural eye it was to hazard everything on the chance of battle, to have no retreat, and to run the risk of losing everything.

The same crisis comes in one way or another to all the redeemed —that intense crisis of the soul in which we are forced to the supreme choice whether there shall be an utter once-for-all abandon of ourselves to the will of God, so that henceforth God is absolutely first in the soul's love and life, or whether we shall take what seems to be the easier way, that is, of continuing in the Christian life, but with a reservation in our love to God. It is one thing to take Christ as Saviour from the guilt of our sin. It is another thing to make Him absolute Master of our will and life. It is one thing to be brought out from the Egypt of our unregenerate life and to join God's redeemed Israel. It is another thing altogether to bury all our self-born aims and desires in Jordan's swift-flowing flood, and to pass through to that higher life where no desires or purposes are tolerated but those of our blessed Lord Himself. It was one thing for Abram to leave Ur of the Chaldees and go out in faith at God's behest. It was another thing—a far bigger and costlier and sublimer thing—for him to climb Moriah and lift the knife to slay his beloved Isaac. Yet the crisis must be. There was no other way of decisively determining whether God was to be supreme in the life and love of the soul. There was no need for further testing after that; and God said: "By Myself have I sworn, because thou hast done this thing, and hast not withheld thy son, thine only son, that in blessing I will bless thee, and in multiplying I will multiply thy seed as the stars of the heaven and as the sand which is upon the sea shore." Abraham's Moriah and Israel's Jordan are the same crisis under different names. There is an Isaac to be sacrificed, a Jordan to be crossed, in the history of every redeemed soul. Abraham yielded his Isaac. Israel crossed the Jordan. What of you and me? This is faith's major crisis; and this is what we have in this third chapter of Joshua—the *crisis* of faith.

Chapter iv.—Memorials raised.

A faith that goes all the way with God leaves many a beautiful "Ebenezer" in its wake. The Jordan memorial stones were faith's witness to the power and faithfulness of God. There were two of these cairns or monumental piles—one on the west bank of the river, at Gilgal (verse 3), and the other in the river itself (verse 9), each consisting of twelve great stones representing the twelve tribes of Israel. The pile on the Canaan side of the Jordan witnessed to the *faithfulness* of God in His bringing Israel at last into the land promised to their fathers. The pile in the river itself witnessed to the *power* of God in holding back the swollen flood and cleaving a pathway across the river bed for the great host. In this fourth chapter, then, we have the *witness* of faith.

Those two memorial piles are symbolic. They witness to God's bringing His people right through the river and into the place of blessing. That preposition "through" really comprises the two ideas of "in" and "out" both in one. There must be both a going *into* and a coming *out of* to make the meaning of "*through.*" Now the two memorial heaps in this fourth chapter of Joshua bear witness both to the going into and the coming out of the Jordan. Israel actually went down into that river basin; otherwise, how explain that submerged pillar of great stones amid stream? Israel actually came out on Canaan's side; hence that erection at Gilgal. Here is symbolic witness to a great truth: never does a soul go down into that *other* Jordan—the death and burial of "selfism"—to find itself deserted. As surely as there is the "*into*" there is the "*out of.*" God brings the now-sanctified soul right through to the resurrection ground of "the heavenlies" in Christ.

Chapter v.—*Gilgal occupied.*

Here we see the *sealing and chastening* of faith. Strange as it might seem, the first experience in the land of blessing is one of pain, though the pain is soon over. Before ever the covenant people draw the sword against the foe, God draws the knife upon *them*. Israel has at last crossed the dividing line, and is now entering in a new way into the purposes of God. Therefore, that which has been neglected during the forty years' wandering now becomes imperative. Circumcision is re-enjoined, as the seal of the covenant between God and Israel. Israel's sons were to carry in their very persons this mark of their separatedness. Moreover, although much of the symbolic and typical meaning of things in the Israelite economy must have been unperceived by the Israelites themselves, they were left in no doubt as to the moral and spiritual significance of circumcision. Moses himself had exhorted them: "Circumcise therefore your heart, and be no more stiffnecked" (Deut. x. 16). "The Lord thy God will circumcise thine heart . . . to love the Lord thy God" (Deut. xxx. 6). Passages like Colossians ii. 11–13 make the New Testament interpretation quite clear. It is that "putting off" of "the flesh," that sharp pruning of the natural desires, which accompanies God's chastening in the soul.

Yes, Jordan must be followed by Gilgal. Even the Jordan

by itself is not enough. The Israelites must carry Gilgal's abiding mark of their fuller separation. Even so with ourselves, that soul-crisis of death and burial to selfism, of which Jordan is the type, must be perpetuated by that continuous denial of "the flesh" of which circumcision speaks. This may mean a pang at first; but it is soon over, for God's deeper work in us when we come through the crisis-burial of Jordan strikes a fundamental blow at inbred sin, and so renews the desires of the heart that the first sharp pang of "daily dying" to "the flesh" is quickly lost in the thrill of new fellowship with God on the resurrection ground of "entire sanctification."

Following Israel's circumcision at Gilgal comes the Passover Feast, speaking of this new fellowship with God in the place of blessing (verse 10). Then comes the change-over of Israel's diet from the manna to the produce of Canaan (verse 12). Both the manna in the wilderness and the corn of Canaan typify Christ; but Christ will be the one or the other to us according to where we are spiritually. He can only be to us as the rich produce of Canaan when we have crossed the Jordan and come into the place of complete separation to Himself.

So then, in these first five chapters we have—

Chapter	i.	Joshua charged	— the *warrant* of faith.
,,	ii.	Jericho spied	— the *prudence* of faith.
,,	iii.	Jordan crossed	— the *crisis* of faith.
,,	iv.	Memorials raised	— the *witness* of faith.
,,	v.	Gilgal occupied	— the *pruning* of faith.

Part II. OVERCOMING THE LAND (vi.–xii.)

In this second group of chapters we see faith's warfare and victory. Israel is now in the place of blessing, and goes forth "conquering and to conquer" in the might of the invisible Captain. Vital spiritual lessons are pictured in these chapters.

Chapter	vi.—The Fall of Jericho.
,,	vii.—The Sin of Achan.
,,	viii.—The Sack of Ai.
,,	ix.—The Guile of Gibeon.
,,	x.–xii.—The Rout of the kings.

Chapter vi.—The Fall of Jericho.

This remarkable chapter sets forth in graphic type the principles by which faith works and wars and waits and wins. Faith's first rule of action is to ascertain the will and word of God. Faith's second rule of action is to obey that will and word implicitly. Faith's final rule of action is to reckon on that word, and count the thing as good as done, giving glory to God in anticipation—as the Israelites gave their mighty shout of victory before the walls of Jericho had actually fallen. Faith's principles of action, therefore, cut right across those of natural reason.

We note four things about the procedure of faith in the conquest of Jericho: (1) the seeming folly of it, (2) the inner wisdom of it, (3) the deeper meaning of it, (4) the utter triumph of it. As for the seeming folly of it, nothing could seem more useless to the natural eye than that harmless winding round and round the city walls to the blowing of rams' horns. As for the inner wisdom of it, nothing could really be wiser than to do just what God Himself had directed, however strange it might seem. As for the deeper meaning of it, nothing could be more significant than the fact that here we see God and man in *co-operation* for the pulling down of a Satanic stronghold. As for the utter triumph of it, nothing could be more marked, for with one fell blow the city was laid low, without a single Israelite casualty. Here is triumph indeed. This is the emphasis in this sixth chapter—*the triumph of faith.*

Chapter vii.—The Sin of Achan.

Alas, there is a swift lapse which, though it is soon put right, is not without cost. It is not that Israel's faith breaks down; but a secret compromise temporarily *disables* it. The men of Israel turn their backs on the foe; and thirty-six of them fall. In all the seven years' war this was the one loss. The cause of the failure is carefully exposed so that the lesson may be clearly learned. The electric wire of fellowship between God and Israel had been cut by "a trespass in the accursed thing"; and the current of power therefore ceased to flow. Israel's first inclination was to attribute blame to God instead of looking *within*. But anon the ugly deed was forced into the open; confession was made, and judgment executed upon it. Achan's smuggled loot was of little

material value; but the taking of it was of deep spiritual seriousness. It was a grievous compromise with that which was forbidden. It must have been a sorrow to Jehovah to inflict the Ai
reverse upon His people; yet Israel must learn by necessary pain
that both for their own sake and the sake of Jehovah's holy
name sin must be judged and put away. Any defeat which we
sustain in the land of blessing is due entirely to some such failure
within ourselves. It need never be; and our great Captain grieves
over it more than we do ourselves. We must learn the lesson of
this seventh chapter—that parley with sin, or permitted compromise, cuts the vital cord of communion and disables faith.

Chapter viii.—The Sack of Ai.

In this chapter we see faith re-empowered and going forth
in renewed triumph. Sin confessed and judged and put away
restores the cord of communion, and the Divine power begins
to flow again. The invisible Captain of Jehovah's host now says
to Joshua: "Fear not, neither be thou dismayed: take all the
people of war with thee, and arise, go up to Ai. See, I have given
into thy hand the king of Ai and his people and his city and
his land." The remainder of the chapter speaks for itself. It is
the picture-lesson of *faith re-empowered* after self-judgment.

Chapter ix.—The League with Gibeon.

Here behold the wiles of Satan. The Gibeonites, realising
that they could not stand against such a power as that which
operated through Israel, resorted to a trick of deception. A group
of them, forlornly attired as wearied travellers from a distant
land, came to the camp of Israel, saying: "From a very far
country thy servants are come because of the name of Jehovah
thy God; for we have heard the fame of Him and all that He did
in Egypt . . . therefore now make ye a league with us." So clever
was the disguise, so reasonable the story, so reverential the
reference to Jehovah, so pitiable their plight, that Israel's com-
passion overflowed. Believing that these men were not of the
Canaanites who were under the curse, and with whom no leagues
were to be made, Israel made a covenant with Gibeon. Three
days later the trickery was exposed.

Note: the most significant thing in this incident is that Israel
"*asked not counsel at the mouth of the Lord*" (verse 14). We need

not only the *power* of the Spirit against giants, but the *wisdom* of the Spirit against serpents! Satan is far easier to strike down as a son of Anak in warrior's armour than as a disguised Gibeonite in some pity-evoking beggar's attire. Satan's subtle wiles are more dangerous than his open assaults. He is more dangerous as "an angel of light" than as "a roaring lion." The league with these Canaanites held evil possibilities. It imperilled Israel's faith. It was not made because of any breakdown of Israel's faith at the time; but faith had been thrown off guard. Here in this ninth chapter is *faith endangered* by the failure to refer everything to God.

Chapters x.–xii.—The Rout of all Foes.

Joshua's plan of campaign here becomes clear. In first striking at Jericho and Ai, he had driven a wedge into the centre of Canaan. Now, in chapter x. he forks south, and then in chapter xi. he strikes up north. Thus we have the *central* campaign (vi.–ix.), the *southern* campaign (x.), the *northern* campaign (xi.); while chapter xii. completes the account by giving a summary of all the kings and major cities which fell before the sword of Israel. Inter-tribal quarrels between the peoples of Canaan were shelved in the presence of the one foe common to all—Israel. Those who had been each other's deadly foes now quickly made common cause against the awe-inspiring invader. Military alliances were hastily struck, and united resistance was offered. But it was all of no avail. The most formidable coalitions were no match for that supernatural power which operated through Israel. Down they went one after another—cities, kings, giants, confederacies, until it could be written:

"So Joshua took the whole land, according to all that the Lord said unto Moses; and Joshua gave it for an inheritance unto Israel according to their divisions by their tribes." (xi. 23).

We group chapters x.–xii. together because whereas the overthrow of Jericho and Ai and the league with Gibeon are depicted in fuller detail, the campaigns in these further three chapters are more summarily described. And what do they show us in a spiritual sense? They shew us *faith all-victorious.* Enemies are vanquished. Israel is victor. Canaan is won. And "this is the victory that overcometh the world, even our faith."

THE BOOK OF JOSHUA (4)

Lesson Number 23

NOTE.—For this present study read again chapters xiii. to xxiv.

THE BOOK OF JOSHUA

THE VICTORY OF FAITH

I. ENTERING THE LAND (i.–v.)

i.	Joshua charged	—the warrant of faith.
ii.	Jericho spied	—the prudence of faith.
iii.	Jordan crossed	—the crisis of faith.
iv.	Memorials built	—the witness of faith.
v.	Gilgal occupied	—the pruning of faith.

II. OVERCOMING THE LAND (vi.–xii.)

vi.	Fall of Jericho	—faith triumphant.
vii.	Sin of Achan	—faith disabled.
viii.	Sack of Ai	—faith re-empowered.
ix.	Guile of Gibeon	—faith endangered.
x.–xii.	Rout of all foes	—faith all-victorious.

III. OCCUPYING THE LAND (xiii.–xxiv.)

xiii.–xix.	Division of Canaan	—faith rewarded.
xx.	Cities of Refuge	—faith protected.
xxi.	Portion of Levites	—faith preserved.
xxii.	Altar of Witness	—faith unifying.
xxiii.–xxiv.	Farewell of Joshua	—faith continuing.

THE BOOK OF JOSHUA (4)

PART III. OCCUPYING THE LAND (xiii.–xxiv.)

THIS FINAL group of chapters is rich with matters of interest, yet it can yield but a thin harvest to a casual reading; for since it deals mainly with names and places and boundary lines, it requires to be studied with map in hand. A detailed geographical tracing-out is rather beyond our present treatment of the book; but there are two or three guiding factors which we ought to note carefully.

First: it requires little imagination to see that the division of the land among the nine and a half tribes and the Levites was no simple task, but a complicated one which demanded careful direction and considerable time.

Second: the dividing of the land was by "casting lots before the Lord" (xviii. 6)—a way of doing which would commend itself because of its impartiality, while at the same time it left the sovereign Lord Himself to settle the tribes in the areas best suited to them. The same blend of impartiality and sovereignty is seen in the administration of spiritual gifts by the Holy Spirit in the Church of Christ.

"Now there are diversities of gifts, but the same Spirit. And there are differences of administration, but the same Lord. And there are diversities of workings, but it is the same God which worketh all in all. But the manifestation of the Spirit is given to every man to profit withal. For to one is given by the Spirit the word of wisdom, to another the word of knowledge by the same Spirit, to another faith by the same Spirit, to another the gifts of healing by the same Spirit, to another the working of miracles, to another prophecy, to another discerning of spirits, to another divers kinds of tongues, to another the interpretation of tongues; but all these worketh that one and the selfsame Spirit, dividing to every man severally as He will" (I Cor. xii. 4–11).

Third: we should mark well the *principle* which governed Israel's occupation of the land, because the same principle operates in our own appropriation of the inheritance in Christ. This principle is seen if we bring together two seemingly contradictory verses. In chapter xi. 23 we read: "So Joshua *took the whole land*, according to all that the Lord said unto Moses." Yet now in chapter xiii. 1, God says: "There remaineth yet very much land *to be* possessed." These two statements in reality are not contradictory but complementary. They are two aspects of the one situation, and both are true. There was a real sense in which "the whole land" had been taken; and there was a real sense in which "very much land" yet remained to be taken. The decisive blow had been struck. The key cities had been sacked. All opposing alliances had been crushed. Any remaining foes were well within the power of Israel's individual tribes to destroy. It only remained for them now to see to it that there was a pressing home of that initial victory to the last detail.

It is the same with ourselves. The decisive blow has been struck at sin and Satan and the powers of darkness by our heavenly Captain; and thereby the entire inheritance of "all blessings in the heavenlies in Christ" is ours; but we must now apply that victory, carrying it through the whole realm of our thought and life, and pressing it home to the last detail. Especially in our prayer-life should there be a pressing forward in the power of this decisive victory. The powers of darkness can never recover from the mortal blow inflicted on them at Calvary; and even though, through the apostasy of the organised Church, they have found increasing opportunity to rally sufficiently for the waging of bitter warfare against God's spiritual Israel, they still quail before the believer who presses forward in the power of the Cross.

Yes, "the whole land" is taken, yet there remains "very much land" to be possessed. It has been aptly observed that there is a difference between the "inheritance" and the "possession." The "inheritance" is the whole land given by God, whereas the "possession" is only that part of it which is appropriated by faith. The ideal is for the possession to measure up to the full inheritance. Our *inheritance* in Christ is what He is to us potentially. Our *possession* in Christ is what He is to us actually, according to the measure of our appropriation by faith.

And now let us glance quickly at the chapters in this section. The key passage is chapter xxi. 43-5.

"And the Lord gave unto Israel all the land which He sware to give unto their fathers; and they possessed it, and dwelt therein. And the Lord gave them rest round about, according to all that He sware unto their fathers: and there stood not a man of all their enemies before them: the Lord gave all their enemies into their hand.

"There failed not ought of any good thing which the Lord had spoken unto the house of Israel. All came to pass."

Note the three things which God gave to Israel—

"The Lord gave unto Israel all the LAND,"
"The Lord gave them REST round about,"
"The Lord gave all their ENEMIES into their hand."

"All came to pass"—and thus was Jehovah's faithfulness amply exhibited. Israel at last was realising the promised inheritance, the promised rest, the promised victory.

The chapters in this final section of Joshua run thus:

Chapter xiii.–xix.—The Dividing of Canaan.
,,   xx.—The Cities of Refuge.
,,   xxi.—The Portion of Levi.
,,   xxii.—The Altar of Witness.
,,   xxiii.–iv.—The Farewell of Joshua.

Chapters xiii.–xix.—The Dividing of Canaan.

In these chapters we have the distribution of the land among the tribes. First, in chapter xiii., the settlement of Reuben, Gad, and half the tribe of Manasseh in Gilead is homologated. In chapter xiv. staunch old Caleb is planted in Hebron. In chapters xv. to xvii. we see the areas committed to Judah, Ephraim, and the remaining half of the Manasseh tribe. Then in chapters xviii. and xix. comes the setting up of the Tabernacle at Shiloh, followed by the allotments to the remaining seven tribes. Following out our spiritual interpretation of the book, we see in these chapters the *appropriation* of faith.

Chapter xx.—The Cities of Refuge.

Here we have the six "Cities of Refuge"—Kedesh, Shechem, and Hebron, on the west of the Jordan; and Bezer, Ramoth, and Golan on the east. These six were among the forty-eight cities given to the Levites (Num. xxxv. 6, 7). Their purpose is clearly explained in Numbers xxxv. and in this present chapter. They were a merciful provision to protect those who had committed certain wrongs unintendingly or by mistake. Many a man of sincere intent and godly faith might have perished but for the horns of the altars in those cities of refuge.

Thus we have here the Divine recognition of the difference between *sins* and mistakes. The holiest of men are fallible, and can make mistakes; but mistakes are not sins, and they therefore do not disqualify us for the faith-life or deprive us of our inheritance in Christ. The little girl who lovingly but ruinously put her mother's shoes in the oven to warm on a wintry night had made a mistake, but had not committed a sin! A man may have a perfect heart without having a perfect head. Sanctification can dwell with a defective memory. Let us be quick to perceive such distinctions and compatibilities.

Even when we are "in the land" we may do many things that are wrong without *realising* they are wrong. In strict justice the law of God cannot but pursue us as guilty. Yet there is provision made for this in the blood of Christ. Mistakes, inadvertences, "sins of ignorance," unintentional wrongs, are provided for in the Atonement. Christ Himself is our "City of Refuge"; and by holding to Him we are protected and covered, so that the maintaining of the faith-life in our spiritual Canaan is made possible. See in this the *protection* of faith.

Chapter xxi.—The Portion of Levi.

Here is the portion of the Levites in the land; forty-eight goodly cities with their suburbs. This distribution of the Levites through the tribes is of obvious significance. "They permeated the whole land with the hallowing influence of Shiloh. What a halo of sacred interest must have gathered round the man whose lot it was to enter into the Tabernacle of God and burn incense at the solemn hour of prayer! Then multiply this a thousandfold, and consider what a wide and wholesome effect must have been produced throughout the country, especially when Levi fulfilled the lofty possibilities of this high calling. Moreover, the teaching of the Law was a special prerogative of the Levites, who appear to have travelled through their apportioned districts. They taught

Jacob His judgments, and Israel His law; as well as put incense and whole burnt-offering on the altar. They caused the people to discern between the unclean and the clean, and in a controversy stood to judge. They acted as the messengers of the Lord of Hosts" (Deut. xxxiii. 10).

The distribution of the Levites was the Lord's provision for the preservation of Israel's faith in the land. They had entered by faith. They had overcome by faith. That faith must now be maintained in the place of blessing by the teaching of God's word. Maintained faith was the condition of maintained blessing. Faith's food is God's word. So is it always.

Chapter xxii.—The Altar of Witness.

A schismatic altar in Israel! Had not the book of the Covenant emphatically declared that there should be but the one national altar of sacrifice before the Tabernacle—at Shiloh? What then of this "great altar" erected by Reuben, Gad, and the half tribe of Manasseh hard by the Jordan? Is it to be wondered at that the other tribes, shocked and angered, gathered together against them?

But a new complexion is given to the apparent breach when the builders of the altar explain that it is meant to be not an altar of sacrifice but of *witness*—a witness to the unity of the two and a half tribes east of the Jordan with the rest of Israel.

How many there are who, like these two and a half tribes, want to feel quite sure that they have their part with God's Israel, yet are content to live just outside the land!

No doubt this altar "Ed" was well meant; but was it not *needless* if the Divine command were obeyed that three times each year all the males of Israel should appear before the Lord, in Shiloh?

Was it not also *presumptuous*? No pattern for its shape had been given of God, and no direction for its construction. Nor, apparently, had the counsel of the Lord been as much as thought of!

Now here is a noteworthy lesson concerning *the unity of faith*. Had Reuben, Gad, and the half tribe of Manasseh settled west of the Jordan with the other tribes, in the promised place of blessing, no such artificial monument of their oneness with Israel would have been required. True unity is not outward but inward. It is not achieved, nor even preserved, by external memorials. It consists in a oneness of inward and spiritual experience. The trend among the various denominations in the organised Church of today is to seek an imposing outward union by the formulation of a common creed and the inclusion of all sections in some single visible body with impressive proportions and social prestige. This is the building of a modern "altar Ed." It is the confusing of unity with mere uniformity.

The only true unity is that of a common inward life, a common spiritual experience, and a common heart-loyalty. Those who are really living "in the land," in the enjoyment of that spiritual Canaan which is in Christ, are conscious of their spiritual oneness with all the elect of God in Christ, whatever outward denominational differentiations may exist between them.

Speaking of this true unity, the late Dr. F. B. Meyer, in a fine passage, says: "Coming from all points of the compass, fired by the same hopes, suppliants at the same meeting-place, reliant upon the same blood, the common attraction establishes an organic unity like that of the tree, the multiplicity of whose parts is subsidiary to the one life-force; or like that of the body, the variety of whose members is subordinate to the one animating soul.

"The nearer we get to Christ, the more clearly we discern our unity with all who belong to Him. We learn to think less of points of divergence, and more about those of agreement. We find that the idiosyncrasies by which each believer is fitted for his specific work do not materially affect those depths of the inner life which in all saints abut on the nature of the living Saviour. As the scattered sheep browse their way up towards a common summit, they converge on each other, and there is one flock, as there is one Shepherd.

"It is the supreme vision of the Bible, granted to the most eminent saints, that though the new Jerusalem comprehends the names of the tribes of Israel and of the Apostles of the Lamb, is garnished by jewels of many hues, and has gates facing in all directions, it yet is one, 'the Bride, the Lamb's wife.' What wonder, then, that the world, and sometimes the professing Church, supposes that the Lord's prayer is not fulfilled, and that the unity has yet to be made? The unity is made; but only the spiritual with spiritual discernment can detect its symmetry."

We cannot *make* spiritual unity. The unity of the sanctified in Christ is a spiritual reality wrought by the Holy Spirit Himself. The secret of Christian unity lies in our being west of Jordan— with the baptismal burial of that Jordan flood passed through, and the experience of the Spirit's fulness entered into. Give us back that Canaan experience of spiritual fulness which came at Pentecost, and then the overflowing consciousness of spiritual unity among Christ's own will submerge all artificial barriers. Israel's true unity lay in a common life and a common experience of God which found concentrated expression in that one altar of sacrifice at Shiloh. Even so, the true unity of the Lord's own today lies in—and is only realised *according to*—their common experience of life in Christ, finding its vital centre in the Cross and person of the Redeemer. Let this twenty-second chapter of Joshua, then, speak to us its message on the true unity of faith.

Chapters xxiii.–xxiv.—The Farewell of Joshua.

Finally, we have the parting counsels of the now aged Joshua. We must not linger over the touching scene. The faithful leader's words unveil the concern of his heart for the privileged nation. For some years now, Israel had been enjoying the rest and plenty of Canaan. What of the future? All depended on whether or not Israel would continue faithful to the covenant. Joshua's words do not conceal his apprehensiveness. Seven times he refers to the idolatrous nations still left in Canaan. He knew the snare they would be to Israel; and he therefore prescribed three safeguards.

First, there must be brave *adherence to God's word* (xxiii. 6).

Second, there must be a vigilantly continued *separation* from the Canaanite nations (xxiii. 7).

And, there must be a cleaving to the Lord with real and fervent *love* (xxiii. 8–11).

This is the gist of these closing chapters; and these are the three indispensable conditions (just as truly today as in Joshua's day) for a *continuing* in the experience of the "fulness of bless-ing." There must be (1) a living close to the word of God; (2) a consistent separation from all known wrong; (3) a cleaving to

God with the best love of the heart. Truly, in the words of I John v. 3, "His commandments are not grievous," and they who fulfil them find indeed a Canaan of spiritual blessing, of peace and joy in the Holy Spirit, of heavenly fellowship and treasure, which this world can neither give nor take away.

In these last two chapters, then, the emphasis is upon the need and the way of *continuance*. Thus, in this third part of the Book of Joshua, we have:

Chapter xiii.–xix. Partition of Canaan — faith *rewarded*.
      ,,   xx. The Cities of Refuge — faith *protected*.
      ,,   xxi. The Levite's Portion — faith *preserved*.
      ,,   xxii. The Altar of Witness — faith *unifying*.
      ,,   xxiii.–iv. Farewell of Joshua   — faith *continuing*.

And now it may be helpful to see the whole book set out in analysis, with special reference to its spiritual message which we have traced through the chapters (see page 264).

FIND OUT THE WEAK SPOTS!

1. What are the main divisions of Joshua?
2. What is the key thought of the book?
3. Is Canaan a type of Heaven? If not, why not?
4. How do Joshua and Ephesians correspond?
5. Chapter i. may be summarised as "Joshua charged." What of the other chapters?
6. What does the crossing of Jordan typify?
7. Where was Israel's first camp in Canaan?
8. What was the guile of the Gibeonites, and where is it mentioned?
9. How many cities fell to the Levites, and how many were cities of refuge?
10. What was the altar "Ed," and where is it mentioned?
11. What are the three emphases in Joshua's farewell exhortation?
12. In Chapter i. we have the *warrant* of faith. What are the characteristics of faith suggested by the other chapters?

END OF VOLUME I